Relations between East and West in the Middle Ages

Relations between East and West in the Middle Ages,
edited by Derek Baker

At the University Press, Edinburgh

© EDINBURGH UNIVERSITY PRESS 1973
22 George Square

ISBN 0 85224 237 8

North America
Aldine · Atherton Inc.
529 South Wabash Avenue, Chicago

Library of Congress
Catalog Card Number 73-76361

Printed in Great Britain by
R. & R. Clark Ltd, Edinburgh

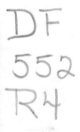

Preface

With one exception the papers presented here were delivered in March 1969 at the second colloquium in medieval history to be held at the university of Edinburgh. The colloquium was organised by the department of History in association with the Institute for Advanced Studies in the Humanities.

Dr Riley-Smith's paper arose out of the discussions which accompanied the colloquium papers, and the volume has been completed by the addition of Professor Nicol's introductory study.

DEREK BAKER   *University of Edinburgh*

Contents

Contributors

ANTHONY BRYER
Reader in Byzantine History,
University of Birmingham

R.H.C.DAVIS
Professor of Medieval History,
University of Birmingham

W.H.C.FREND
Professor of Ecclesiastical History,
University of Glasgow

JOSEPH GILL S.J.
Lecturer in Church History,
Campion Hall, Oxford

KARL LEYSER
Magdalen College, Oxford

DONALD M. NICOL
Koraës Professor of Modern Greek and
Byzantine History, Language and Literature,
King's College, London

JONATHAN RILEY-SMITH
Queens' College, Cambridge

R.W.SOUTHERN
President, St John's College, Oxford

DEREK BAKER, *Editor*
Lecturer in Medieval History,
University of Edinburgh

Abbreviations

ACO = *Acta Conciliorum Oecumenicorum*, 4 vols in 12,
    ed. E. Schwartz (Berlin/Leipzig 1914–40)
Byz = *Byzantion* (Brussels/Boston 1924–)
BZ = *Byzantinische Zeitschrift* (Leipzig 1892–)
$CSCO$ = *Corpus Scriptorum Christianorum
    Orientalium*, ed. J.B.Chabot and others
    (Paris/Rome etc 1903–)
$CSEL$ = *Corpus Scriptorum Ecclesiasticorum
    Latinorum* (Vienna 1886–)
$CSHB$ = *Corpus Scriptorum Historiae Byzantinae*
    (Bonn 1828–97)
DOP = *Dumbarton Oaks Papers* (Cambridge, Mass., 1941–)
HE = *Historia Ecclesiastica*
Hefele-Leclercq = K.J.Hefele and H.Leclercq,
    Histoire des Conciles, 8 vols in 16 (Paris 1907–21)
Mansi = J.D.Mansi, *Sacrorum conciliorum nova et
    amplissima collectio*, 31 vols (Florence/Venice
    1757–98); new impression and continuation ed.
    L.Petit and J.B.Martin, 60 vols (Paris 1901–27)
MGH = *Monumenta Germaniae Historica inde ab a.
    c. 500 usque ad a. 1500*, ed. G.H.Pertz etc.
    (Berlin/Hanover 1826–)
    SRG = *Scriptorum rerum germanicarum*
    SS = *Scriptores*
PG = *Patrologia Graeca*, ed. J.P.Migne, 161 vols in
    166 (Paris 1857–66)
PL = *Patrologia Latina*, ed. J.P.Migne, 217 + 4 vols
    (Paris 1841–64)
PO = *Patrologia Orientalis*, ed. J.Graffin and F.Nau
    (Paris 1903–)
RHC = *Recueil des Historiens des Croisades*
    (Paris 1841–)
RHE = *Revue d'Histoire Ecclésiastique*
    (Louvain 1900–)
RS = *Rerum Britannicarum Medii Aevi Scriptores*,
    99 vols (London 1858–1911) *Rolls Series*

Introduction

DONALD M. NICOL

The essays here gathered together were the intellectual wines poured out at a symposium held at Edinburgh in 1969. Its theme was East-West contacts in the Middle Ages. The title was taken to apply to relations between eastern and western Europe, or between the eastern and western parts of the old Graeco-Roman world, and not to contacts between, for instance, France and Far Cathay.

To the founder of the Roman Empire and his successors relations between East and West meant relations between the eastern and western parts of a whole, the *pars orientalis* and the *pars occidentalis* of the unified structure of the empire. Roman poets liked to boggle the minds of their listeners by talking of a dominion that extended from the barbarous Britons at one end to the perfidious Parthians at the other. But the dominion was one. Jupiter, if Vergil is to be believed, granted to Romulus and his Romans an *imperium* without limits and without end.[1] Augustus nevertheless wisely decided that his empire should have manageable territorial boundaries. But within the limits that he set Roman, Greek, Jew, Christian and Gentile could live under the same law. Romans of the old school sometimes complained about the corrupting influence on their city of Greeks and orientals, of the Orontes flowing into the Tiber. But they employed Greek tutors to educate their sons. People did not think of the eastern and western parts of the empire as being separate entities whose relations with each other must be the object of careful study.

Even at the moment of the empire's birth, however, there was already a clear idea of where the Latin West ended and the Greek East began. The Roman historian Appian tells us that when, in 44 BC, Octavian and Mark Antony divided the world between them, they drew a line down their map from north to south. The line passed through the Dalmatian town of Scodra on the Adriatic Sea. Everything to the east of that line, as far as the Euphrates, was to belong to Antony; everything to the west of it, as far as the Atlantic Ocean, was to belong to Octavian.[2] It was a remarkably realistic division. When the structure of the Roman Empire cracked in later centuries, the crack appeared more or less down that seam; and in the Middle Ages it was across that line that Byzantines and westerners maintained their tenuous contacts. Most of what lay to the west of Scodra was lost to the Roman world in the fifth century. Yet the emperors reigning in Constantinople regarded the loss as being only temporary. Barbarians had unhappily usurped authority in the West. But the empire had not fallen apart; and in God's good time the barbarians would either come to learn or to be forcibly taught their rightful place in the imperial scheme of things. Justinian, as a true successor of Augustus, Trajan and Constantine, made it his lawful business to restore order to the world by re-establishing Roman rule over the western provinces. Given the means and the opportunities to do so he had no option. He would have been failing in his imperial duty if he had not seized those opportunities; and, as Professor Frend points out in the first of the essays in this volume, most of Justinian's subjects probably shared the common pride in the enterprise of reconquest. But the cost of that enterprise, in terms of human suffering as well as of hard cash, was more than the empire could sustain; and even by Justinian's time reintegration of the empire had already been rendered almost impossible by reason of the differences among its members in matters of theology and ecclesiology. Christianity proved to be an even more potent factor than language, culture, or barbarian conquest in the division of the structure.

In the early centuries of the Christian Roman Empire the rivalry between the Old Rome of the West and the New Rome of Constantinople was tempered by the reactions of the great cities and patriarchates of Antioch and Alexandria. After the Arab conquest of Syria and Egypt, however, the field was clear, for Antioch and Alexandria were no longer in the running; and authority in the Church as in the world was effectively narrowed down to the twin poles of Rome and Constantinople. The erosion by new barbarians of the territory that lay between them produced a physical separation of East from West which helped to accentuate and foster their differences. The Slavs descended on the Balkan peninsula and Greece and thus drove a wedge of barbarism down the middle of the Graeco-Roman world. The Magyars arrived in the ninth century to block the last land route between eastern and western Europe. Thus by the tenth century, as Dr Leyser makes clear in his paper, the division between East and West had become a matter of harsh physical reality, adding substance to the ideological gulf which had already appeared between them. For by then the Greek East and the Latin West, Byzantine Orthodox and Roman Catholics, had gone their own ways and developed their own ideas for too long; they had begun to take up the positions of mutual incomprehension which had become second nature to them by the time of the crusades.

The establishment of an alternative 'empire' in the West, first by

Charlemagne and then by Otto the Great, which seemed to be so momentous in the history of western Europe, appeared to the Byzantines as a deliberate affront to the universal sovereignty of the one true Roman emperor in Constantinople. Inside every Byzantine emperor there was a Justinian trying to get out. It was taken for granted, even in the tenth century, that the western provinces belonged by right to the heirs of Augustus in Byzantium. The fiction of a single, universal *imperium* was maintained by all manner of devices. The Byzantine emperor was said graciously to permit lesser kings and princes to reign over portions of his sundered provinces as his 'spiritual' sons, brothers, nephews, or cousins. He was the *paterfamilias* of a great family of Christian rulers.[3] It was particularly distressing when western kings began to style themselves 'emperors'. But even then Byzantine diplomacy and ingenuity were able to make the best of a bad job by rephrasing the theory of a single *imperium*. It was touch and go whether Charlemagne married the formidable empress Eirene; it was a fact that Otto 11 married the Byzantine princess Theophano. In both cases there were high hopes that intermarriage might in some way mend the torn garment of the Roman Empire. But such devices could not turn back the differing processes of historical and cultural development which made the Byzantines and the westerners the men and women they were.[4]

So long as East and West were restricted to communicating by sea their contacts were necessarily limited. From time to time the Byzantines would show the flag in their province in South Italy and its satellite principalities. As late as 1025 the emperor Basil 11 was preparing an armada for the reconquest of Sicily. There were formal exchanges of embassies and many negotiations about marriages between Byzantine princesses and Latin princes. Westerners like Liudprand of Cremona were, however, rare visitors to Constantinople. They were not very welcome, at least on their own terms; nor did they much care for the high-handed manner in which they were sometimes treated. But the re-opening of the overland route from West to East through Hungary early in the eleventh century changed the whole picture, as Dr Leyser observes. The conversion of the Magyars to Christianity in 975 and then the annexation of Bulgaria to the Byzantine Empire in 1018 meant that relatively cheap, if arduous, communications between East and West were again possible. The trickle of fairly evenly balanced exchanges of select representatives gave way to an indiscriminate flood of humanity moving from West to East. The flood was mainly composed of pilgrims on their way to the Holy Land. All of them had to pass through Constantinople to make the only short sea crossing on their route. Relations between easterners and westerners, between

Greeks and Latins, became a matter of fact, and neither party much enjoyed the experience of discovering the realities.

In the course of the eleventh century the catalogue of differences between the two societies lengthened and their respective positions hardened. The western world and the Roman Church began to find new sources of strength and confidence. The Byzantine world began to sink into a decline after the glorious era of its soldier emperors. Its falling fortunes are sadly symbolised by the events of the year 1071, when imperial armies were humiliated at either extremity of the Empire, at Manzikert by the Seljuq Turks, at Bari by the Normans. The realities of East-West relations are symbolised by the event of 1054, when the Churches of Rome and Constantinople openly admitted that a state of schism existed between them. The schism in the Church was a symptom of a deeper malaise in the body of Christendom. The balance of power was shifting from East to West. The westerners were full of new ideas and new vitality. But the Byzantines could not bear to think of them as equal partners; nor could they go back on their own past by renouncing their claim to be the only true heirs of the Christian Roman Empire.

The misunderstandings engendered by the crusades were almost without number. The Norman leaders of the First Crusade soon showed that they had little intention of honouring any agreements they made with the emperor in Constantinople. The Byzantines accused them of perjury. They retaliated by accusing the Byzantines of treachery. Every failure of their adventures in the Holy Land could be attributed to the double-dealing of the Greeks. Prejudices on either side were reinforced. Tolerance and patience were at a premium. There were, however, a few who tried to bridge the gap as 'contact men'. William of Tyre, about whom Professor Davis writes, was a perfect example of the species. Born in the crusader kingdom of Jerusalem, versed in both Greek and Arabic, widely travelled, a visitor to Byzantium, and remarkably if not wholly impartial, William of Tyre had every qualification to bridge the gap. Yet the gap which he perceived and described was not really that ancient and recurring division between the Greek East and the Latin West. As a member of the community of Latin colonists who had moved into the Levant on the wave of the crusades, William's real concern was to manage relations between western Christians and oriental Muslims to the advantage of the former. The Byzantines were rather on the fringe of his perceptions and activities, for all that he sought their co-operation and played down their reputation for treachery. To William, the 'East' signified the countries surrounding the Holy Land. As Professor Davis writes, 'he did not consider himself as part of the East but rather as a western Bishop in the East'.

A 'contact man' of another kind was the Byzantine emperor Manuel I Komnenos. William of Tyre was among the guests at a fashionable double wedding that took place in Constantinople in 1179. Amid scenes of brilliant pageantry and sumptuous festivities, which William records with admiring detail, the emperor Manuel gave his daughter Mary in marriage to Rainier of Montferrat and his son Alexios in marriage to Agnes, daughter of King Louis VII of France. The weddings celebrated an ideal of Byzantine-Latin relations which the emperor did his best to nurture and to put into practice. But the subsequent fate of the two western spouses is perhaps instructive. Rainier of Montferrat fell victim (along with Manuel's widow, Mary of Antioch) to the backlash of anti-Latin reaction that swept the Byzantines out of their senses in 1183. Agnes of France, on the other hand, though still only twelve years old, was coerced into marrying the ring-leader of that reaction, the usurper Andronikos Komnenos, who had murdered her Byzantine husband. After he too had been violently deposed, she married for a third time and settled down to the Byzantine way of life. When in 1203 the leaders of the Fourth Crusade first entered Constantinople, they enquired after the young princess from France who had been so long in exile. They expected a warm welcome as compatriots and friends. But Agnes of France had long since become Anne of Byzantium. She gave them a chilly reception and refused to talk to them except through an interpreter.[5]

The emperor Manuel's efforts to undo the damage done to Byzantine-Latin relations by the crusades earned him the derogatory name of a 'Latinophile' among his subjects. His own personal friendship with some of the westerners was remarkable. With Conrad III of Germany, for instance, he had a sincere understanding. The spectacle of the Byzantine emperor nursing the German king back to health in Constantinople in the winter of 1147 ought to have been an example of Greco-Latin co-operation for the rest of the world.[6] But such cases of fellow-feeling were isolated and exceptional; and Frederick Barbarossa, who succeeded Conrad in 1152, would never put himself out to cultivate the friendship of one whom he regarded simply as a king of the Greeks who ought to know his place. In the realm of ideas, culture, literature and the arts, the Latinophile policy of Manuel I had little effect, perhaps less than has sometimes been suggested, as Dr Bryer argues. The effects of the exchange of ideas and customs are naturally harder to assess than those of recorded personal relationships between members of the Greek and Latin ruling classes; though it may be fair to say that the introduction of jousting to the Byzantine court by Manuel in the twelfth century made less permanent impact than

B

the introduction of the fork to Venice by Maria Argyrou, who married the doge at the beginning of the eleventh century.[7]

For tangible evidence of East-West contacts, however, one must look to the geographical meeting-points between Byzantines and westerners – to Hungary, to Serbia, to the areas between the Greek and Turkish spheres of influence in Anatolia, where several western adventurers found scope for their talents, or to South Italy and Sicily. It was in these 'areas of overlap', as Dr Bryer calls them, that Greeks and Latins had occasion to associate or, more normally, to ignore each other. A common culture was never likely to be forged through exchanges of ambassadors or ecclesiastical legates. But at a humbler level some forms of hybrid cultures or sub-cultures were born out of circumstances, in the ports of the Levant, for example, where Venetians, Pisans, Genoese, Jews and Greeks had no escape from each other and evolved a *modus vivendi* and a *lingua franca* in which to conduct their common affairs, in the kind of environments described by Dr Riley-Smith.

But such people were usually the by-products or the victims of the policies of their leaders; and the leaders of Church and State, by reason of their having been born into a ruling class, were all too ready to presume their own more expert knowledge of what was best for the world. Sometimes, as in the case of the First Crusade, their initiative struck an immediate answering chord in the hearts of a multitude. Sometimes, as in the Fourth Crusade, they created an opening for the realisation of a great variety of half-formed or latent aspirations, fantasies and ambitions, religious, political, commercial, or selfish. The Fourth Crusade was a turning-point in East-West relationships. Many in the West had been hoping for such an eventuality; many in the Greek East had been half expecting it, and their rulers had unwittingly prepared the ground. But when it came it was a fearful shock, and when it had spent its force nothing could ever be the same again.

The Fourth Crusade was more than a simple exercise in conquest and colonisation of Byzantium by the Latins. It came to be a deliberate act of chastisement visited upon the Byzantines by the Christians of the West for their obstinate refusal to admit their perversity and 'return' to the fold of the Roman Church. Pope Innocent III, who had inspired it, and who had bitterly condemned its immediate consequences in the appalling sack of Constantinople in 1204, quickly came round to the view that it was after all part of God's plan for the reintegration of Christendom. Its leaders, as he himself wrote, were the agents of providence in punishing the Greeks for their refusal to accept the supremacy of the Holy See. But it can have been little comfort to the Byzantine bishops in Greece, whom the Latins evicted for declining to take the oath of

obedience or subservience to the pope, to be told that he only required it of them because it was within the power and the right of
the successor of St Peter, and in the power of no one else, to do so.
The Fourth Crusade, and its moral justification by the papacy *post
eventum*, brought home to the Byzantines the practical significance
of the papal claims to universal jurisdiction and supremacy over
the world which their ancestors had first encountered as a theory
propounded by Cardinal Humbert in 1054. They had rejected its
implications then. They suffered under its application in the years
after 1204. The ideological gulf between East and West was irre-
mediably widened by the pope, for all that he was motivated, as
Fr Gill demonstrates in his paper, by the highest ideals and the
truest traditions of his office. Even Byzantines like the fourteenth-
century statesman Demetrios Kydones, who were well disposed to
Latin culture and to Catholic doctrine, found it especially hard
to stomach the pronouncement of Pope Innocent III, quoted by
Fr Gill, that 'the Roman Church is the head and mother of all
Churches not by the decision of some council but by divine ordinance'.[8] For the authority of the oecumenical councils was paramount to the Byzantines, and no one bishop, however exalted his
see, could add to or subtract from their decisions and decrees without consulting the representatives of the whole body of the faithful in council. The confrontation of Innocent III and his successors with the patriarchs and bishops of the Orthodox Church was,
therefore, no less awkward than that between the ambassador of
Otto the Great and the emperor Nikephoros Phokas. Just as the
Byzantine emperor in the tenth century knew instinctively that
authority over the Christian world was his by divine ordinance,
so the pope in the thirteenth century knew, as Fr Gill puts it, that
'he did not have to seek authority. He possessed it.'

The crusades, which had been directed against the Muslims for
the rescue and protection of the Christians and their holy places,
in the end did more damage to Christendom than to Islam. The
Muslims ultimately triumphed with the conquest of Asia Minor,
of the Balkans, and of Constantinople itself in 1453; and there
were those in the western world who said, even as early as the
fourteenth century, that the Orthodox Christians got what they
deserved for their continuing refusal to abjure their errors, repent
of their devious practices, and admit their inferiority. The Byzantines were aware of their faults, though they were not the faults
imputed to them by the Latins. The triumph of Islam in the shape
of the Ottomans, for instance, was readily explained by Byzantine
churchmen and others as a direct consequence of the falling standards of the Christians and the wickedness of their priests. The
Muslims, it was said, were in many ways their moral superiors.[9]

In this respect at least the churchmen of East and West seem to have spoken with a common voice. For, as Professor Southern points out, 'the responsibility of a vicious Christian clergy for the rise of Islam was a favourite theme of western critics of the church in the fourteenth century'. It was popularly believed in Dante's day that Saladin himself had been deterred from becoming a Christian only by the vices of the Christian clergy. Saladin therefore qualified for the category of those with 'the baptism of desire' and was set by Dante not in Hell but in Limbo.

It appears that even Dante had limits to his vision and his horizons. Professor Southern demonstrates that he was largely indifferent to the Muslim world. 'He was a wholly western man.' One might add that he was no less indifferent to and ignorant of the Byzantine world. He was aware, because Lorenzo Valla had not then unmasked the 'stupendous lie' of the Donation of Constantine, that Constantine the Great had made over Italy to the pope and set up imperial house 'as a Greek' in Constantinople.[10] But he was totally unaware that, at the time that he was composing the *Divina Commedia*, the successors of Constantine were already battling for the possession of the Asiatic portion of their empire against the new influx of Turks. It is only fair to say that the Byzantine poets and scholars of the same age, though hardly to be compared to Dante, were almost as totally indifferent to and ignorant of the western world. Theodore Metochites and his pupil Nikephoros Gregoras, the two great luminaries of the revival of Greek scholarship in the early fourteenth century, were both contemporaries of Dante. But neither had heard of him. Neither knew a word of Latin, nor did they think it worth the trouble to learn it. They were both wholly eastern men, or perhaps wholly Byzantine men.

The cultural contacts between East and West were of course to burgeon and grow in the later fourteenth and fifteenth centuries, as the desire to learn Greek became more widespread in Italy. There were even Byzantine scholars who swallowed their pride and learnt Latin so that they could translate Augustine, Boethius and Thomas Aquinas into their own language. Italian scholars like Francesco Filelfo went to Constantinople to study. They made a welcome change from the long procession of papal legates and Catholic theologians who had visited the capital over the centuries, to bludgeon the emperor into submission or to lecture the patriarch on the errors of his faith. Byzantine scholars like Manuel Chrysoloras went to live and teach in Italy. But these were contacts on a very sophisticated and rarefied level, however momentous their consequences may be thought to have been for the future of western learning and humanism. And in any case, by then it was too late. The Byzantine Empire *had* no future. Its days were already numbered.

It is sad to have to conclude that the kind of relationship that might have reunited the sundered halves of the ancient Roman Empire and the Christian Church which was born in that empire was never established. The people, the ordinary inhabitants of the Greek and Latin worlds, never came together in a great imperial *oikoumene*, as envisaged by Justinian, or in a great society of Christendom, as envisaged by Pope Innocent III. The crusades, which brought them together by force of circumstance, proved disastrous to their understanding. The Fourth Crusade made any hope of real reconciliation almost unthinkable. Contacts there were, through commerce, through western colonisation of the Levant and appropriation of Byzantine provinces, through embassies political and ecclesiastical, through intermarriage in high places, and occasionally through artists and scholars. But the sum total of these contacts never added up to anything that might be called mutual understanding on the scale required; and at the eleventh hour of Byzantium the lack of any fruitful relationship between East and West was tragically demonstrated by the inability of Greeks and Latins to co-operate in the Christian venture of stemming the infidel tide in Asia, in eastern Europe, and finally at the walls of Constantinople.

NOTES

1   Vergil, *Aeneid*, 1. 278–9: 'His ego nec metas rerum nec tempora pono,/ Imperium sine fine dedi'. Cf. Horace, *Carmina*, III, v. 2–4: 'Praesens Divus habebitur/Augustus, adiectis Britannis/imperio gravibusque Persis'.
2   *Appiani Historia Romana*, ed. L. Mendelssohn and P. Viereck (Leipzig 1905) v. 65 : 11, p. 576.
3   See F. Dölger, 'Die "Familie der Könige" im Mittelalter', in Dölger, *Byzanz und die europäische Staatenwelt* (Ettal 1953) pp. 34–69; G. Ostrogorsky, 'The Byzantine Empire and the Hierarchical World Order', *Slavonic and East European Review*, XXXV (1956) pp. 1–14.
4   R. Jenkins, *Byzantium. The Imperial Centuries* (London 1966) pp. 109–10, 293–5.
5   William of Tyre, *Historia Rerum in Partibus Transmarinis Gestarum* (RHC, *Historiens Occidentaux*, 1) pp. 1066–7. Cf. C. M. Brand, *Byzantium confronts the West, 1180–1204* (Cambridge, Mass., 1968) pp. 19, 22–3, 45–7, 72–3. The tale of the crusaders' interview with Agnes of France is told by Robert of Clari, *La Conquête de Constantinople*, ed. P. Lauer (Paris 1924) 52–4, pp. 81–90.
6   Cf. S. Runciman, *A History of the Crusades*, II (Cambridge 1954) pp. 270–1.

7   On Maria Argyrou, see S. Runciman, in *Cambridge Medieval History*, IV : *The Byzantine Empire*, part ii, ed. J. M. Hussey (Cambridge 1967) p. 368; L. Bréhier, *La Civilisation byzantine* (*Le Monde byzantin*, III, 2nd ed. : Paris 1970) pp. 51–2.
On tournaments in twelfth-century Byzantium, see Niketas Choniates, *Historia*, ed. I. Bekker (Bonn 1835) pp. 142–4 (description of a tournament held at Antioch in which the emperor Manuel I took part); and in general, C. Diehl, *La Société byzantine à l'époque des Comnènes* (Paris 1919) pp. 13ff, 23ff.

8   See the letter of Demetrios Kydones to Barlaam of Calabria (Latin text), in J. P. Migne, *P G*, 151, cols 1291–2.

9   See, for example, the remarks of Alexios Makrembolites in the mid-14th century, and of the patriarch Neilos (1379–1388) about the moral and religious decadence of Byzantine society when compared with that of the Turks. I. Ševčenko, 'Alexios Makrembolites and his "Dialogue between the Rich and the Poor"', *Zbornik Radova Vizantološkog Instituta*, VI (Belgrade 1960) pp. 196–7; I. Dujčev, 'Le Patriarche Nil et les invasions turques vers la fin du XIVᵉ siècle', *Mélanges d'Archéologie et d'Histoire*, LXXXVIII (1966) pp. 207–14, especially p. 213 (reprinted in Dujčev, *Medioevo Bizantino-Slavo*, II (Rome 1968) pp. 253–61, 609–10, especially p. 258).

10   Dante, *Paradiso*, XX.57 : 'Per cedere al pastor si fece greco'. Cf. P. Toynbee, *A Dictionary of Proper Names and Notable Matters in the Works of Dante*, revised by C. S. Singleton (Oxford 1968) p. 202, under 'Costantino'.

Old and New Rome in the Age of Justinian

W.H.C.FREND

For those who believe that 'a week is a long time in politics', Byzantine history is a wearisome business. For generations the same problems of theology and ecclesiastical precedence are argued between Rome and Constantinople without any apparent progress being made, while for centuries after the event Coptic and Syrian historians were treating the Council of Chalcedon with as much abuse as though it had only met the previous day. From the West, in his requisitory against Michael Cerularius, Cardinal Humbert did not fail to point out that six hundred years before, the see of Constantinople had abused its powers by consecrating Maximus as patriarch of Antioch without notifying the see of Rome.[1] No wonder Gibbon was exasperated with Byzantium, for such concern for the rights and wrongs of the remote past tended to ossify thought and action. Whether one turns to the art of war, to political thought or historical writing the evidence for the backward-looking tendency in Byzantium is clear. It must be accepted as one of the factors that led to the extinction of its empire and itself.

We begin near the origins of the great crisis in European history symbolised by the formal breach between Rome and Constantinople in 1054. The reign of Justinian (shared at first with his uncle, Justin, 519–27) 527–65 marks the climax of the first period of Byzantine history. Justinian and Theodora peer down the ages from the mosaic walls of San Vitale challenging romantic and historian alike, for their reign and their era had the attributes of greatness in struggle, endeavour and ultimate failure. In purely material terms the achievement of the emperor in the first ten years of his reign as sole ruler 527–37 was impressive. In a series of sweeping military successes, Africa, Sicily, Dalmatia and southern Italy, including Rome had been reconquered and reality given once more to the idea of the 'Roman world'. Old Rome and New Rome were united politically and ecclesiastically. The road taken by his predecessors Zeno and Anastasius in accepting the Acacian schism had been demonstrated to be false. Moreover, these reconquests had not been the results of mere greed for power. Given the western orientation of Justin and Justinian, it is difficult to see how the latter could have reacted differently to the situation presented by the progressive collapse, first of the Vandal kingdom in Africa and then of Ostrogothic power in Italy and the Balkans. Moreover, this was combined with powerful Catholic appeals, especially in Africa, for intervention, and it was the western Catholic 'lobby' in Constantinople that according to both Zacharias Rhetor and Procopius was mainly responsible for Justinian's decision to send Belisarius's expedition to Africa in 533.[2] Its amazing success, like other similar military situations, then developed a momentum of its own. Twenty years later Procopius could point out how pre-occupations in the West had denuded the Danube frontier for the benefit of the Huns and Slavs, but this was hindsight which few shared at the time. Most of Justinian's subjects probably shared the pride which John Lydus and Cosmas Indicopleustes voiced in the imperial restoration.[3]

The restoration of the Roman world, based on the Catholic religion as defined in the first four general councils and interpreted by the emperor himself as intermediary between God and the human race, is the keynote of the reign.[4] It is no accident that the first years should see at one and the same time a ruthless drive against pagan-ism and heresy of all sorts, and the accomplishment of a revision and codification of the law. There was to be one Church and one standard of Christian law for humanity. In fourteen months during 529–31 Tribonian revised the *Codex Theodosianus* and the subse-quent legislature extending over a century to produce the *Codex Justinianus*, as a single code of law for the whole empire, and by 534 had established in the *Digest* and *Institutes* a complete revision of the *ius antiquum*. As a visible climax of the endeavour of his age the vast, new and imposing church of Sancta Sophia rose slowly but steadily from its foundations, between 532 and 537. It won Pro-copius' praise as providing 'so brilliant a vision, that one might say that instead of being lit by the sun's rays, it enclosed the source of light within itself', and that 'when one entered it to pray, one looked upon it as a work of the wisdom of God rather than the handiwork of men'.[5] The example was taken up all over the By-zantine world. 'Église paléo-chrétienne' means more often than not a church with mosaics built in the first decade of Justinian's reign. Symbolic, too, of the direction of Justinian's thought, the dedications were more often to the *Theotokos* than to Christ Himself.[6]

In the spring of 532 Justinian had summoned six of the Mono-physite leaders to Constantinople to discuss their differences with an equal number of champions of Chalcedonian orthodoxy, in the hope that reconciliation could be achieved on the basis of an ac-knowledgement of the Council of Chalcedon of 451. The discus-sions, according to Zacharias Rhetor, lasted for rather over a year, but the results were inconclusive.[7] The Chalcedonians were able to point to inconsistencies in their opponents' case relating to the origins of the dissension. They were, however, unable to rebut the counter-claim that the doctrinal definition of the Council of Chalcedon represented a novelty, in the sense that it added to the Creed of Nicaea which all in the East agreed was the sole criterion of orthodoxy. Even the emperor's personal pleas had not prevented a breakdown. Justinian had been unable to unite his eastern dominions in a single faith before he turned his energies towards the reconquest of the former western provinces.

The Monophysites by now held the key to any restoration of religious, and ultimately political, unity between the east and west Roman worlds. The issues that divided them and the orthodox were already a century old and they concerned fundamentals of doctrine and ecclesiastical life. The Council of Chalcedon in 451 had resulted in major realignments. It had defined the Person of Christ as 'made known to us in two natures' inseparably united, rejecting by implication the view that Christ incarnate was formed 'out of two natures' one. In doing so, the bishops had indicated that they preferred a definition associated with Pope Leo, and set down by him in a letter (known as the *Tome* of Leo) to the erstwhile patriarch of Constantinople, Flavian, to that upheld by Cyril of Alexandria and his successor, Dioscorus.[8] There was, however, an element of ambiguity. The bishops at Chalcedon, apart from the papal legates, were all easterners. They had been willing to accept a definition which in fact meant little to them in order to rid themselves of the tyranny of Dioscorus, but they had no intention of abandoning the theology of Cyril. The *Tome* of Leo had been accepted even with enthusiasm because it could be argued that 'it agreed with Cyril'. Faced with the alternatives 'Leo or Dioscorus' by lay commissioners who presided over the council, the bishops had opted for Leo, but it was always Cyril's doctrine that was regarded as the yardstick against which all else had to be measured. Yet only by tearing fragments of certain of Cyril's letters from their context could his doctrine be made to accord even verbally with that of Leo. This had no doubt been realised, for many bishops at the council explicitly refused to accept the doctrinal definition as a Symbol of Faith, to be placed on the same level of importance as the Creeds of Nicaea and Constantinople and the decisions of the first Council of Ephesus in 431.[9] It was a statement of lesser value, something to be employed in baptismal interrogations and as a shield against the twin heresies of Eutyches and Nestorius. For the West and Pope Leo, however, the Definition represented a binding document beyond all discussion and negotiation,[10] and here East and West were to part company.

The dangers implicit in this divergence of interpretation became clear immediately, for Leo treated all those who had reservations over the Definition as heretics. At this time the 'hesitants' or *Dia-koinomenoi*, as they came to be called, comprised a large proportion of the bishops throughout the Byzantine world as well as the majority of the ordinary provincials, represented by the monks, who were later to form the backbone of the Monophysite movement. In addition to the doctrinal issue, Chalcedon had focussed attention on the ecclesiastical standing of the capital, Constantinople, or as it was more usually known, 'New Rome', and this also was to be a lasting bone of contention.

At the end of the council, partly to protect the capital from aggression on the part of Alexandria but equally as a general tidying up of existing practice, it was agreed that New Rome should enjoy ecclesiastical privileges next in rank to Old Rome. In the view both of the bishops and the lay commissioners, Rome was one, and it was unthinkable that New Rome should not enjoy the same dignities and honours as her venerable sister on the Tiber. Moreover, the canon said no more than what the Fathers had agreed at the Council of Constantinople, and its decision corresponded to reality. For the previous half-century Constantinople had been the court of appeal to which aggrieved clerics from all over the east had brought their cases, while the patriarch had similarly been represented at important hearings, such as that of Ibas, metropolitan of Edessa, tried at Berytus in 448 for heresy and peculation in the eastern provinces. Old Rome, however, could still assert the primacy congruent with its status as elder partner. This decision, known as the 28th canon, while acceptable to the eastern bishops aroused the strongest opposition in Rome, on the grounds that Constantinople had no canonical standing.[11] It was not an apostolic see and at the time of Nicaea when the precedence of the major bishoprics had been laid down, it was only a suffragan bishopric of the metropolitan see of Thrace, namely Heraclea. Leo refused to ratify the decision of the council and for the next six hundred years this grievance against Constantinople was never far from the minds of the popes.

Behind the matter of ecclesiastical precedence lay, however, a far deeper divergence of view concerning the role of the state, and the emperor as its representative, in the life of the Church. The Council of Chalcedon had been summoned by the emperor Marcian. He and his consort Pulcheria had been present at some of the more crucial of its deliberations. Through the lay commissioners who presided, he had been responsible for the terminology of the *Tome* of Leo being accepted in the Definition of Faith, and once he had given his views there was nothing left for the bishops but to applaud the 'new David' and 'new Constantine' and to obey.[12] Marcian was a professional soldier with none of the theological training of his predecessor Theodosius II, or of Justinian, but he accepted automatically the theological view of kingship derived from Constantine. To him, as to his successors, his 'common oversight' over his realm involved concern for both the religious and material welfare of his people. He would have had little hesitation in agreeing with Theodosius II that 'the stability of the state depends on the religion by which we honour God', though he would have disagreed with him regarding his definition of right religion.[13] In any event, however, the initiative in matters of religion lay in his hands, and if any ecclesiastic disobeyed his edicts, then resignation and despatch into exile was all that he could hope for. It was in this tradition that Justinian built. His caesaro-papism was simply an explicit continuation of the ideas of Constantine and Constantius II.

This view of the emperor's prerogatives also rested on a long tradition. Ultimately, it could be traced back to the ideal of the 'godly monarchy' propounded by Philo in the time of Augustus, and elaborated by generations of Greek Christian apologists from Melito of Sardis to Eusebius. The emperor was not only 'the friend of God', but also the reflection of the Divine Word, the ruler of the universe, the herald of God's command throughout the inhabited world, and hence the supreme authority in matters religious as well as political.[14] In the West, however, no such ideas were accepted. The Church remained a gathered community of the elect whether in suffering as under the pagan emperors, or in triumph as under Constantine and his successors, but however much the Church might benefit by the favour of the state, its goal remained distinct. The emperor, far from being arbiter over its affairs, was a layman, within the Church and not above it, and as an indication that this was no idle pretence Ambrose of Milan had humbled even Theodosius I. 'Render unto Caesar . . .' was the touchstone of western ecclesiastical philosophy towards the Roman Empire. If the government of the world could be represented by the metaphor of the 'two swords', that wielded by the Church was the more effective, and that of the state could be better described as an executioner's axe.[15] These views were fully accepted by the popes. Though Leo accepted the emperor's right to summon a Church council, his views of the emperor's function in ecclesiastical affairs were well expressed in a letter to Marcian, namely that he must repress the disorders that emerged and in particular use his executive power against all heretics.[16] This was to be the role reserved for Justin and Justinian by Hormisdas.

If one looks back at the evidence, it would seem almost incredible that eastern and western Christendom remained in any degree united for as long as they did. The secret was that pope and emperor believed in the oneness of Christendom represented by Rome, whether symbolised by Old Rome or New Rome. The issue was where the power lay, in the hands of the descendant of the Fisherman, or in those of the descendants of Constantine. For the question to become a practical one required, however, an emperor at New Rome to be both determined and able to maintain his rule in both halves of the empire. Marcian, or rather, Pulcheria, did attempt this. His successor Leo I began as though he did, but gradually changed course, especially after the failure of the attempt in 468 to reconquer Vandal Africa. Zeno and Anastasius clearly saw the future of the empire as lying with the eastern provinces. It was Justin and Justinian who tried to turn back the tide and revert to the policies of Marcian.

Their accession on the death of Anastasius in July 518 found the religious differences between East and West already developed and hardened. The effective ending of the Roman empire in the West in 476 as well as the common ties of religion, culture and trade that bound the eastern provinces to Constantinople had concentrated the attention of the emperor and his advisers on the religious problems of the East. Though opposition to Chalcedon was strongest in Egypt, where the fall of Dioscorus and the slight on Cyril's Christology were never forgiven, it was lively in all the eastern provinces, but particularly wherever the monks were in evidence, for example in east Syria and Pamphylia.[17] There, congregations had turned on their bishops returning from Chalcedon with bitter reproaches of having betrayed the true doctrine.[18] Though ultimately the One-Nature Christology was to emerge as the religion of clearly defined territories, including most of Syriac-speaking Syria and Coptic Egypt and become the national religion of Armenia, Nubia and Ethiopia, it would be a great mistake to think of it originally as a movement of independence, or even one whose leaders thought in terms of provincial or regional particularism. An Egyptian in the fifth and sixth century regarded himself as a 'citizen of Jerusalem', that is of the capital of the whole 'race of Christians' and not as a Copt. His opposition to Chalcedon was not an eastern form of Donatism. Centuries after the ending of Byzantine rule in Syria, the Monophysite historian, the patriarch Michael of Antioch, was criticising Marcian because Chalcedon divided the empire in secular and religious matters alike and thereby contributed to its ruin.[19] One-Nature Christology implied the analogy of one Christendom and one empire, and the main objective of the successors of Dioscorus at Alexandria, Timothy the Cat, and Peter Mongus, had been not separation of Egypt from the rest of the empire but to secure the rejection of Chalcedon by the emperor himself. Their aim like that of Cyril and Dioscorus had been to vindicate the primacy of Alexandria as the 'city of the orthodox'.

In the twenty months' successful usurpation of Basiliscus, 475–6 the Alexandrians had nearly achieved their goal, for the Encyclical that Basiliscus promulgated had done just this, and upheld the doctrines of Cyril and the Egyptian Church as contained in Cyril's *Twelve Anathemas*. They failed, however, because Acacius, the patriarch of Constantinople, had realised that the outright rejection of Chalcedon would spell the end of the primatial jurisdiction of his own see. The alliance of primate, pillar-saints and populace of Constantinople, backed on this occasion by the papacy, had proved too much for Basiliscus and Timothy. The emperor Zeno on his return from exile in December 476 had solemnly reconfirmed Chalcedon and the rights of the see of Constantinople.[20]

The matter, however, could not be left there. Acacius saw that the eastern provinces would not accept the *Tome* of Leo and Chalcedon as the basis of their religion, and Zeno himself came from a province, Isauria, where opinion was strongly anti-Chalcedonian. Above all, he was anxious not to go on his travels again. Using a formula that had originally been suggested by Martyrius, patriarch of Jerusalem, in 478, Acacius drafted a letter to the Church in Egypt setting out a compromise.[21] The *Henotikon* of Zeno, as it came to be called, of 28 July 482 did everything but condemn Leo and Chalcedon outright. It laid down as the basis of the faith of the empire the first three oecumenical councils together with Cyril's *Twelve Anathemas*. It proclaimed Jesus Christ as consubstantial with God and man, that he was in nature 'one and not two', and it condemned 'every person who has thought or thinks anything else either now or at any time, either in Chalcedon or in any synod whatsoever'. The effect of this was to demote Chalcedon to the level of a local and somewhat suspect synod whose condemnation both of Eutyches and Nestorius could, however, be accepted. It restored communion between the patriarchs of Alexandria and Constantinople on the latter's terms. It accepted by implication the emperor's right of pronouncing on doctrinal matters, and it had nothing to say to Rome or to western theology whatsoever.[22]

The *Henotikon* remained the official standpoint of the empire through the rest of the reign of Zeno and that of his successor Anastasius. Both these emperors regarded the eastern provinces as of greater moment than the West, including Italy, where both were prepared to accept a shadowy suzerainty first over Odoaker, and then Theodoric. Ecclesiastically the quasi-harmony of the four eastern patriarchates was more important than communion with Rome. Rome for its part had reacted with extreme anger against the *Henotikon*, hostility to its doctrinal provisions being reinforced by a belief in the personal duplicity of Acacius. In July 484 a

Roman synod solemnly excommunicated Acacius and all who were in communion with him. An ally of Rome in the person of one of the Sleepless Monks pinned the sentence to the pallium of Acacius as he was celebrating the eucharist in Sancta Sophia. For the next thirty-five years Rome and the eastern Roman provinces were not in communion with each other.

In the East, however, the *Henotikon* was regarded as a compromise.[23] On the one hand, there began to develop a school of theologians, predecessors of Leontius of Byzantium, who were prepared to accept Chalcedon, provided always that its definition of faith could be reconciled with the theology of Cyril.[24] On the other, the anti-Chalcedonians found two brilliant leaders in the person of Severus (patriarch of Antioch, 512–18) and Philoxenus of Maboug (Hierapolis). These men show how opposition to the council attracted individuals of entirely different background, outlook and race. Severus was the son of a rich landowning family in Pisidia in Asia Minor, whose grandfather had been at Ephesus in 431. He was a cosmopolitan, equally at home in the capital, Antioch or Alexandria, who admired the philosophy of Libanius almost as much as the Trinitarian theology of the Cappodocians, and accepted Cyril as providing in a manner of genius the only Christology compatible with the Creed of Nicaea and its development by the Cappodocian Fathers. His world was the world of Hellenistic philosophical theology with, as he says, every word of Cyril 'canonical'.[25]

Philoxenus, on the other hand, was a Persian by origin, a Syriac-speaker and writer, whose major theological contribution was a Syriac translation of the Bible.[26] He was a man of the people, harsh, uncompromising and turbulent, but who spoke for the monks of the province of Euphratesia, a vital province for the defence of the south-western approaches of Armenia on whose loyalty depended to a large extent the security of the whole of Rome's eastern frontier. No emperor could afford to ignore the opinion of the representatives of popular Christianity there, namely the monks.

Between them Severus and Philoxenus had brought about a revolution in the religious situation in the East in the first twenty years of the sixth century. The one by his great dialectical skill, and his insistence on 'accuracy' in doctrinal belief, meaning the exclusion of all thought of the Incarnate Christ existing in Two Natures, had gradually transformed the *Henotikon* from being a document of compromise to a means by which Chalcedon could be rejected, without calling into question the jurisdictional rights of Constantinople. The other, by his ability as an agitator, united the monks of Syria against the patriarch Flavian, himself loyal to the *Henotikon*, to drive him from office in November 512 and make way for Severus to become patriarch of Antioch. The emperor Anastasius was personally opposed to Chalcedon and in 510 he had denounced the council in a document known as the *Typos* drafted by Severus while in the capital. Next year, again at Severus's prompting, he had deposed the patriarch of Constantinople, Macedonius, for alleged 'Nestorianism', and had permitted the introduction of an addition to the Doxology, 'Holy God, Holy and mighty, holy and immortal have mercy upon us', the words 'who was crucified for us', which interpreted in the One-Nature sense meant that Christ as God suffered and died on the Cross.[27] Thus in 511 the east Roman world was to all intents and purposes Monophysite.

Anastasius had, however, forgotten that even the empire over which he ruled contained Latin-speaking provinces, and in proportion as the patriarchate of Antioch, comprising Syria and southern Asia Minor, swung towards Monophysitism, the Balkan provinces of Illyricum turned towards Rome. There the Acacian schism had brought three main developments, first, a hardening of doctrinal thinking towards the presentation of a Two-Nature Christology, in which the theology of Cyril played no part, secondly, the rejection of any participation in ecclesiastical affairs by the emperor, and thirdly a contempt for the Byzantine clergy as 'heretical Greeks', and above all for Acacius and his successors. All these tendencies were blatantly demonstrated in the correspondence between Pope Gelasius (492–6) and Anastasius, and the efforts by him and successive patriarchs of Constantinople to end the schism on terms which would not damn the memory of Acacius were rebuffed with contempt.[28]

In the final period of Anastasius's reign, the situation between East and West both in its religious and political aspects had become hopelessly confused. The middle way of the *Henotikon* had visibly failed to reconcile the conflicting parties. Alexandria and Antioch were Monophysite, while Constantinpole and Jerusalem were tending once more to accept the canonical status of Chalcedon. The Illyrian provinces and, significantly, the Greek cities of Syria Secunda had turned to Rome, and Roman and Chalcedonian orthodoxy was being forced on the reluctant court by the rebellion of the *Comes foederatorum*, Vitalian the Goth. This was the legacy to which Justin and Justinian succeeded on 9 July 518.

To all outward appearances the policy of the new rulers was a complete reversal of the old. Within a week of Anastasius's death, the crowd in Sancta Sophia were demanding the proclamation of the Council of Chalcedon, within a month a synod at Jerusalem had restored the council to the diptychs, on 7 September Justin and Justinian wrote to Pope Hormisdas informing him of their intention of restoring communion between Old and New Rome, and on 16 September Severus fled his patriarchal see of Antioch, never to return. Early in the new year, after some months of negotiation, the papal legates were making a triumphant progress through Illyricum to end the Acacian schism on their terms.[29] The scene on 28 March 519 when the patriarch Timothy signed the papal *libellus* and accepted the papal condemnation not only of Acacius, Timothy the Cat and Peter Mongus, but of his three predecessors, including the saintly Macedonius, and the emperors Zeno and Anastasius to boot, has been regarded as a great catastrophe for the Church in the East.[30] It certainly coloured the whole of the ecclesiastical policy of Justin and Justinian, and had a permanent effect on the relationship between the capital and the Monophysites in Syria and Egypt. A closer look, however, at what happened suggests that the papal triumph may be overstressed.

The initiative for the ending of the Acacian schism came from the emperor himself.[31] Justin's aim had been simply the restoration of unity between the two Romes, and in this he had been supported by his patriarch. The latter wrote to Pope Hormisdas on 28 March 'I accept that the two most holy Romes, that is to say, your Old Rome and our New Rome are one, and I admit that that see of St Peter and this see of the Imperial City are one'. He granted, as his predecessors had, precedence to Old Rome, and accepted the condemnation of Acacius and his successors, but the man who was the first patriarch of Constantinople to use the title 'ecumenical patriarch' shows no sign of humility or humiliation.[32] He wrote to Hormisdas as a colleague with whom he was glad to be in communion once more. The all-important 28th canon of Chalcedon had not been renounced. The view of the emperor and his nephew was still more significant. On 7 September 518 in the letter informing the pope of his intention to end the schism Justinian had written to Hormisdas telling him to come to Constantinople without delay; it was an order just as Vigilius was to be ordered a generation later.[33] Old Rome and its patriarch were to be brought once more into the orbit of the empire as a whole. The emperors had timed the move perfectly. People, as Procopius of Caesarea said, were tired with arguments about 'senseless doctrines', and if Christ was composed of Godhead and manhood as all agreed, was this not 'two natures'?[34] What was the difference between the essential union of the two making One, and the inseparable union of the two, making Two? Might not, in any event, Chalcedon be accepted as a disciplinary council condemning Eutyches and Nestorius? People were as bored with Severus and his 'accuracy' as they were with Philoxenus and his fighting monks.

The policy of Justin and Justinian was to ensure the religious unity of the Roman world under their aegis. The basic principle of their government was enunciated by Justinian in Novel 7, 'The priestly power and royal power are not widely separated, and sacred property is not far removed from that which all mankind hold in common, or from that which is owned by the state, because the churches are endowed with all their material resources and their status by the munificence of royal power . . .' In so many words this meant that Church and state were complementary aspects of one imperial rule; there might be *regnum* and *sacerdotium*, but no Two Swords. Moreover, if the exercise of right religion was necessary for the prosperity of the empire and its people, the decision of what that right religion was, and its enforcement, lay with the emperor. In this Justinian followed in the footsteps of Constantine, Theodosius I and II, Marcian, Zeno and Anastasius. The only difference with his two predecessors was that his concept of Roman unity entailed the acceptance of four oecumenical councils and not three; but the four were to be accepted in their totality including those canons that upheld the dignity of the see of Constantinople.

Very soon Justinian realised, like Zeno and Anastasius before him, that no unity could be built between East and West on the *Tome* of Leo. To the great majority of the Christian provincials this represented a vindication of Nestorius's 'two Christs', one before and one after incarnation, only one of whom was worthy of worship. If the *Henotikon* was to be abrogated it must be replaced by something very similar, and Justinian found his answer in the Theopaschite idea.

As with the preparation of the *Henotikon*, we find the patriarchate of Jerusalem playing a considerable role in preparing the Theopaschite formula.[35] Jerusalem was in a peculiar situation, the Holy Places being a centre of international pilgrimage, but with Christians only a bare majority of the total population, and the patriarchate ultimately dependent on the goodwill and power of the capital. These factors outweighed any leanings the monks may have had towards their Egyptian and Syrian counterparts, but though Chalcedonian in loyalty, the Palestinians were also Cyrillian in their theology and ready bridge-builders between the Monophysite and Chalcedonian positions. So, when the Scythian monks of the capital proposed a Christology which combined the Chalcedonian formula with the affirmation 'one of the Trinity suffered in the flesh' they could count on immediate support, including that of Justinian himself. This was Monophysite in its expression of piety, but lacked the associations of 'who was crucified for us'. The *Tome* plus Cyril was to become the orthodoxy of Justinian's age.

The papal legates, however, had come to the capital with no

c

wish to compromise with anyone; their loyalty was to the *Tome*, and to the *Tome* alone. If Justinian aimed at restoring unity between Old and New Rome, the pope was concerned only with the restoration of Petrine authority. That, and not the will of the emperor, represented orthodoxy. For Hormisdas as for Leo and Gelasius before him, the emperor was a son of the Church whose particular duty was to execute the Church's orders against heretics and schismatics.[36]

Between 519 and 521 first the legates and then Hormisdas himself insisted on the forceful repression of anti-Chalcedonian opinion in the East as the price of the restoration of communion. Though they found themselves politely thwarted in the capital, in the provinces no less than 55 bishops were deposed and, what was more fateful, there was a wholesale expulsion of Syrian monks from their monasteries. This act more than any other sowed the seed for the establishment of a Monophysite hierarchy in rivalry to that of Chalcedonian orthodoxy.

It is just possible that but for the 'ten years of exile' to which the monks and Monophysite clergy were subjected between 521 and 531, Justinian's theology might have succeeded at least as well as the *Henotikon*. Hormisdas (d. 523) had more pliable successors and John 11 accepted it; in the West, the Severan Monophysites were regarded as 'Theopaschites' and Severus himself in exile, ageing and tormented by the growing division among his followers, between the Julianists and himself, might in time have accepted. The conferences with the orthodox leaders in 532 had shaken some of their arguments against Chalcedon, and their self-confidence.[37] For Justinian too, these four councils were no longer associated with the *Tome* of Leo but with the doctrine expounded in the patriarch Proclus' *Tome* to the Armenians of 435, which all parties in the East accepted as orthodox. If there was ever a chance of Justinian reconciling East and West in one religious and political realm under his own sway it was on the eve of Belisarius's expedition to Vandal Africa in 533.

The Acacian schism, however, had left too strong a legacy. Severus and his colleagues were still loyal to the person of the emperor, despite years of exile and hardship. Striking evidence for this may be seen in the letter which they sent to Justinian in the spring of 532 outlining once more their objections to Chalcedon while accepting an invitation to a conference in the capital. They prayed daily for the emperor's majesty, they declared, 'and for their own sins; and now they cried blessings of every sort on his name and on that of the empress for the destruction of all rebellion' – the reference was to the Nika riot – before expounding their faith.[38] Even so, trust was ebbing away. Before he himself left for the capital in the winter of 534–5 Severus let it be known that he had no real confidence in the outcome of any discussions there. 'Don't be deceived. In the lifetime of these emperors no means of peace will be found, but so that I do not appear to hinder or oppose it I will go through with heartsearchings. I will return without anything being accomplished'.[39] Meantime, he had authorised the first steps towards the creation of an independent Monophysite hierarchy through the ordination of presbyters by his lieutenant John of Tella.

Justinian for his part could not afford a complete break with Severus. The latter's supporters dominated not only Egypt, but the vital north-east frontier area with Persia, and the striking success of the first Monophysite ordinations, for which multitudes of candidates presented themselves, could not be denied. 'Hundreds of people' came to John of Tella 'like a flooded river that has burst its banks.'[40] This had contributed to the emperor's resolve to call the conference of 532. There was, too, the personality of Theodora. Whatever her origin and early life she was a powerful personality and a woman of the people, who shared the basic Monophysitism of the popular faith and she interpreted this accurately in her career as empress. Already in 523 she had interceded on behalf of the deposed bishop of Amida, and until her death in 548 she threw all her considerable influence on the Monophysite side. She was responsible for two events which ensured the perpetuation of the Monophysite movement. First, she ensured the election of the deacon Theodosius to the see of Alexandria after the death of Timothy IV in February 535, and secondly by giving him asylum in the palace of Hormisdas in the capital she enabled him to direct the entire Monophysite movement, including its missions and the consecration of a new hierarchy, for thirty years.[41] Justinian could never afford to ignore its existence.

Whatever may have been the emperor's own leanings, and his gradual move towards the Aphthartodocetism of the Julianist Monophysites suggests that at heart he may always have agreed with Severus's theology, politically there was no uncertainty. In the crisis caused by the patriarch Anthimus's conversion to Monophysitism in 535, as well as in the affair of the Origenist monks, and later in the Three Chapters controversy he never moved from the position that the religion of the empire must be based on the acceptance of the four councils and the union of the five patriarchates. He personally ordered the condemnation of Anthimus by the Home synod as a heretic. From 536 onwards, however, he was no more able to win the acceptance of the West to his ideas than he had been the Monophysites. Once again, the problems were those of the traditional theological positions combined with a lack of personal confidence between the principals.

Ostensibly, he could not have had a more favourable combination of political situations and personalities. Rome was under his direct authority, there was now a papal *apocrisarius* in the capital so that effective diplomatic contact could be maintained. In Vigilius, who became pope in December 537, he had an ecclesiastic who owed his position to his subservience to the emperor and Belisarius. Yet whatever the personal equation it was impossible for Old and New Rome to deviate one iota from previously fixed positions. Vigilius's pathetic intrigue in 538 in which he told Theodora that, 'we do not confess two natures in Christ, but that Christ was from two natures, one Son, one Christ and One Lord', was speedily withdrawn to limbo,[42] and by 547 Menas of New Rome and Vigilius were excommunicating each other.[43] Paradoxically, Theodora's last recorded public act before she died was to reconcile the warring prelates.

A similar pattern underlay the events surrounding the ten-year controversy (543–53) leading to the condemnation of the Three Chapters. The question was essentially one that affected the eastern patriarchates alone, how far could the Two-nature Christology defined by Chalcedon be watered down without denouncing Chalcedon itself, in order eventually to reconcile the Monophysites and the Origenist monks in Palestine. The latter, though loyal to Chalcedon by interest and emotion, were strongly opposed to the Two-nature Christology represented by the Antiochene theologians Theodore of Mopsuestia and Ibas of Edessa. The man behind the moves that culminated in the Fifth General Council and Vigilius's humiliation was Theodore Askidas, the *éminence grise* of the second half of Justinian's reign, who had ousted the papal representative at court at the moment when the latter looked like being able to regain for Rome its traditional influence in Alexandria.[44]

Vigilius himself seems to have had no great qualms about falling in with the emperor's views and condemning the Three Chapters. The sequel to the *Judicatum* of 548 showed, however, that theological traditions and language and cultural boundaries were stronger than the personal inclinations of pope and emperor. The long-term political effects of Justinian's military successes fifteen years before were becoming clearer. The restored Catholic Church in Africa felt little gratitude to Justinian, though many of its bishops may have owed their freedom and even their lives to the emperor's generals.[45] Looking back, it becomes clear how the African theology of Grace and the Augustinian doctrine of the Trinity which emphasised the factor of will and love as the union between the Persons of the Trinity and man's relation to God, would tend naturally towards the theology of Antioch and would not easily have reconciled itself to its outright condemnation. In addition, the Africans retained to a surprising degree the sense of independence and separation of Church-State relations that had characterised their outlook throughout the fourth century. After its restoration in 535 the Church had simply re-started where it left off with the onset of the Vandals a century before. In the archdeacon Liberatus, and Bishop Facundus of Hermiane it combined the theology of Theodore and Nestorius with the anti-imperialism of Donatus of Carthage. The Latin-speaking Illyrians proved trusty allies. In 550 their combined pressure forced Vigilius to withdraw the *Judicatum*. Three years later, though willing to attend the Fifth General Council, they disputed its findings hotly. Liberatus's *Breviarium* and Facundus's *Pro defensione trium Capitulorum* demonstrate western theological and political independence of the East, even at the apparently triumphant climax of Justinian's reign : in 553 not only Italy, but one third of Spain became his.

The Fifth General Council resulted, in effect, in the emergence of three different theologies in Christendom. The West, consolidated round the papacy, accepted Chalcedon and the *Tome* of Leo as the sole norm of orthodoxy : Vigilius was from time to time compelled to imitate at least the language of Leo. At Constantinople, however, it was Chalcedon, but craftily interpreted by Leontius and others so as to rid it of reliance on the *Tome* of Leo and replace this with the whole panoply of Cyrillian Christology. In Egypt and Syria, the latter only was accepted, and Chalcedon, because it also accepted the *Tome*, was instinctively rejected.

This triangle of incompatible interest was to persist in one form or another so long as the Byzantine empire existed. It is doubtful whether anything but total capitulation by one side or the other would have availed for a settlement. In 519 Justin and Justinian had made what appeared to them to be a supreme effort to achieve reunion with Old Rome and its patriarch, only to find that Hormisdas's terms were too steep even for them, while the 'Nestorianism' of the *Tome* of Leo and its representatives was intolerable to the Greek Christian populace. In its turn, the attempt to placate the papacy by persecuting the Monophysite monks led directly to the establishment of a rival Monophysite hierarchy whose existence then made reconciliation among eastern Christians impossible. Strong though Justinian's position was, and ably as he might manœuvre, he could never reconcile the conflicting interests of Constantinople, Rome and Alexandria. Chalcedon proved the stumbling block, and after Justinian had passed from the scene, there were never again men or conditions capable of removing it.

NOTES

1   See Leo, *Ep.* 119.3, *PL* 54, and A. Michel, 'Die römische
     Angriffe auf Cerullarios wegen Antiocheia 1053/1054',
     BZ XLIV (1951) pp. 419–27.
2   Zacharias Rhetor, *HE*, ed. and tr. E. W. Brooks, *CSCO*,
     Scriptores Syri, Series III, VI (Louvain 1919–24) IX.17 and
     Procopius, *Wars*, III.10.19.
3   John Lydus, *De Magistratibus* III.39, ed. R. Wuensch, pp.
     126–7, and Cosmas Indicopleustes, *The Christian Topography*,
     ed. E. O. Windstedt (Cambridge 1909) p. 80. See W. E. Kaegi,
     Byzantium and the Decline of Rome (Princeton 1968) p. 143.
4   The best account of Justinian's religious policy is still that of
     E. Schwartz, 'Zur Kirchenpolitik Justinians', *Sitzber.*
     Bayerisch. Akad. der Wiss., phil-hist. Abt. (1940) pp. 32–81;
     also Ch. Diehl, *Justinien* (Paris 1901) ch. vii and B. Rubin, *Das*
     Zeitalter Justinians (Berlin 1960).
5   Procopius, *De Aedificiis*, 1.1. Compare Evagrius, *HE*, IV.3,
     ed. Bidez/Parmentier (London 1898).
6   See G. H. Armstrong, 'Fifth and Sixth Century Church-
     building in the Holy Land', *Greek Orthodox Theological Re-*
     view, XIV (1969) pp. 17–30, at p. 23. A useful survey also, of
     the veritable explosion of church-building in Justinian's
     reign and the reasons for it.
7   Zacharias Rhetor, *HE*, IX.15. For an account of one of the
     major confrontations written from a Chalcedonian stand-
     point, see the letter written by Innocentius of Maronia to
     Thomas, a presbyter in the Church of Thessalonica, *ACO*,
     IV, 2, pp. 169–84.
8   See R. V. Sellers, *The Council of Chalcedon* (London 1953)
     pp. 103ff.
9   At Chalcedon the bishops protested against any suggestion
     that they were being called upon to draw up an expression
     of the faith, see Mansi, VI, col. 953. In 457 Epiphanius,
     bishop of Perga, described the Definition as 'veluti scutum
     eam contra haereticos opponentes et non mathema fidei
     existentem', Codex Encyclius, *ACO*, II.5, p. 59.
10   For instance, in *Ep.* 145 of 11 July 457 to the emperor Leo I,
     'quia in illo concilio per sanctum spiritum congregato tam
     plenis et perfectis definitionibus cuncta firmata sunt, ut nihil
     ei regulae quae ex divina inspiratione prolata est, aut addi
     possit aut minui.'
11   Leo, *Epp.* 104, 105, 106 and 114–16. See, T. O. Martin, 'The
     Twenty-eighth Canon of Chalcedon, a background note,'
     Das Konzil von Chalkedon, ed. Grillmeier/Bacht (Würzburg
     1953), II, pp. 433–58, and E. Schwartz, 'Der sechste
     nicaëmschen Kanon auf der Synode von Chalkedon,' *Sitzber.*
     Berliner Akad. der Wissenschaften (1930) pp. 611–40.
12   Mansi, VII, col. 173; compare Zacharias Rhetor, *HE*, III.1.
13   Theodosius to the Council of Ephesus I, Mansi, IV, col.
     1112. Compare Zeno's statement of his motive in writing
     the *Henotikon* to the bishops and monks of Egypt in 482
     'cum sic igitur immaculata fides et nos et Romanam servet
     rempublicam.' Cited by Liberatus, *Breviarium*, XVII, *ACO*, II.5.
14   See E. Peterson's classic essay, *Der Monotheismus als politisches*

Problem (Leipzig 1935) and N.H.Baynes, 'Eusebius and the Christian Empire', *Mélanges Bidez*, II (1934) pp.13ff.

15 See S.L.Greenslade's summary of the western position in *Church and State from Constantine to Theodosius* (London 1954) pp.45ff.

16 Leo, *Ep.*106.

17 For Pamphylia as Monophysite, see John of Ephesus, *HE*, ed. E.W.Brooks, *CSCO*, CV–CVI, *Script. Syri*, Ser.III, 3 (Louvain 1935–6) V, 6 and Severus of Antioch, *Select Letters*, ed. E.W.Brooks (London 1902) IV.3.

18 See the instances catalogued by John Rufus *circa* 500 under the title of *Plerophoria*, Ed. F.Nau, *PO*, VIII.

19 *Chronicon*, ed. J.B.Chabot (Paris 1901) II, p. 122.

20 *Codex Justinianus*, 1.2.16. The best account of this period remains E.Schwartz, 'P[ublizistische] S[ammlungen zum Acacianischen Schisma]', *Abhandlungen der Bayerischen Akad. der Wiss.*, phil-hist. Kl. (1934) pp.170.

21 For this episode see, Zacharias, *HE*, V.6.

22 Complete text published by E.Schwartz, 'Codex Vaticanus, graecus 1431, Eine antichalkedonische Sammlung aus der Zeit Kaiser Zenos', *Abhandlungen Bayerisch. Akad. der Wiss.*, XXXII, Abhang VI (München 1927) pp.52ff. Eng. tr. in P.R.Coleman-Norton, *Roman State and Christian Church* (London 1966) III, pp.924–33.

23 Severus of Antioch, *Select Letters*. p.1. For the events see E.Schwartz, *PS* pp.202–10, and L.Duchesne, *The Early History of the Church*, III, pp.346–59.

24 See Ch.Moeller, 'Un représentant de la christologie néo-chalcédonienne au début du VIᵉ siècle en Orient, Nephalius d'Alexandrie,' *RHE*, XL, (1944/45) pp.110ff. and 'Le Chalcédonisme et le néo-chalcédonisme,' in Grillmeier/ Bacht, *Chalkedon*, I, pp.637–720.

25 *Select Letters* 1.9. See the *Life* of Severus by Zacharias Scholasticus, his contemporary, ed. H.Kugener, *PO* II, and for his doctrine the studies of J.Lebon, 'La Christologie du monophysisme syrien,' in Grillmeier/Bacht, *Chalkedon* I, pp.425–580.

26 Compare Michael the Syrian, *Chronicon* IX.9 '[Philoxenus] was versed in everything contained in our writings and in our language.'

27 For this period see E.Honigmann, 'Évêques et évêchés monophysites d'Asie antérieure au VIᵉ siècle, ' *CSCO*, CXXVII, and E.Schwartz, *PS* pp.242–3 (on the addition to the Trishagion).

28 See in particular, Gelasius's *Epp.*3, 10 and 12, ed. A.Thiel, *Epistolae romanorum pontificium genuinae* (Braunsberg 1868) and E.Caspar, *Geschichte des Papstums* (Tübingen 1933) II, pp.65ff.

29 For the narrative of events, see [A.] Vasiliev, *[Justin the First]* (Dumbarton Oaks 1954) pp.136–60.

30 *Coll[ectio] Avell[ana]*, *Ep.* 216, ed. O. Guenther, *CSEL* XXXV and CCXXIII. For discussion, see Vasiliev, pp.174–8.

31 See for instance, *Coll. Avell. Ep.* 161, p.612, 'adunationem sanctissimis ecclesiis sapientissime comparavit (Iustinus).' Compare ibid. *Ep.*147 (Justinian to Pope Hormisdas).

32 *Coll. Avell., Ep.* 159.

33 Ibid. *Ep.* 147.

34 Procopius, *Anecdota*, XI, 25.

35 On the role of the Palestinians in winning the court's accep-
    tance of the Theopaschite formula, see Philoxenus, *Letter
    to the Monks of Senoun*, ed. A. Halleux (1963) pp. 62, 66. For the
    Theopaschites, see L. Duchesne, *L'Eglise au VIᵉ siècle* (Paris
    1924) pp. 59–69, and the documentation, *ACO*, II.4, pp. 3ff.

36 Hormisdas to Justin, *Coll. Avell., Ep.* 168.3, of 9 July 519,
    'Haec prima sunt vestri fundamina principatus, deum placasse
    iustitia et asciusse vobis excellentissimae maiestatis auxilia,
    dum adversarios eius velut proprios comprimitis inimicos.'
    Compare ibid. *Ep.* 238 of 26 March 521.

37 One of their leaders, Philoxenus of Doliche in Syria, a friend
    of Severus, went over to the Chalcedonian side after the
    conferences. This, however, was to be cancelled out in 536 by
    the adhesion of Anthimus of Trebizond, who had been on the
    Orthodox side, to the Monophysite cause.

38 Zacharias, *HE*, IX.15.

39 Severus, recorded by John of Ephesus, *Lives of Five Patriarchs*,
    ed. E. W. Brooks, *PO*, XVIII, p. 687.

40 John of Ephesus, *Lives of Eastern Saints*, PO, XVIII, p. 518.

41 John of Ephesus describes her as 'desirous of furthering
    everything that would assist the opponents of the synod of
    Chalcedon,' and states that she was responsible for the con-
    secration of James Bar'adai and Theodore as bishops in 542,
    Life of James and Theodore, ed. E. W. Brooks, *PO*, XIX, p. 154.

42 The text of two letters allegedly written by Vigilius 538–40
    are preserved in Victor Tonnunnensis (*Chron.* ad ann. 542)
    and Liberatus, *Breviarium* XXII. Discussed by E. Schwartz,
    Zur Kirchenpolitik Justinians, p. 58. For Vigilius's confession
    of orthodoxy, see *Coll. Avell., Ep.* 92 of September 540 to
    Justinian, and *Ep.* 93 to Menas of Constantinople.

43 Theophanes, *Chron.*, A.M. 6039 (Bonn ed.) pp. 349–50.

44 On Askidas's motives, see Liberatus, *Breviarium*, XXIV, and on
    his influence over Justinian, see Evagrius, IV, 38. For the fifth
    general council, see the narrative in Hefele-Leclerq,
    III.I, pp. 1ff.

45 See R. A. Markus, 'Reflections on Religious Dissent in North
    Africa during the Byzantine period,' *Studies in Church History*,
    III (Leiden 1966) pp. 140–50.

The Tenth Century
in Byzantine-Western Relationships

KARL LEYSER

Let us first of all look at the physical conditions of Byzantine links with western Europe and especially the continental core of it, north of the Alps. The land-route was blocked. The Magyars who poured into the Danubian Basin and Pannonia during the last years of the ninth century, had seen to that.[1] It was not to open again until the first quarter of the eleventh as Rodulf Glaber described in a famous passage of his *History*. 'At that time', when the Hungarians under their king Stephen had turned to conversion, 'nearly all those from Italy and Gaul who wanted to visit the Lord's sepulchre in Jerusalem abandoned the usual sea journey and travelled through this king's country.'[2] He suggests that even the Italians preferred the new route by land. The embassies which the emperor Basil I had sent to the East-Frankish king, Louis the German, in 871 and 873 always met him at Regensburg and they could well have travelled overland.[3] It was the time of the great missions to Moravia and Bulgaria and of almost uninterrupted peace between the empire and its northern neighbours. For much of the ninth century moreover the far-flung south-eastern marches of the East-Frankish Carolingians and their Slav client lordships bordered upon the Byzantine spheres of influence in Dalmatia and Serbia.[4] The arrival of the nomad warriors and the destruction of the great Moravian principality which was their first deed in Central Europe thus created for Venice that near-monopoly of communications between Constantinople, Lombardy and the Rhineland which she seems to have enjoyed throughout the tenth century. This in itself gives the period a certain claim to be considered as a distinct moment in east-western relationships. If the Venetians were well-prepared for the opportunities which events in the Danubian plain presented to them early in the century, the chrysobull they gained from the emperors Basil II and Constantine in 992 makes it clear that they had used them to the full. By this time they had become agents and carriers on behalf of third parties and picked up much business on their way to Constantinople.[5]

Venice not only controlled the passenger-traffic between north-alpine Europe and Byzantium, she also handled the post. There is an important ducal *decretum* of 960 which enjoined that no Venetian was to carry letters from Lombardy, Bavaria or Saxony or any other places to Constantinople either to the emperor or to any other Greek. Only the customary correspondence from the doge's palace was to pass as usual. For it had happened that letters from the Italian kingdom, Bavaria and Saxony addressed to the emperor had given great offence and that the displeasure they caused was visited also on the carriers, the Venetians.[6] The *decretum* spoke of all this as a recent evil and it is worth remembering that Otto I's envoy, Liudprand, was in 960 detained by the Byzantine authorities at Paxos and unable to reach Constantinople.[7] It is by no means clear why Romanus II and Otto were on bad terms at this moment. Could the Byzantine government have got wind of the Saxon king's missionary plans, the consecration of a Latin bishop who was to be sent to Kiev?[8] It is even less certain why the Italian kings, Berengar II and his son Adalbert, should have sent offensive letters to the emperors Constantine VII and Romanus II as the *decretum* complained and as Liudprand later asserted in one of his acrimonious conversations with Nikephoros Phokas.[9] Though their relations with the Macedonian dynasty had been bad they needed allies now against the coming invasion from the north.

The *decretum* about the posts between Venice and Byzantium carried a large number of *signa* headed by the doge's and besides the patriarch of Grado and his bishops, sixty-five laymen gave it solemnity and force. Its tenor suggests that there could be correspondence between the princely courts of the West and the emperor's without the trouble and expense of embassies, or even messengers. Berengar and Adalbert, who, if Liudprand is to be believed, had a reputation for meanness, may have sent their letters to Constantinople by private Venetian channels rather than their own envoys. In 968 the bishop of Cremona, on the mission made famous by his polemic, expected to be able to communicate with the Ottonian court from Constantinople either by letter or by courier.[10] Venice sometimes also transmitted news from the East to the distant centres of the Franco-Saxon kingdom. It was one of her doges, Petrus Candidus II, *imperialis consul et senator*, who in 932 addressed a letter to King Henry I and Archbishop Hildibert of Mainz with the news of some strange and miraculous events in Jerusalem which were to lead to the conversion of the Jews. Petrus Candidus's call for their baptism or expulsion came as from an imperial dignitary and a synod at Erfurt in 932 duly took notice of it.[11] In distant Ottonian Saxony the place of Venice in all dealings with the East is sometimes casually reflected in the chronicles. Under the year 1017 Thietmar of Merseburg entered into his *Chronicon* with his own hand a note that four great Venetian ships, loaded with spices and dye-stuffs, had been lost at sea.[12]

This by no means exhausts Venice's role as the successful broker and agent of Byzantium's relationships with the West in the tenth century. Once at least, in 967, Otto I used a Venetian, Dominicus, perhaps the *presbyter et cancellarius* of the 960 *decretum*, as his envoy to Nikephoros Phokas, who later told Liudprand of Cremona that the ambassador's promises had caused him to abandon a planned expedition against the Ottonian invaders of Byzantine territories in southern Italy. He was already marching through Macedonia. Liudprand reveals that Dominicus had exceeded his instructions and given away too much so that the Saxon emperor repudiated his engagements.[13] Such tactics would not have been uncharacteristic of Otto who had employed them before. If Nikephoras really meant what he said about his campaign-objective in 967, Dominicus would have done Otto I a signal service in deflecting the basileus with promises. For as the Byzantine conquests advanced in the tenth century the distances between the Asiatic and the European theatres of war grew larger. More than ever campaigns had to be planned far in advance and once abandoned could not be easily resumed. How much the services and goodwill of the Venetian ducal palace were in demand both amongst the Ottonians and the Macedonian emperors can be seen from the pages of John the Deacon's chronicle, especially his account of Peter II Orseolo's reign. Otto III belatedly became the *compater* of the doge's son Peter who at his confirmation in Verona in 996 took the name Otto and when the emperor visited Venice secretly in 1001 he stood godfather to one of his daughters.[14] To counter this invasion of his sphere of authority Basil II in 1005 insisted that Peter Orseolo's most important son John, who had in 1004 become his father's colleague, should marry a Byzantine princess, an Argyros, at Constantinople and reside there for a season. He himself, a kinsman of the bride, furnished the wedding feast.[15] Now the spiritual relationship of *compaternitas* created bonds not only between godchild and godfather but also between the latter and the child's parent. After 996 Peter Orseolo appears as Otto III's *compater* in the diplomata which the Saxon emperor gave to the doge, and John the Deacon, the adroit manager of their connections, made much of this relationship in his chronicle.[16] In 1004 moreover, Henry II, Otto's successor, took care to renew it when he sponsored the confirmation of another ducal son who then became his namesake.[17] This happened at Verona and the parallel with the act of 996 is very striking. The great Byzantine marriage of the Orseoli in 1006 therefore must be seen as a challenge to all this Ottonian *compaternitas*. Basil II did more still. Whereas in the past the sons and successors of doges on their visits to Constantinople had only been given the court rank of *protospatharios*, the

young John Orseolo was made a *patricius*. At the same time the
emperor was ostentatiously less generous to his younger brother,
the godchild of Otto III.[18] There was already something strained
in the links which tied Venice to Byzantium and John the Deacon
wrote that this festive journey and the marriage took place only
after many entreaties from the emperor so that in the end the
Orseoli had to accept the invitation.[19]

Travellers of whatever kind then between western Europe and
Byzantium in the tenth century went by sea for a good part, if not
the whole of the way. The only time when a doge's son – it was in
913 – tried to return overland from the customary visit to the imperial palace was not an encouraging experience. As he was about
to enter Croatian territory, Michael, the ruler of the Zachlumi,
captured him, seized all the rich presents which stood for both his
importance and his clientage in Byzantine eyes and, worst of all,
handed him over to Symeon of Bulgaria.[20] He could be recovered
at a price. Yet the sea-journey too was not to be chanced lightly or
for pleasure. It took at least twenty-four days, the recorded best
time in this period (Liudprand's in 949) and at worst, Liudprand's
return in 968/9, well over three months. Leo, the *synkellos* and
later metropolitan of Synada, in the second letter he wrote from
his embassy to Rome and Otto III's court in 997, mentioned that
he had suffered ship-wreck in mid-sea and Bishop Bernward of
Würzburg, Otto III's envoy to Basil II in 995, according to one
source succumbed to an epidemic on board ship on his way to
Constantinople. By other accounts he and a large number of his
companions died on Euboea.[21] Liudprand of Cremona had to en-
dure contrary winds at Lepanto but suffered far worse delays at the
hands of imperial officials and agents along his route in 968. Their
chicanery and ill-will wrung from him many a tear and curse and,
if we can accept his story, greatly aggravated the dangers and increased the expenses of his way home to the Ottonian court and
his see.[22] Yet this too must be counted as one of the risks of the
journey. Whether the route led through Thessaly or hugged the
coasts and islands, the Byzantine authorities controlled travellers
and meted out facilities according to the quality of their papers and
recommendations. When the doge Peter Orseolo's sons and the
Argyros bride returned home they received help and attentions all
along so that they must have had an exceptionally well-favoured
and easy journey.[23]

For aristocratic and exalted churchmen like Archbishops Gero
of Cologne, Arnulf of Milan and Bishop Werner of Strassburg to
be sent to Constantinople by the Ottonian and Salian emperors
was perhaps an honour, certainly an opportunity to acquire new
relics for their sees but also a possible sentence of death. Liudprand

himself may have died on the mission which was to bring Theophano, John Tsimiskes's niece, to Italy for her wedding with Otto II.[24] In 1027 Bishop Werner of Strassburg set off for Constantinople as Conrad II's ambassador in search of another marriage alliance. The land-route through Hungary was by this time open but not for him and his large train of attendants and livestock which he had collected for the journey. Refused entry by King Stephen he had to cross the Alps and attempt the uncongenial sea journey from Venice after a long delay in the march of Verona. He had a wretched passage down the Adriatic and died in Constantinople in October 1028 without having visited Jerusalem as he had hoped to do with the *basileus*'s help. With Constantine VIII's death shortly afterwards the embassy finally lost its purpose for the Salians and the letter with the golden bull which Bishop Werner's colleague, Count Manegold, brought home with him was thus dearly bought.[25]

So far we have looked mainly at the agents and means and it is time now to look at the heart and substance of Byzantine-western relationships in the tenth century. The Greeks had seen Charlemagne's empire come and go. It had made a profound impression on them, much deeper than Theophanes's ironical and caricaturing description of Charles's coronation and anointment at Rome in 800 would suggest. 'Rome', so he dismissed the distasteful business, 'is now in the power of the Franks', and this meant barbarians.[26] More than three centuries later John Cinnamus with greater bitterness and anger echoed and enlarged on this theme. Yet the '*basileus* of the Franks', as Theophanes called Charlemagne once and once only, left a legacy that could not be ignored. Barbarians though the Franks were, they and their heirs differed, ever since the creation of the Carolingian *Reich* and its church, from the barbarians of the steppes and the German peoples of the migrations that had once been, and were still, so to say, on the books of the empire, Leo VI's *Tactica* for instance. For although Charlemagne's Italian and East-Frankish successors were by now far less dangerous than the Bulgars, their place amongst the *ethne*, the peoples surrounding Byzantium, remained a problem to the Byzantine authorities. In the *Kletorologion* of Philotheos of 899, for instance, it appears at first sight that Frankish envoys ranked below Bulgarian ones at the imperial court but the *atriklines*, the official responsible for protocol at state banquets, had to distinguish carefully between Franks holding appointments (*cheirotonias*), in the first place bishops, and those who did not (*paganoi*). The former were to be called and seated as befitted their rank.[27] In a scheme of gradations otherwise so clear, here was a trace of vagueness.

The Franks' special relationship with the papacy, of which the *basileis* owned themselves to be the spiritual sons, was founded on new ideas and uses of late-Roman antiquity that were wholly irreconcilable with the divine mission and universality of the one Roman Empire the Byzantines knew to be theirs and theirs alone.[28] Much of Byzantine policy towards the West in the ninth and tenth centuries was concerned not so much with territorial interests and frontiers or alliances against the Arabs in the central Mediterranean as with finding some acceptable theory or formula, some idiom from a vast arsenal of diplomatic devices by which the ideological challenge could be fitted into the traditional but vigorous political philosophy of the Christian Roman Empire of Constantine's heirs. Frontiers were negotiable and legal fictions for letting barbarians keep possession of them always at hand, provided the intruders conformed in other and more important ways to the scheme of things and values in the Byzantine world. Most of the *ethne* accepted the conventions of an ideal order of relationships between the emperor and themselves which the Greeks had fashioned; only the Franks, encouraged by the papacy, had begun to dissent.[29] There is some irony in the Franco-Byzantine settlement of 812 when it was Charlemagne who made territorial concessions: he abandoned Venice which he could not have held in any case but insisted on addressing his hard-pressed Byzantine opponent as 'brother' and on receiving from Michael I Rangabe's ambassadors an endorsement of the *nomen imperatoris* and the *laudes* which belonged to it.[30] The scars of this great breach struck into the wall of Byzantine self-consciousness can be traced in the tenth-century compilations of the emperor Constantine Porphyrogenitus. The heirs of the Carolingians, now once more local kings but still with larger horizons and sense of opportunities, the 'king of Saxony', the 'king of Bavaria' or of 'Gaul' and 'Germany', all these were still addressed as spiritual brothers and letters to them began with a solemn invocation. Against this the *basileus Bulgarias* remained a spiritual son.[31] To the Byzantines the latter meant a warmer relationship and closer dependence on the Roman Empire, to the Franks their spiritual brotherhood spelt an ascent towards equality.[32]

German scholarship has devoted much ingenuity to interpret all these forms of address collected in Book II, ch. 48 of the *Book of Ceremonies* and to identify the situations and embassies when they may have been employed.[33] By the early tenth century their term *rex* had come to denote for the Greeks in the main one of the Christian rulers of the Frankish kingdoms as against the *archontes* of, say, the Magyars or (before 927) the Christian Bulgars, but was it applied also to the dukes who were gaining kingly powers in some regions of the former Carolingian *Reich*? For the history of the new political order in the West and its ties with Byzantium this is of some importance. What then are we to make of the 'king of Bavaria', seemingly the most incongruous and unaccountable *inscriptio* in the list of addresses? It could not well have been the emperor Arnolf (887–99) for he was more than a local *rex* in a fraction of the Frankish *Reich*.[34] For a time at least he became once more something like a king over 'Great Francia', as the Byzantines called it, who forced his way into Italy and Rome to be crowned by Pope Formosus. The embassies sent to him in 894 and 896 speak for his importance in Leo vi's calculations.[35] Possibly the *rex Baioure* was the Liutpolding Duke Arnulf (907–37), Henry i's rival. In 933 he invaded northern Italy, called by the count and bishop of Verona in search of a new king. Although Hugh of Arles drove him out he threatened to come back and this alone might have persuaded the emperor to take notice of him.[36] Most likely however the 'king of Bavaria' in the *Book of Ceremonies* was none other than Otto i's own brother, Henry, to whom he gave the Bavarian *ducatus* in 947. By 952 Henry had acquired a large stake in Italy, the marches of Aquilea and Verona. Above all his daughter Hadwig was meant to become the second western bride of the young emperor Romanus ii, Constantine's son. Henry's regal ambitions were not only made manifest in two great risings against his brother but they received also a kind of recognition in Ottonian house historiography and even from Otto i himself. When the duke of Bohemia was forced to submit in 950 he was placed under Henry's lordship.[37] Otto, so Widukind wrote, 'made peace and concord' with his brother (947) and he has them both rule together harmoniously, advancing the *res publica* and fighting enemies. They shared a *paterna potestas* over their *cives*.[38] Bavaria was and remained a *regnum* in the usage of Ottonian writers. Some of this must have been known in Constantinople and the Byzantine embassies sent to the *Reich* in 949 and 952 may well have brought letters to Henry, the possible father-in-law of a Macedonian emperor, addressing him as king. Was he not said to have been 'formidable even to the Greeks' in Ruotger's *Life of Brun*? It seems as if Ruotger in this very phrase alluded to some special honours which the Byzantine envoys paid to Otto's brother.[39] The Greeks preferred many *reges* in *Francia* to a single, all-powerful one. However those historians who have made the indivisibility of kingship the foundation-stone of a new *regnum Teutonicorum* rising under the Saxon rulers, may find some comfort in a famous passage of the *De Administrando Imperio* (30/73) where the White Croats were described as subject to Otto, 'the great king of *Francia* and Saxony.' Yet to the Byzantines a *megas rex* like a *megas basileus* might have kings of lesser rank under him.[40]

Too much weight should perhaps not be placed on every expression the learned emperor used. When he enlarged on the family history of his son's first wife, Bertha-Eudocia and of her father King Hugh, he mentioned that Berengar I had enjoyed a *basilea* in Italy (though he shared it with Rudolf of Burgundy) and that the elder Bertha, Hugh's mother, had ruled 'imperially' for ten years after the death of her husband, Margrave Adalbert of Tuscany.[41] These were ambiguous terms. The fragmentation of Carolingian kingship, the murderous wars between the kins and affinities of its representatives from 875 onwards and more still after the death of Arnolf in 899, seemed to restore Byzantium to her former place in the West of their own momentum. At least they offered her great opportunities to re-unite western Rome and perhaps the whole Italian kingdom with Constantinople. It is characteristic for the empire's orientation in the tenth century that it never made any exceptional or all-out effort to seize these openings. There were several good reasons for this. At first the shattering aggressive power of the Bulgarians under Symeon confronted it with greater necessities nearer home and then the progressive decline of the caliphate of Baghdad with far greater chances and hopes in Asia. What was happening along the empire's frontiers in Asia Minor and Armenia did not altogether differ in kind from the splintering of lordship and the diminution in the size of armies typical of the late- and post-Carolingian West, especially Italy. In the East too the Empire's enemies tended to become less formidable. Local dynasties, like the Buyids and the Hamdanids, took over positions at the centre which they could not fully hold so that authority and government broke into smaller and less resilient shares for untrustworthy subordinates and military adventurers. The empire only needed a few determined and active rulers, such as it found in Romanus I Lecapenus, Nikephoros Phokas and John Tsimiskes, to seize the territorial spoils. By comparison the situation in Italy was far less tempting. For despite the emperor Basil's gains in Apulia and Calabria between 876 and 886, Byzantium's South-Italian stake had been much reduced by the loss of nearly all Sicily and the unending attacks of the Arabs against the coasts of the mainland, especially Calabria.[42] The Greeks were fighting on more than one front here. Their Italian subjects suffered much and many coastal settlements had to be abandoned for the safer hill-tops. Sometimes even the capital of the Calabrian theme, Reggio, where the Fatimite general and emir of Sicily, Hasan, in 952 enforced the building of a mosque, had to be evacuated. The population did not love its Byzantine governors and their soldiery. The satellite principalities to the north, especially Capua-Benevento and Salerno, were unreliable although their cultural and social bonds with

Constantinople remained close.[43] Their rulers received court ranks and mandates (*keleuseis*) rather than letters (*grammata*) from the *basileus* but the empire's standing with these princes rested on its successes and failures against the Arabs and here much depended on naval supremacy. To Otto I's ambassador Nikephoros Phokas could indeed boast that he alone possessed maritime power and skills, but in the fighting round Calabria and Sicily the units of the Byzantine fleet often came to grief, not least of all his own in the Straits of Messina in 964.[44] His attempt to save the last Greek stronghold in Sicily, Rametta, ended in disaster. It was in this direction that his great successor, Basil II, near the end of his life wanted to lead an expedition in person, not against the Lombard principalities and the outposts of the Ottonian *Reich*.[45]

Yet even if none of the tenth-century masters of Constantinople wanted to fight Justinian's wars over again, they never ignored or wholly neglected the corrupt and seedy, but at the same time sophisticated, struggles for possession, both in the *regnum Italicum* and at Rome. The resources they employed were modest, but they could always count on a large clientage on the spot. Until the Ottonians and their mixed armies of Saxons, Slavs, Lotharingians, Suabians and Bavarians arrived, Byzantine influence and management were paramount however much a Berengar of Friuli, Hugh of Arles and the Roman *princeps* Alberich sought to be masters in their own houses. For it must be said that if the Greeks had not forgotten Charlemagne nor had these hardfaced and unscrupulous contenders for the Italian kingdom and for Rome, their margraves and counts, all recruited from the Carolingian immigration aristocracy.[46] Berengar I's panegyrist, writing shortly after 915, lost no time in presenting his hero as Charlemagne's descendant and he had the last emperor Charles (*ob* 888) on his deathbed point to Berengar as his true successor in Italy and Rome to whom the great would submit. At his Roman coronation he and Pope John X could be likened to Constantine and Sylvester, only the times had changed for the worse.[47] Hugh of Arles did everything in his power to gain imperial coronation and effective control over the city which Berengar never had, first by marrying the foremost of the Theophylacts, the *senatrix* Marozia, and when this failed, by ceaseless military pressure. Even Charlemagne's embassies and exchanges with the Abbasid caliphate found a strange echo in this small circle of Carolingian descendants and their affinity. Early in the tenth century Hugh of Arles's mother, the elder Bertha, of whom Constantine Porphyrogenitus wrote with so much respect, sent a letter by a Moslem captive to the caliph al-Muqtafi (902–8) with overtures for an alliance against Byzantium. In it the margravine of Tuscany spoke of Rome as part of her lordship and claimed

D

that her forces were stronger than those of the empire. Bertha's envoy conveyed the secret substance of her message by word of mouth, as was customary. She received a gratified, if guarded reply.[48]

Judicious deployment of their naval squadrons in the Tyrrhenian and above all diplomacy were the means by which the emperors secured their influence during the first half of the tenth century and maintained a footing in Rome even during the second. King Hugh's match with Marozia in 932 crossed a plan to ally her daughter to one of Romanus Lecapenus's sons.[49] This might almost have restored Byzantine authority in Rome had not both schemes been thwarted by the revolt of Marozia's son Alberich. He in turn however sought a Greek marriage. To impress his future bride and her escort and perhaps also to have hostages from the insurgent Roman aristocracy he seems to have conscripted a number of noble girls from Rome and the Sabina to serve in his household.[50] When Alberich's son and heir to his regime in Rome, Pope John XII, wanted to shake off Otto I's protection, he turned to Constantinople.[51] In 997 Basil II's envoy, the *synkellos* Leo, writing to friends and dignitaries in Constantinople, claimed that the elevation of Johannes Philagathos as anti-pope had been his work.[52] Johannes, a Greek from Rossano, was a protégé of the Ottonian court-circle for many years and owed the abbey of Non-antula and the see of Piacenza to its favour but the expelled pope, the Salian Gregory V, was Otto III's kinsman, his own choice for the Holy See and his *coronator*. The *synkellos*'s letters do not reveal either his doings or his designs very clearly but in one of them, addressed to the patriarch of Constantinople, he boasted that Rome was now in the hands of the great sublime emperor [Basil II] and that God had moved the heart of the Crescentius who was responsible for Gregory V's expulsion.[53] Johannes Philagathos had become the instrument of the Roman ruling family which had already in 974 and again in 984 seized control of the papacy through a clerical henchman and ruffian, the deacon Franco. The Crescentii, like their predecessors, seem to have maintained useful and close connections with Byzantium. When Franco as Pope Boniface VII found the Holy See untenable in 974 he fled to southern Italy and after another abortive coup in 980, to Constantinople. With Byzantine money he was able to make a further attempt in 984, after Otto II's death and this time he held the papacy for over a year.[54] The popes whom he and the Crescentii captured, imprisoned and killed were sanctioned or chosen by the Ottonians. That Philagathos and Crescentius II Nomentanus had been the agents of Byzantine designs in 997 was the view of Arnulf of Milan and Benzo of Alba in the eleventh century.[55] The Greeks were thus able to create difficulties for the new masters of Rome at all times and the Saxon emperors' hold there remained precarious. It might be argued that neither side could harm the other very much at the furthest distance and limit of power from its native centre. Yet Rome was for both more than a frontier city in central Italy.

Let us return to the less devious and more public dealings of Byzantine diplomacy with the Rome of the West. In the collections of the *Book of Ceremonies* the reception of embassies sent by the Roman patriarch and the *princeps* Alberich to Constantinople, holds an important place. It heads the chapter dealing with the arrival of envoys. At the presentation audience the *princeps* of Old Rome had to be referred to as *endoxotatos* by the logothete.[56] In Philotheos's *Kletorologion* this epithet belonged to the order of the *magistroi* which was listed immediately before the dignities reserved to the imperial family.[57] When the greetings on behalf of the reigning pope, his bishops and clerks had been spoken by the envoys, the Roman *princeps* and his *archontes*, the allied nobles who shared offices and power under him had their 'most faithful services' (δούλωσιν) presented to the emperor. Nothing could express the purposes and suit the proprieties of Byzantine state ceremonial and the ideas behind it better. Underneath these formalities it is clear that from time to time Roman aristocratic society in the tenth century still looked to the court of Constantinople for favours and help. Its new autonomy was not wholly irreconcilable with a distant membership of the empire.[57a]

The same impression is conjured up by another text in the *Book of Ceremonies*, the *état* of the fleets and military missions which were despatched by Romanus Lecapenus in 934 and 935 to overawe the rebellious princes of Salerno and Benevento and the disloyal subjects of the theme Langobardia and also to secure King Hugh's alliance and help.[58] The *patrikios* Kosmas came with a mixed squadron of ships, including seven Russian transports and his force consisted of small detachments from every kind of unit in the imperial army. There were horsemen from the themes Thrakesion and Macedonia as well as guards and almost all the *gentes* in the empire's service for pay contributed a few score men: Pharganoi, Chazars, African Moslems and Sicilians, Magyars and some Armenian volunteers. There were also a few engineers.[59] This glittering variety of armament, dress and tongues served a purpose. Together they displayed the universality and cosmocratic horizons of imperial rule. The grandiose spectacle which normally awaited foreign envoys in Constantinople was here exported from the palace to show the local Italian rulers where they belonged. The account of the *protospatharios* Epiphanios's mission to Hugh of Italy in 935 listed the presents intended for the king and then those which were to be given to the margrave of Spoleto, seven counts and six bishops.[60] Hugh's entourage and his treacherous vassals received as much attention as their master and again there is a strong suggestion of clientage in the munificence and also in the make-up of the gifts which included items of Byzantine court dress.[61] Epiphanios carried with him an additional store of presents which he could employ on his expedition, perhaps to gratify important insurgents when they made their submission. He accounted for what he had spent and returned the rest.[62] These tactics of diplomacy and bribery, combined with a demonstration of force, seem to have been successful: the disaffected princes were pacified, the provincials of the theme subdued. In 938 Epiphanios, the *patrikios* Kosmas and the *strategos* of Langobardia can be found at Benevento making a grant to its bishop.[63]

It has been thought that only those occidental rulers who had interests or aspirations in Italy and Rome were flattered by these imposing Byzantine diplomatic missions which later the Ottonians and Salians had to repay in kind if they wished to be seen as equals of the *basileis*. Their ambassadors could not appear in any less splendour and lavishness.[64] Now it is true that between 899, the year of the emperor Arnolf's death, and 945 we hear nothing of Greek embassies to the East-Frankish kingdom with but one possible exception. In Widukind of Corvey's *res gestae Saxonicae* there is a stray note about one of the abbots of his house, Bovo II (900–16): he earned fame because he was able to read and translate a Greek letter for King Conrad I.[65] W. Ohnsorge believed that it was brought to the East-Frankish court by envoys of Leo VI in 912.[66] It is not easy to see however what the ageing and ailing emperor can have wanted from the successor of Louis the Child who, at the very beginning of his reign, faced desertions and a diminution of his kingship. He could not have done much to help Leo's Carolingian protégés and kinsmen by marriage, Louis the Blind and his son, Karl Constantine.[67] We have seen that Venetians sometimes carried correspondence from the East-Frankish kingdom to Byzantium and, no doubt, also in the reverse direction. Could it not be therefore that Conrad received an imperial letter brought by a returning traveller, a merchant perhaps, rather than an emissary of rank from the court of Constantinople?[68] The Byzantine chancery's *grammata* to foreign rulers were often documents of great solemnity and splendour but it is questionable whether this one was more than a fleeting incident in the troubled reign of Conrad I which but for Widukind's interest in abbot Bovo's scholarship stirred no memories.[69] Although one or two Greek monks and guests can be found at Reichenau *c.* 920, Byzantine links with Francia were at this time tenuous. Henry I received no embassies from the empire nor do we know how the doge's letter was presented to him. Perhaps his acquisition of the Holy Lance in 935 and his planned journey to Rome were to prepare his entry into this larger world of cultural riches and superior political skills, presided over by Byzantium. When the first Greek envoys did arrive at the Ottonian court, on October 31 945, they aroused much interest. They came *cum muneribus*, as ambassadors should.[70] Otto I had for some time given shelter to a dangerous enemy of King Hugh of Italy, margrave Berengar of Ivrea and Hugh's daughter was now the wife of Constantine's son. More likely however the embassy wanted to make known the Porphyrogenitus's sole rule after the removal of the Lecapenoi and to treat with the Saxon king about the Magyars who were raiding the lands of the empire. Other envoys, as we have seen, followed in 949 and 952 and again in 956 when Widukind of Corvey, in the best Carolingian tradition, recited their gifts, not to make Otto appear as the client of the Greeks but to proclaim the fame of his victories and the *dilatatio* of his empire.[71] Perhaps the more fulsome of the two protocols for letters addressed to Frankish kings in the *Book of Ceremonies* was revived to greet Otto on this occasion. In the *intitulatio* it enlarged on the supremacy of the Roman emperors but in the rich flow of honorific predicates for the addressee it recognised the new possessor of Charlemagne's or at least Arnolf's inheritance.[72] As the husband of Adelaide, the widow of King Hugh's son Lothar, Otto was the incoming master of Italy and already in 951 the deprived bishop of Verona, Rather, saw in his invasion a hallowed purpose with an imperial undertone: Otto had aspired to the Italian kingdom only to end injustices (like Rather's expulsion) and to bring back the *rectitudo Christianae legis* and this by imperial *potestas*.[73]

Yet it would be mistaken to confine Byzantine interests and spheres of influence in the West to the horizons of Italy. The forms and style of imperial diplomacy, the all-important flow of precious commodities, works of art and relics which was so much part of them, directly or indirectly, reached the whole of occidental Europe. In the course of the tenth century the ruling families there, new and old, came to accept this style as the norm, the only correct idiom of kingly converse. There is as yet no evidence of any Byzantine embassies visiting either the conquering successors of Alfred or the later Carolingian kings of France fighting for survival.[74] The first known initiative to forge new links between the West-Frankish kingdom and Byzantium came from Hugh Capet. Early in 988 Gerbert drafted a letter for him addressed to the emperors Basil and Constantine. In it Hugh asked for a Byzantine princess, a *filia sancti imperii* which he duly called the Roman

Empire for his son Robert. Neither Gaul nor German – and he meant by them Otto III's men – would harass the empire's frontiers if the alliance came about. This was to be Hugh's main service in return for the bride, besides the expressions of respect and awe the *basileis* always liked to hear from a Frankish king.[75] Here lay indeed new possibilities for the older empire to pare down the claims of the Ottonians, yet no serious negotiations followed this overture. Robert almost immediately afterwards married nearer home.[76] Later his relations with Byzantium seem to have been momentary: a Jerusalem pilgrimage of Bishop Odalric of Orléans gave him the opportunity to exchange amicable messages and presents with the emperor Constantine VIII.[77]

Long before this time however both the Capetians and the kings of Wessex had shared and imitated the usages of Byzantine diplomacy in their dealings with one another. William of Malmesbury in the *Gesta Regum* has described amongst the glories of Athelstan's reign the eagerness with which foreign princes sought the hands of his sisters in marriage. His account, as he himself made clear, closely followed a tenth-century panegyric poem which he both quoted and paraphrased. The suitor of Athelstan's sister Eadhild was Hugh the Great whom William mistakenly called *rex Francorum*.[78] There follows a full list of the presents offered to the king of Wessex by Hugh's princely envoys at Abingdon in 926: perfumes hitherto unknown in England, precious stones, an onyx vase with carved scenes, the sword of Constantine with a nail relic, a banner of St Maurice and a lance, once Charlemagne's which had always brought him victory and was rumoured to have been that of Longinus. There was also a jewelled crown. The relics and their distribution amongst English sanctuaries have left a greater imprint on monastic traditions and histories than the secular gifts.[79] They suggested that the divine favour and the *virtus* that had once been Charlemagne's had now been transferred to Athelstan. Very sacred relics, like particles of the cross, were also amongst the gifts which the emperors sent to western rulers but they were never unaccompanied by articles of secular luxury and display of Byzantine manufacture.[80] Here Duke Hugh's presents to Athelstan clearly reflected the all-pervasive fashions of Byzantine diplomacy. It is likely that his onyx vase was a classical piece which had once belonged to a Carolingian treasure, but an onyx cup was also one of the gifts entrusted to the *protospatharios* Epiphanios for the king of Italy in 935. A remarkable number of onyx chalices of the tenth and eleventh centuries in the treasury of St Mark's, Venice testify to the Greeks' superb craftsmanship and near monopoly in this medium.[81] William of Malmesbury's list of exotic presents had other features in common with Widukind of Corvey's and the *état* in the *Book of Ceremonies*.[82] Ambitious western rulers now had to be seen to possess and to be able to exchange such gifts if their *amicitia* was to be worth courting. Athelstan was said by William of Malmesbury to have sent back to Duke Hugh offerings of almost equal value and renown together with the bride.

How well aristocratic society in the West had come to know and like the gold and the luxurious artefacts of Byzantium appears also from the mid-eleventh-century epic poem, *Ruodlieb*, written at Tegernsee. The author, however, may have been a *monachus palatinus* of Henry iii's clerical entourage for he described the courts of kings and what passed in them in a manner far from hackneyed and commonplace. When the hero of the poem after many signal services takes leave of his lord, the *rex maior*, he received rich gifts including minutely and accurately described Byzantine gold coins and a piece of jewellery closely resembling the so-called necklace of the empress Gisela found at Mainz.[83] Boekler and others have distinguished between the classical, the Carolingian and the Byzantine sources of Ottonian art, and the Mainz treasure has been categorically assigned to Byzantine models.[84] It had the shape of a *loros*, a pendant sash worn by the *basileis* and their empresses which appears in more than one place and form on Ottonian full-page illuminations and ivories. The later Saxon emperors and their Salian successors seem to have adopted it and made it their own just as occasionally they liked to be shown crowned by Christ in their gospel books and sacramentaries.[85]

The precious objects which Greek ambassadors brought with them to gratify and overawe the acquisitive kings of the post-Carolingian West could nurse new styles and artistic experiments. The arrival of a Byzantine princess to marry one of them could do this even better and more besides. Most of the matrimonial projects mooted and endlessly negotiated between the court of Constantinople and Carolingian, Ottonian and Salian rulers came to nothing and this makes the marriage between Otto i's son and *co-imperator*, Otto ii and Theophanu in 972 all the more important. The bride, it is true, was not a *porphyrogenita* and there were men who advised the old emperor not to receive her into his family.[86] She came with a large following and treasure and their presence gave to the Ottonian court a much closer view of its great rival in the East than it had ever possessed before.[87] It did not change the character of relations already well established through diplomacy but it enlarged them. It opened new avenues for Byzantine influence in the small and select circle of the Liudolfing house, their affinity, their favoured prelates and monasteries. The evidence is ubiquitous: the ivories, enamels, jewellery, goldsmith work, illuminated manuscripts and seals of the later Ottonians could not have been commissioned and created without Byzantine models, nor are they belittled by the direct uses, imitations and adaptations of Greek exemplars.[88] For it is equally characteristic of the late tenth-century *Reich* that it had already experienced and absorbed Byzantine teachings in many spheres, not least of all the visual representation of emperorship.[89] These lessons had now become part of its own make-up and so paradoxically strengthened it in its dealings with Basil ii and his successors. The Byzantine influence did not lessen but it encountered increasingly self-conscious and self-reliant native traditions. Yet it could still happen in the middle of the eleventh century when many German *scriptoria* and work-shops had two or three generations' experience behind them that a gold and purple letter which the emperor Constantine ix Mono-machos sent to Henry iii was simply used to decorate an altar in the Salian ruler's new foundation, St Simon and Jude, at Goslar.[90]

With Otto iii the emulation of Byzantine imperial thinking en-tered a new phase, but it was short-lived. Otto, following the *basileis* and traces of the Roman past, conferred offices and titles of rank on Saxon, Italian and unreliable Roman nobles.[91] Amongst the traditions which gathered round his meeting with Boleslas Chrobry at Gnesen in 1000 are some which suggest that he too wanted to found an *oikoumene* and a family of rulers tied to him by brotherhood or *amicitia*.[92] When his cousin Brun whom he had so recently imposed on the Roman Church crowned him in 996, Otto had at least temporarily taken something away from the con-stitutive powers of the papacy in the making of a western emperor. In his palace at Rome he could be seen from time to time dining alone at an elevated semi-circular table.[93] But it was difficult to turn a Saxon king's clerical and lay *comitatus* into a hierarchy of office-holders. In between the solemn crown-wearings and other occas-ions when they wished to stand for the majesty of Christ, the Ottonians had to be very approachable and live informally, not to say gregariously, with those who enjoyed their *familiaritas*. When Thietmar of Merseburg described Otto iii's march to Gnesen only a few years after the event he wrote: 'there came with him Ziazo who was then *patricius*.'[94] We know Ziazo as an East-Saxon noble, most probably a forbear of the Wettins. Otto's titles sat lightly on those who received them and were soon forgotten.

To discover the Byzantine heritage of Theophanu's son we must perhaps look in another direction. The empress's Greeks may have had a share in his early upbringing though it is hard to prove. Certainly Otto possessed something more than a mere spark of that Greek diligence and finesse which in a famous letter he invited Gerbert to rouse and cherish.[95] In the Byzantine world it was very common for a powerful and highly placed layman, even emperors, to have a monk as a spiritual counsellor and friend, a guide with whom to communicate. The charisma of the gifted ascetic who had the vision of God would ensure that he gave the right advice to a troubled penitent.[96] In western monasticism this relationship which often by-passed *ex officio* authority was rare. Here rulers, founders and benefactors wanted to be associated with a monastic community, its prayers and its saints. Most of the monastic reform movements of the tenth and eleventh centuries moreover sought to strengthen the rule, the common life of the institution and to reduce the individuality of its members. The only man in the West who caught something of the spirit of these intimate bonds between Greek monks and great men of the world was Otto III. His short life is full of encounters and close personal associations with monastic saints and spiritual mentors: Ramwold of St Emmeran, Adalbert of Prague, Brun of Querfurt, St Nilus and St Romuald.[97] In the *Lives* of these men, or in the case of Brun his own writings, Otto was an important figure and severally they wanted to claim him as their own and draw him away from his more mercurial clerical friends and counsellors. The emperor sought and followed the rigours of their penitential advice and it is perhaps significant that his relations with abbot Odilo of Cluny, who often visited his court, were friendly but not as close.[98] Here no less than in other respects Otto III was half a Byzantine to whom it had fallen to rule the Saxon *Reich*.

These personal traits and the general enhancement of Byzantine influence in the Ottonian environment were not admired and welcomed by everyone. They aroused both resentments and controversies. Men looked upon Otto III's doings at Rome with mixed feelings as Thietmar dryly observed.[99] Already Widukind of Corvey had held up Greek deceit and trickery when he wanted to explain one of Otto I's military setbacks in Apulia.[100] The infant Otto III's Byzantine descent could be used as a justification to desert his cause in 984 and to accept his cousin, Duke Henry II of Bavaria, as king instead.[101] The empress Theophanu had enemies in the Ottonian family circle, notably her mother-in-law Adelaide and Bishop Dietrich of Metz who seems to have suspected her loyalty when Otto II invaded Byzantine Calabria in 982 and fought disastrously against the Sicilian emir.[102] It was a catastrophe that called for culprits. Liudprand of Cremona was not alone when he attacked the cultural pre-eminence of the Greeks in his *Legatio* by a mixture of grotesque caricature and belittlement. Otloh's *Liber Visionum* and one of the codices containing the *Life of Bernward of Hildesheim* record the vision of a nun to whom Theophanu had appeared and lamented her torments in hell. They were her punishment for introducing noxious Greek luxury, jewellery and fashions into the *Reich* where they had hitherto been unknown. She had led other women into sin because they now desired such things and here lay the burden of her offence. Against this however the emperor Henry III wanted to link his descent with Theophanu's name and for this very reason imitate Byzantine manners and styles.[103]

The princess and her following were not, of course the only Greek immigrés north of the Alps in the tenth century. There is scattered evidence of Greek monks and sometimes refugee bishops not only at Reichenau but also in Lotharingian monasteries and sees, at Dijon and at Cologne.[104] The court of Edgar, whose kingship had imperial overtones, attracted foreigners as that of a ruler over many peoples should. Not only Flemings, Danes and continental Saxons but also a Greek bishop whom the Ely tradition branded as a clerical go-getter, can be found in his entourage.[105] For the most part, however, knowledge of and contact with Byzantium were in the tenth century the privilege of only a few in the West and they prided themselves not a little, as did Liudprand of Cremona, on their expertise.[106] The relationships of the East-Roman and Ottonian courts which had so markedly shaped the tastes and the ambitions of the later Ottos, Henry II and their circle, were exclusive. Diplomacy was the main channel of communication, if not the only one. With the opening of the land route through Hungary in the first decades of the eleventh century all this changed. For it made possible and encouraged the movement of many more pilgrims to the Holy Sepulchre than the sea-journey had attracted in the tenth and all these overland travellers to Palestine had to pass through Constantinople and the imperial provinces on their way. Many of them stayed in the capital to refresh themselves and see the sights. The easier route alone may not explain the rising cult of the Jerusalem pilgrimage as an act of penance and sanctification but its appeal could not have spread without it.[107] The old-established relations between the imperial courts, the solemn embassies, as we have seen, did not come to an end but they were overshadowed now by a far more continuous and extensive traffic of pilgrims from regions, especially France, which had hitherto possessed very little first-hand knowledge of the Greek world. If men had once visited Byzantium in scores, they now did so in their thousands and this created a new atmosphere.[108] An age of diplomacy and highly privileged trade gave way to an age of mass contacts. Gregory VII's famous plan to come to the rescue of Constantinople and the Christian brethren in the East becomes more understandable when it is remembered that his call to arms in 1074 was addressed to princes and nobles quite a few of whom had been there and visited the sanctuaries and relics of the capital.[109] Rodulf Glaber who sang the praises of the new route also saw the new urge to visit the Holy Places as a movement, something unheard of in the past.[110] Moreover it seemed to him that it had begun with the humble, the *ordo inferioris plebis* and spread upwards towards higher ranks of society before reaching the princes and, lastly, women.[111] Rodulf's impressions were faulty in detail but right in the round. A few aristocratic ladies had now and again ventured to Jerusalem in the tenth century but perhaps many more did so in the eleventh.[112] There is some evidence of poor men like the wandering priest Haimerad, of obscure Suabian origin, making the journey at his own prompting.[113]

A few of the more literate pilgrims, especially if they came from Lotharingia or Bavaria, could have read what Liudprand of Cremona had written about the eastern Empire in his *Antapodosis* and *Legatio*. His works spread across the Alps and enjoyed literary success notably in Lotharingia and however much his feelings towards the Greeks changed they became an important source of knowledge about Byzantium.[114] Modern historians here only follow in the footsteps of a Sigebert of Gembloux and other eleventh-century scholars. Yet paradoxically Liudprand's angry polemic, the *Legatio*, belonged to a single moment of the empire's relations with the Roman Church and the Ottonians, a moment that was soon past even for him.[115] It set out to create tensions where there had been little before and it contained also an element of personal vindication. For in the *Legatio* Liudprand has been shown to have joined Pope John XIII's side in the debate about the meaning and purpose of Otto I's imperial coronation.[116] He addressed the Ottonians, father and son, as *imperatores Romanorum* who had toiled for the restoration and exaltation of the Roman Church while the pretended Roman emperor, the *basileus*, slept. Their past services to St Peter had earned him, Liudprand, his safe return home from the dangerous embassy and he called upon them to do more still: Nikephoros Phokas and his patriarch were to be summoned and judged by a papal synod. Otto I and Otto II, both now crowned emperors, should carry out the sentence.[117] Did Liudprand wish to make some amends for his own conspicuous role in the depositions of John XII and Benedict V?

The target of the bishop of Cremona's venom and abuse was Nikephoros Phokas first and foremost and certainly not the Macedonians, the young emperors Basil and Constantine, then under the military ruler's tutelage. In more than one place Otto I's ambassador appears almost as a camp-follower of the legitimist interest.[118] For Liudprand in 968 had friends and contacts in Constantinople from his earlier embassy in 949 and some of the gifts he had to distribute were intended for them. Nikephoros Phokas

paid Otto's ambassador much attention but he also sought to
isolate him and have him watched by his police. It is possible that
the covert purpose of the bishop's mission was to befriend discon-
tented circles, enemies of Nikephoros Phokas's regime in Constantinople, under the guise of conducting official negotiations which
at this moment he and Otto I knew could not succeed.[119] Otto's
policies and campaign in southern Italy had reached an impasse
and here lay a possible way out. Lastly the *Legatio* was written also
to court the interest and loyalty of Italian nobles and clergy who
were accustomed to Byzantine influence, gifts and patronage as the
Liudprand of the *Antapodosis* had been himself. If Nikephoros
Phokas appears as a bad paymaster who despised and mistrusted
his Italian allies, led by the dispossessed Adalbert of Ivrea, it was
because Liudprand hoped to persuade the remaining adherents of
the king that the Greek alliance could no longer be counted on.[120]
The very vehemence of the *Legatio* reveals how delicate and fragile
the beginnings of Ottonian rule in Italy really were.

Against Liudprand's freshness and novelty it is striking that
much of the contemporary Byzantine information about the *gentes*
in the West, the Franks and the Lombards we meet in the emperor
Leo's *Tactica* and in Constantine Porphyrogenitus's *De administrando imperio*, was old and somewhat out of date. It is doubtful
whether Nikephoros Phokas knew or cared about the enhanced
fighting skills of Otto I's mounted warriors as he knew and cared
about the military capabilities of the empire's northern and Muslim
neighbours. All policy is self-regarding, but Byzantium's relationships with the West were inward-looking in a very special way.
Rather than come to terms with changing situations they were
often more concerned with preserving and insulating the exalted,
ideal status of the empire against contamination. This attitude was
quite logical, given that the *basileus* had been entrusted by God
with the direction of the *oikoumene* in earthly life. It belongs not
only to later centuries of economic failure and political powerless-
ness when emperors and their courtiers clutched tenaciously at
the straws of ceremonial and form to safeguard the substance of
the imperial idea. It held good also in the century of Byzantium's
greatest aggressiveness and material gains. In the West it was increasingly resented and here Liudprand may have been influential.
His anger about slights and supposed slights had even been anti-
cipated by Notker of St Gallen in the late ninth century who, like
Liudprand, presented the treatment of Charlemagne's envoys in
Constantinople as inhospitable and humiliating.[121] The literature
of the eleventh-century pilgrimage to Jerusalem liked to dwell on
the sufferings and hardships that had to be endured and overcome
on the way. The German bishops and lay nobles who took part

in the great overland journey to Palestine of 1065 seem to have counted Greek *imperialis arrogantia* as one of these hardships.[122]

NOTES

While being prepared for publication this paper has put on a certain amount of weight. I am indebted to Mr Peter Brown of All Souls College, Mr James Howard-Johnstone of Corpus Christi College, Oxford, Dr Jonathan Alexander of Manchester University and Mr James Campbell of Worcester College for their kind interest, advice and suggestions over points of detail.

1   Constantine Porphyrogenitus, *De Administrando Imperio cc.* 40/31–4 and 42/15–18, ed. Gy. Moravcsik and translated by R. J. H. Jenkins (Budapest 1949) pp. 176 and 182 and vol. II, *Commentary* ed. R. J. H. Jenkins (London 1962) pp. 153ff. For the route from Thessalonica to Belgrade mentioned by the emperor see C. J. Jirecek, *Die Heerstrasse von Belgrad nach Constantinopel und die Balkanpässe* (Prague 1877) pp. 75ff.

2   Rodulf Glaber, *Historiarum Libri Quinque*, III, 1, 2 ed. M. Prou, *Collection de Textes pour servir à l'étude et à l'enseignement de l'histoire* (Paris 1886) p. 52 : 'Tunc temporis ceperunt pene universi, qui de Italia et Galliis ad sepulchrum Domini Iherosolimis ire cupiebant, consuetum iter quod erat per fretum maris omittere, atque per huius regis patriam transitum habere'.

3   *Annales Fuldenses*, ed. F. Kurze, *MGH, SRG* (Hanover 1891) pp. 75 and 81 and [F.] Dölger, *Regesten [der Kaiserurkunden des oströmischen Reiches von 565 bis 1453]*, I, *Regesten von 565–1025* (Munich/Berlin 1924) nos. 489, 491.

  This was also the time of the greatest insecurity along the Dalmatian coastal tracts when Muslim and Slav piracy made the sea-journey especially hazardous. The sea route, however, appears to have carried most of the diplomatic traffic between Charlemagne and Louis the Pious and the Byzantine court. Cf. Charlemagne's letter to the emperor Michael Rangabe in 813, *MGH, Epistolae Karolini Aevi*, II, ed. E. Dümmler (Berlin 1895) p. 556 : 'cum primum oportunum navigandi tempus adveniret, legatos nostros ad tuae dilectae fraternitatis gloriosam praesentiam mitteremus'. The embassy sent in 838 to Venice proceeded to Louis the Pious at Ingelheim in 839.

4   See E. Klebel, 'Die Ostgrenze des Karolingischen Reiches' in *Die Entstehung des deutschen Reiches*, Wege der Forschung, I (Darmstadt 1956) pp. 1–41 and esp. p. 21.

5   [*Urkunden zur älteren Handels- und Staatsgeschichte der Republik Venedig*, I. Theil (814–1205)] ed. [G. L.] Tafel and [G. M.] Thomas, *Fontes rerum Austriacarum, Diplomataria et Acta*, XII (Vienna 1856) no. XVII, pp. 36ff. The text has survived in an atrocious Latin translation. It is noteworthy that in the preamble the Venetians are classified as *extranei*. In general, see [W.] Heyd, [*Histoire du commerce du Levant au Moyen-Âge*], I (repr. Leipzig 1923) pp. 114ff and [A.] Schaube,

[Handelsgeschichte der Romanischen Völker des Mittel-meergebiets bis zum Ende der Kreuzzüge] (Munich/Berlin 1906) pp. 17ff. W. Heinemeyer, 'Die Verträge zwischen dem Oströmischen Reiche und den italienischen Städten Genua, Pisa und Venedig vom 10. bis 12. Jahrhundert', *Archiv für Diplomatik* . . . III (1957) pp. 79ff, and F. Dölger and J. Karayannopulos, *Byzantinische Urkundenlehre, Byzantinisches Handbuch im Rahmen des Handbuchs für Altertumswissenschaft*, III.i.1 (Munich 1968) pp. 94ff.

6   Tafel und Thomas, no. XIII, pp. 17ff. The *decretum* also legislated against the slave-trade but here it only enlarged on an older ordinance of duke Orso's (864–81). For its contents and purpose see also Heyd, p. 112ff, Schaube, p. 16, and R. Cessi, *Venezia Ducale*, (Venice 1940) I, pp. 343ff who suggested that the decree's aims were to thwart anti-Venetian propaganda and the intrigues of exiles no less than postal traffic between the two empires (strictly speaking there was as yet no empire in the West). G. Luzzatto, *An Economic History of Italy*, trans. P. Jones (London 1961) p. 52, thought that only private letters were banned by the decree but that official ones from Lombardy, Bavaria and Saxony could be carried. The text does not encourage this distinction, rather the ducal government wanted to check the enterprise of its subjects who conveyed 'foreign' correspondence to Constantinople, if only for the time being and as a gesture to appease the imperial court.

7   Liudprand, *Antapodosis*, III, 1, in *Die Werke Liudprands von Cremona*, ed. J. Becker, *MGH, SRG* (Hanover/Leipzig 1915) p. 74, and [R.] Hiestand, *[Byzanz und das Regnum Italicum im 10. Jahrhundert, Geist und Werk der Zeiten]*, Heft 9 (Zürich 1964) pp. 211ff, who cannot quite account for the envoy's detention. W. Ohnsorge, 'Otto I und Byzanz', *Mitteilungen des Instituts für österreichische Geschichtsforschung*, Ergänzungsband XX, i. p. 115 and in two papers, collected in his *Abendland und Byzanz* (Darmstadt 1958) pp. 36 and 272, thought that Liudprand's mission in 960 was to secure Otto I's recognition as *imperator Francorum* from Romanus II and that it succeeded. This view, however, wholly ignores the evidence for friction between the two courts, both in the *Antapodosis* (loc. cit.) and in the Venetian *decretum*.

8   This seems to me to be the most likely explanation of the rift. For the consecration of Libutius at Otto I's Christmas court held in Frankfurt in 959 see the continuator of Regino of Prüm, Adalbert of St Maximin, in *Reginonis abbatis Prumiensis Chronicon cum continuatione Treverensi*, ed. F. Kurze, *MGH, SRG* (Hanover 1890) p. 170 *sub anno* 960. Libutius, a monk of St Alban in Mainz, died in 961 before setting out to Kiev. He was replaced by Adalbert of St Maximin himself.

9   Liudprand, *Legatio*, c. 5, p. 178 where Adalbert alone is referred to. Berengar II had died as Otto I's prisoner in 966 while Adalbert hoped to regain Italy and his kingship with byzantine money and ships. Cf. *Legatio*, c. 29, p. 191 and *infra*, p. 48

10   Liudprand, *Legatio*, c. 1, p. 175 and c. 53, p. 203.

11 *M G H, Constitutiones et Acta Publica*, 1, no. 4, pp. 6ff, and cf. no. 3, where however it is made to appear that the news came via Rome.

12 *Thietmari Merseburgensis episcopi Chronicon*, VII, c. 76 ed. R. Holtzmann, *M G H, S R G*, nova series IX (Berlin 1955) p. 492. Thietmar also prided himself a little on being able to tell his readers something about Greek ships, notably what a *chelandia* was and how it was manned. See *Chronicon*, III, c. 23, p. 126.

13 See the continuator of Regino of Prüm, p. 178 *sub anno* 967 and Liudprand, *Legatio*, cc. 25 and 31, pp. 188ff, 192, B. A. Mystakidis, *Byzantinisch-Deutsche Beziehungen zur Zeit der Ottonen* (Stuttgart 1891) p. 23, and P. E. Schramm, 'Kaiser, Basileus und Papst in der Zeit der Ottonen', in his collected works, *Kaiser Könige und Päpste, Gesammelte Aufsätze zur Geschichte des Mittelalters*, III (Stuttgart 1969) pp. 204ff. This supersedes the article as first published in the *Historische Zeitschrift*, CXXIX (1924) pp. 424ff. For Dominicus cf. Tafel und Thomas, p. 25 : 'Ego Dominicus, Presbiter et Cancellarius, ex mandato domini Petri Ducis, Senioris nostri, complevi et roboravi'. It is possible that Nikephoros was bluffing and had marched into Macedonia only in order to threaten the Bulgarians while his ally Sviatoslav attacked them from the East. For the chronology of his Bulgarian campaigns see [S.] Runciman, *[The First Bulgarian Empire]* (London 1930) p. 305.

14 John the Deacon, *[La Cronaca Veneziana]* in *Cronache Veneziane*, 1, ed. G. Monticolo, *Fonti per la Storia d'Italia* (Rome 1890) pp. 151ff and 163. See also J. F. Böhmer, *Regesta Imperii*, 11, 3, *[Die] Regesten [des Kaiserreiches unter Otto III, 980 (983)–1002*, M.] Uhlirz (Graz-Cologne 1956) nos 1164d and 1407e.

15 John the Deacon, pp. 167ff, and Georgius Cedrenus, *Historiarum Compendium*, ed. I. Bekker (Bonn 1839) 11, p. 452 : 'τὸ ἔθνος οὕτως ὑποποιούμενος' was the purpose of the marriage. This should be set against the motif of Otto III's godfathership in 1001 : 'ad perfecte . . . fidei vinculum confirmandum'. (John the Deacon, p. 163). For the marriage see also G. Schlumberger, *L'Épopée byzantine à la fin du dixième Siècle* (Paris 1900) 11, p. 323. Maria Argyros and Basil 11 were related through the daughters of Romanus Lecapenus, one of whom, Helena, had been married to Basil's grandfather, Constantine VII, while another, Agatha, became the wife of an Argyros. John the Deacon was right when (p. 168) he described the bride as *imperiali editam stirpe* but wrong when, a little later, he made her Basil 11's niece (p. 169). The only child of the shortlived couple was however duly named Basil (ibid.).

16 See *MGH, Die Urkunden der deutschen Könige und Kaiser*, 11, 2, *Die Urkunden Ottos des III* (Hanover 1893) no. 307 of 999 and no. 397 of 1001. No. 165 of 995 has been doubtfully reconstructed out of no. 307. See also John the Deacon, pp. 154, 161 and 163. On the bond of *compaternitas* between the Carolingians and the popes of the eighth century, see E. Caspar, *Pippin und die Römische Kirche* (Berlin 1914) pp. 39ff.

17 John the Deacon, pp. 167 and 171 and S. Hirsch, *Jahrbücher des deutschen Reiches unter Heinrich II* (Berlin 1862) I, p. 305.

18 John the Deacon, (p. 168): 'Ottonem suum puerulum, qui aderat, fratrem muneribus tantum honoravit.' In the event it was Otto who succeeded Peter II as doge.

19 op. cit., pp. 167ff: 'sedula petitione a Vassylio et Constantino imperatoribus coactus.'

20 op. cit., p. 132. On Michael, prince of the Zachlumi, see *De Administrando Imperio*, c. 33 / 16 and *Commentary*, p. 137 and Runciman, p. 162.

21 For Leo's journey see [P. E.] Schramm, 'Zwölf Briefe [des byzantinischen Gesandten Leon von seiner Reise zu Otto III. aus den Jahren 997–998]', in *Kaiser Könige und Päpste*, III, pp. 257ff and also 262ff with German translations pp. 269, 273. Schramm's edition of the letters follows that of J. Darrouzès, *Épistoliers byzantins du Xe siècle*, *Archives de L'Orient Chrétien*, VI (Paris 1960), no. 10, pp. 171ff. For Bishop Bernward's embassy in 995 see Uhlirz, *Regesten*, no. 1146a.

22 Liudprand, *Legatio*, cc. 58–65 (pp. 207–12). For Liudprand's itinerary on the return journey see V. Menzel, *Deutsches Gesandtschaftswesen im Mittelalter* (Hanover 1892) p. 214. According to Menzel Liudprand went by ship to an eastern Greek port and then overland to Naupacte where (cf. *Legatio*, cc. 58, 59, p. 207) he was made to embark on two boats which which were too small for his party.

23 John the Deacon (p. 168): 'cui Grecorum seu aliarum gentium incole ubique usque ad patriam non denegabant impertiri obsequia'.

24 *MGH, SS*, III, p. 267, n. 23.

25 Wipo, *Gesta Chuonradi II. imperatoris*, c. 22 in *Wiponis Opera*, ed. H. Bresslau, *MGH, SRG* (Hanover/ Leipzig 1915) pp. 41ff: 'tandem cum maximo labore per Venetiam mare Adriaticum ingressus navigio calamitoso Constantinopolim pervenit'. For Bishop Werner and Count Manegold's embassy see H. Bresslau, *Jahrbücher des Deutschen Reichs unter Konrad II.* (Leipzig 1879) I, pp. 234–6 and 271–5, H. Appelt, *Regesten des Kaiserreiches unter Konrad II. 1014–1039*, (Graz 1951) nos 116b and 140a and Dölger, *Regesten*, no. 830. The bishop and the count had set out in the autumn of 1027 and the count returned early in 1029.

26 *Theophanis Chronographia*, ed. C. de Boor (Leipzig 1883) I, pp. 472ff.

27 For the text see [J. B.] Bury, *[The Imperial Administrative System in the Ninth Century]*, British Academy Supplemental Papers I (1911) and reprint (New York, no date) p. 156, lines 17–19. Hiestand's translation and interpretation of Philotheos's remarks on the precedence of Frankish ambassadors (*Byzanz und das Regnum Italicum*, pp. 99ff) cannot stand. He takes χειροτονίαι to mean 'letters of credence' and *paganos* 'heathen'. For the correct interpretation of the latter see Bury, pp. 21ff and R. Guilland, *Recherches sur les institutions byzantines* (Berlin 1967) I, pp. 154ff. What Philotheos had to say about the seating of Frankish bishops is, on the whole, borne out by Liudprand of Cremona. In *Legatio*, c. 11 (p.

181) he complained about his own *placement* at the emperor
Nikephoros's table and that his companions had not even
been allowed to dine in the same house. But they were
paganoi, men who held no office or dignity. See also *Legatio*,
c. 19 (p. 186) where his relegation to a place below the
Bulgarian envoy was explained to him : the Bulgarian,
though dirty and wearing a brass chain, was a *patricius* and
ever since the *basileus* of the Bulgars, Peter, had married
Maria Lecapena (927), Bulgarian ambassadors took precedence over those of all other *gentes*. This was not yet the
practice when Philotheos wrote. The Franks mentioned
by him in Bk iv (p. 160, l. 29) appear to have been in the
Empire's service together with other *ethne*. See H. Ahrweiler,
Byzance et la mer (Paris 1966) p. 206, n. 3.

28   For these problems see F. Dölger, 'Die Kaiserurkunde der
Byzantiner als Ausdruck ihrer politischen Anschauungen',
and 'Europas Gestaltung im Spiegel der fränkisch-byzanti-
nischen Auseinandersetzung des 9. Jahrhunderts', in both his
Byzanz und die europäische Staatenwelt (Ettal 1953, and his Wissenschaftliche Buchgesellschaft, Darmstadt 1964) pp. 9ff and
282ff, W. Ohnsorge, *Das Zweikaiserproblem im früheren Mittelalter* (Hildesheim 1947) and his paper 'Byzanz und das
Abendland im 9. und 10. Jahrhundert. Zur Entwicklung
des Kaiserbegriffes und der Staatsideologie', in *Abendland
und Byzanz*, pp. 1ff. O. Treitinger, *Die oströmische Kaiser-
und Reichsidee* (2nd ed. Darmstadt 1956).

29   On this hierarchy and its history see G. A. Ostrogorsky, 'Die
byzantinische Staatenhierarchie', *Seminarium Kondakovianum*,
viii (Prague 1936) pp. 41ff.

30   Einhard, *Vita Karoli Magni*, c. 28, ed. O. Holder-Egger,
MGH, *SRG* (Hanover / Leipzig 1911) p. 33, and Charlemagne's letters to the emperors Nikephoras i and Michael i
in *MGH*, *Epistolae Karolini Aevi*, ii, ed. E. Dümmler (Berlin
1895) pp. 546ff and 555ff. For the *laudes* see the *Annales
regni Francorum* for 812, ed. F. Kurze, *MGH*, *SRG* (Hanover
1895) p. 136. The best recent survey of Charlemagne's and
Pope Leo iii's conflict and peace with Byzantium is P. Clas-
sen's *Karl der Grosse, das Papsttum und Byzanz* (Düsseldorf
1968).

31   *De Cerimoniis Aulae Byzantinae*, ii, c. 48, ed. I. I. Reiske (Bonn
1829) pp. 689ff and p. 691, and cf. the *salutationes*, c. 47, pp.
681ff.

32   F. Dölger, 'Die "Familie der Könige" im Mittelalter', *Byzanz
und die europäische Staatenwelt*, pp. 39ff and also 'Die mittelalterliche "Familie der Fürsten und Völker" und der Bul-
garenherrscher', op. cit., pp. 167ff. The Bulgar ruler Symeon
at times repudiated the spiritual fatherhood of the emperor,
cf. art. cit., pp. 177ff.

33   See O. Meyer, 'Εἰς τὸν ῥῆγα Σαζωνίας', *Festschrift Albert
Brackmann*, ed. L. Santifaller (Weimar 1931) pp. 123–36 and
the review by Dölger, *BZ*, xxxi (1931) pp. 439–42 and
especially [W.] Ohnsorge, 'Drei Deperdita [der byzantinischen Kaiserkanzlei und die Frankenadressen im Zere-
monienbuch des Konstantinos Porphyrogennetos'] *Abendland und Byzanz*, pp. 227ff.

E

34   This against Ohnsorge (op. cit., p. 247) who would identify
     the 'ῥήξ Βαιούρη' with Arnolf.
35   *Annales Fuldenses*, pp. 125, 130.
36   Duke Arnulf seized hostages at Verona and took them back
     with him to Bavaria. Cf. Liudprand, *Antapodosis*, III, cc. 49–
     52 (pp. 100ff) and K. Reindel, *Die bayerischen Liutpoldinger,
     Quellen und Erörterungen zur bayerischen Geschichte*, Neue Folge,
     XI (Munich 1953) pp. 63ff. It could also be argued that if the
     Emperor Alexander, Leo VI's brother, in 912 sent a letter
     announcing his accession to Conrad I, the reputed *rex
     Germanias*, he may also have addressed one to Arnulf. Cf.
     infra, p. 40 and n. 67.
37   Thietmar of Merseburg, *Chronicon*, II, c. 2 (p. 40): 'fratri
     suimet Heinrico, Bawariorum duci, ad serviendum traditus
     est.'
38   Widukind of Corvey, *Res Gestae Saxonicae*, II, c. 36, ed. P.
     Hirsch and H.-E. Lohmann, *MGH, SRG* (Hanover 1935)
     p. 95 : 'dum unanimes res publicas augent, hostes debellant,
     civibus paterna potestate presunt.'
39   Ruotger, *Vita Brunonis*, c. 17, ed. I. Ott, *MGH, SRG*, new
     series (Weimar 1951) p. 16 : 'ipsis etiam Grecis formida-
     bilem.' The editor connected this with Henry's successful
     offensive against the Magyars in 950.
40   *De Administrando Imperio*, p. 142 and *Commentary*, pp. 97 ff,
     megas here means 'great' or 'superior' rather than 'the elder'.
     For 'megas rex' see Dölger, 'Europas Gestaltung', op. cit.,
     p. 286, n. 7 and Hiestand, p. 208 and n. 77 where however
     Otto's designation as a *megas rex* in the *De Administrando
     Imperio*, c. 30 / 73 is made to do duty for a style not found in
     the *Book of Ceremonies*. W. Ohnsorge, 'Drei Deperdita' (pp.
     234ff), categorically rejected a royal *inscriptio* for Henry in
     952. 'In diesem fränkischen Machtbereich Ottos war für ein
     Königtum Bayern nicht Platz' (pp. 236ff). Yet the regal
     character of the Liudolfing *ducatus* in Bavaria was still re-
     membered in the *eleventh* century. Wolfhere, St Godehard's
     biographer (c. 1035), wrote of the Emperor Henry II's
     father, Duke Henry II, 'qui eandem provinciam acsi regali
     sibi dominatione vendicabat'. See the *Vita Godehardi
     Episcopi Hildenesheimensis prior*, c.I, *MGH, SS*, XI, p. 170.
41   *De Administrando Imperio*, cc. 26 / 37 (p. 110) and 26 / 71
     (p. 112) and Hiestand, pp. 110 and 132. That βασιλεύω was an
     ambiguous term is suggested by Dölger, loc. cit.
42   J. Gay, *L'Italie méridionale et l'Empire Byzantin* (Paris 1904)
     pp. 210ff. For the military and political situation on the two
     fronts in the last years of Constantine VII's reign see A. A.
     Vasiliev, *Byzance et les Arabes*, II, *Les Relations politiques de
     Byzance et les Arabes à l'époque de la dynastie Macédonienne*, I,
     trans. and ed. M. Canard (Brussels 1968) pp. 378ff. For a detailed
     but perhaps sometimes too dramatic account of the Byzan-
     tine-Fatimite wars in southern Italy during the tenth century
     see E. Eickhoff, *Seekrieg und Seepolitik zwischen Islam und
     Abendland (650–1040)* (Berlin 1966) pp. 296ff.
43   [V. von] Falkenhausen [*Untersuchungen über die byzantinische
     Herrschaft in Süditalien vom 9. bis ins 11. Jahrhundert]* (Wies-

baden 1967) p. 34. For the distinction between foreign rulers who received letters and satellite princes who were sent mandates from the imperial palace see Ostrogorsky, 'Die byzantinische Staatenhierarchie', p. 49.

44 Liudprand, *Legatio*, c. 11 (p. 182): 'Navigantium fortitudo mihi soli inest'.

45 See Eickhoff, op. cit., pp. 345–51 and pp. 382ff for Basil II's plans in 1025.

46 For this aristocracy and its continuing connections north of the Alps see E. Hlawitschka, *Franken, Alemannen, Bayern und Burgunder in Oberitalien (774–962), Forschungen zur oberrheinischen Landesgeschichte*, VIII (Freiburg 1960).

47 *Gesta Berengarii Imperatoris*, IV, ll. 151–5, ed. P. Winterfeld, *MGH, Poetae*, IV, i, p. 400.

48 For an excellent account of these exchanges see Hiestand, pp. 11off with German translations of the Arabic texts (pp. 225–9) and also Wattenbach-Levison, *Deutschlands Geschichtsquellen im Mittelalter Vorzeit und Karolinger*, IV, rev. H. Löwe (Weimar 1963) p. 424 and n. 161.

49 G. Fasoli, *I re d'Italia (888–962)* (Florence 1949) pp. 120ff, Runciman, *Romanus Lecapenus*, pp. 192 and 195 where however events are misdated. From the tenor of the emperor's letter it seems probable that it was sent when the news of Alberich's coup had not yet reached Constantinople. Falkenhausen, p. 43, however, agrees with Runciman that Romanus treated the proffered marriage alliance coolly. Cf. also Hiestand, pp. 162–9, Dölger, *Regesten*, no. 625 and H. Zimmermann, *Papstregesten 911–1024*, *Regesta Imperii*, II, *Sächsische Zeit* (Vienna, Cologne, Graz 1969) nos 111, 113. For a general appraisal of imperial diplomacy based on the empire's dealings with the peoples of the northern frontier see D. Obolensky, 'The Principles and Methods of Byzantine Diplomacy', *Actes du XIIᵉ Congrès International d'Études Byzantines* (Beograd 1963) I, pp. 45ff.

50 *Benedicti S. Andreae Chronicon*, ed. G. Zucchetti, *Fonti per la storia d'Italia* (Rome 1920) p. 172.

51 Liudprand, *Historia Ottonis*, c. 6, ed. cit., p. 163 and H. Zimmermann, *Papstabsetzungen des Mittelalters* (Graz, Vienna, Cologne 1968) pp. 81ff, also *Papstregesten*, no. 315. For Adalbert, Berenger II's son, seeking Greek aid see *supra* p. 30 n. 9 and *infra* p. 48.

52 Schramm, 'Zwölf Briefe', nos 1, 2 and 3, *Kaiser Könige und Päpste*, III, pp. 256–60 and 'Kaiser, Basileus und Papst', op. cit., pp. 220–8. For Philagathos's movements before his elevation see M. Uhlirz, *Jahrbücher des deutschen Reiches unter Otto II und Otto III*, II, *Otto III 983–1002* (Berlin, 1954) pp. 511–517. On the whole episode see especially Zimmermann, *Papstabsetzungen*, pp. 105ff. For Johannes's earlier career in the royal chapel see J. Fleckenstein, *Die Hofkapelle der deutschen Könige*, II, *Die Hofkapelle im Rahmen der Ottonisch-Salischen Reichskirche*, *Schriften der MGH*, 16/ii (Stuttgart 1966) pp. 73ff. For further references see Zimmermann, *Papstregesten*, nos 784, 801.

53 Schramm, 'Zwölf Briefe', no. 1, pp. 256ff.

54 On the Byzantine connections of the Crescentii see also G.
    Bossi, *I Crescenzi*, Atti della Pontificia Accademia d'Archeo-
    logia, xii (1915) p.36. For Boniface vii see Zimmermann,
    Papstabsetzungen, pp.99–103 and *Papstregesten*, nos 524–6,
    575, 582 and 630 with ample references.

55 *Arnulfi gesta archiepiscoporum Mediolanensium*, i, c.11, *MGH,
    SS*, viii, pp.9ff: '... De quo [Philagathos] dictum est quod
    Romani decus imperii astute in Graecos transferre temp-
    tasset. Siquidem consultu et ope quorumdam civium Roma-
    norum, praecipue Crescentii praedivitis apostolicam sedem
    iam violenter invaserat.' *Benzonis episcopi Albensis ad Heinri-
    cum IV imperatorem libri VII*, i, c.13, *MGH, SS*, xi, p.604:
    'Tercius denique Otto decollavit Crescentium, et cecavit
    papam Sergium [instead of John], eo quod cum Grecis fre-
    quentabant inlicitum commercium.' Cf. also V. Grumel, 'Les
    Préliminaires du schisme de Michel Cérulaire ou la Question
    Romaine avant 1054', *Revue des Études Byzantines*, x (1952)
    pp.5ff.

56 See *De Cerimoniis*, ii, c.47 (p.680) for the *chairetismoi*
    (formulae of salutation) spoken by the envoys from Rome
    at their first audience and the *interrogatio* by the logothete.
    For the reception of ambassadors in general see Treitinger,
    op. cit., pp.197ff.

57 Bury, p.135 (text) and pp.29ff.

57a In Constantine Porphyrogenitus *De Thematibus*, ed. A.
    Pertusi, *Studi e Testi*, clx (Rome 1952) p.94, written in the
    time of Romanus Lecapenus, papal 'self-rule' in Rome was
    still called an innovation. The historical perspectives of the
    emperor were avowedly lofty.

58 *De Cerimoniis*, ii, c.44, pp.660–2. For the dispatch of these
    small, part naval, part military and part 'diplomatic' task
    forces and the history of Byzantine relations with Capua,
    Benevento, Salerno, Naples, Amalfi and Gaeta see Gay, pp.
    210ff, Runciman, *Romanus Lecapenus*, pp.177ff and Falken-
    hausen, pp.120ff.

59 *De Cerimoniis*, loc. cit. For the Pharganoi see Ahrweiler,
    Byzance et la mer, pp.110 and 397, n.3. For the transports,
    (*karabia*), op. cit., pp.114 and 409. On the *patrikios* Kosmas
    see R. Guilland, 'Les Patrices byzantins sous le règne de
    Constantine vii Porphyrogénète (913–959)', *Silloge
    Bizantina in onore di Silvio Giuseppe Mercati, Studi Bizantini
    e Neoellenici*, ix (1957) p.197.

60 *De Cerimoniis*, loc. cit., pp.661ff. Hiestand (p.171) has Kos-
    mas command a large army and suffer an 'annihilating defeat'
    at the hands of Margrave Theobald of Spoleto with far-
    reaching consequences, a 'renversement' of Byzantine alli-
    ances in Italy *c*.935, which he regards as the purpose of Epi-
    phanios's mission. The only source for such a military catas-
    trophe is Liudprand's *Antapodosis*, iv, c.9 (p.108) but the
    frontier warfare he described there stretched over several
    years and his very brief account of it only set the scene for
    one of his more macabre anecdotes (c.10). If Theobald
    really mutilated a large number of captured Greeks, as Liud-
    prand narrated, it is unlikely that Romanus would have
    honoured him with presents only a year later. The story of

the meeting between Kosmas and the defiant Landulf of
Benevento preserved in Cedrenus, II, 355ff does not bear out
the hypothesis of a crushing Byzantine defeat. There is no
mention of any battle and we are very ill-informed indeed
about the course of these hostilities. In general and for his
comment on this passage see P. Lamma, 'Il problema dei due
imperi e dell'Italia meridionale nel giudizio delle fonti lette-
rarie dei secoli ix e x', *Atti del 3° Congresso internazionale di
Studi sull'Alto Medioevo*, Centro Italiano di Studi sull'Alto
Medioevo (Spoleto 1959) pp. 155ff and esp. pp. 226–9.

61   *De Cerimoniis*, loc. cit., for example the *scaramaggia*, given to
high military and civil dignitaries every year before Palm
Sunday and mentioned frequently also in Philotheos's *Kletorologion* as obligatory dress for various official occasions.
For the annual gifts see Liudprand, *Antapodosis*, VI, c. 10
(p. 158) who was invited to watch the ceremony in 950 on
one of his embassies.

62   Op. cit., p. 662.

63   Falkenhausen, pp. 78ff and no. 10 (pp. 164ff) in her *regestae* of
charters issued by the *strategoi* of Langobardia.

64   When Archbishop Arnulf of Milan entered Constantinople
in 1001 to conclude the negotiations for Otto III's marriage
to a *porphyrogenita* his horse was said to have been shod
with golden shoes. Bishop Werner of Strassburg in 927 then
had to imitate this feat. See Schramm, 'Kaiser, Basileus und
Papst', p. 237, n. 98 and Treitinger, p. 200, n. 179. According
to a less legendary source, Archbishop Arnulf 'satis episco-
paliter conversatus est in urbe regia', *Arnulfi gesta archiepiscoporum Mediolanensium*, I, c. 13, *MGH, SS*, VIII, p. 10.

65   Widukind, III, c. 2, p. 106.

66   Ohnsorge, 'Drei Deperdita', pp. 227ff, and 232ff, 'Byzanz und
das Abendland', pp. 34ff, and n. 128, also *Konstantinopel und
der Okzident* (Darmstadt 1966) pp. 212ff.

67   Leo's illegitimate daughter – not a *porphyrogenita* – was the
first Byzantine princess to marry a Frankish king and future
emperor, Louis III of Provence, who was blinded in 905.
Karl Constantine, count of Vienne (*c.* 901–62), were their son.
On this marriage see Ohnsorge, 'Drei Deperdita', pp. 229ff,
and Hiestand, pp. 90ff, who (p. 125, n. 57) advanced good
reasons for thinking that the letter sent to Conrad I came
from Leo's brother Alexander.

68   It is difficult to mark the boundary between long-distance
trade and diplomatic missions in the first half of the tenth
century. The immediate successors of the Carolingians in
Italy and Germany could not afford their expensive eastern
embassies. (Cf. *supra*, p. 30.) Otto I's earliest ambassador to
Constantinople in 949 was a rich Mainz merchant, and an
experienced slave-trader from Verdun took charge of the
presents on John of Gorze's mission to Córdoba in 953. Cf.
Liudprand, *Antapodosis*, VI, c. 4, p. 154, the *Vita Iohannis
Gorziensis*, cc. 116, 117, *MGH, SS*, IV, p. 370 and the pun-
gent remarks on Liudprand of Cremona's own orientation
in G. Arnaldi's 'Liutprando e la storiografia contemporanea
nell'Italia centro-settentrionale', *La Storiografia Alto-
medievale*, Settimane di Studio del Centro Italiano di Studi

sull'Alto Medioevo, XVII (Spoleto 1970) II, pp. 515ff.

69   Neither the indivisibility of the East-Frankish kingdom in
936 nor the claims of Otto I's brother, Henry *quia natus esset
in aula regali* (*Vita Mathildis Reginae*, c. 9, *MGH, SS*, IV, p.
289) need be connected with the arrival of this letter as
Ohnsorge, op. cit., p. 233, n. 30 and Dölger, 'Die Ottonen-
kaiser und Byzanz', *Karolingische und Ottonische Kunst,
Werden, Wesen, Wirkung, Forschungen zur Kunstgeschichte und
christlichen Archäologie*, III (Wiesbaden 1957) p. 53 suggested.
They have perhaps occasionally claimed too much for Byzantine influence, if only to educate the many historians of the
Ottonian period who, before their fine discoveries, neglected
and ignored it. Hiestand (p. 170) thought it significant that
shortly after receiving the Greek letter Conrad was called
invictus in the protocol of one of his diplomata (*MGH,
Urkunden*, I, p. 17) but although it is singular in his reign the
epithet was at home in the East-Frankish chancery of the
ninth century.

70   *Annales Hildesheimenses*, ed. G. Waitz, *MGH, SRG* (Hanover
1878) p. 20 and 'cum muneribus maximis' in the *Annales
Altahenses maiores*, ed. E. Oefele (Hanover 1891) p. 8 and
Mystakidis, p. 17 where however the embassy is dated 944.

71   For the mission of 949 cf. *supra* p. 35 and E. von Ottenthal,
*Die Regesten des Kaiserreichs unter Heinrich I. und Otto I. 919–
973* (Innsbruck 1893, Hildesheim 1967) no. 174a. For 952
see Liudprand, *Legatio*, c. 5, pp. 178ff. For 956 see Widukind
of Corvey, III, c. 56, p. 135.

72   *De Cerimoniis*, II, c. 48, p. 691, ll. 13–20 and cf. p. 689, ll. 4–12.
On the differences between the two protocols see Ostro-
gorsky, 'Staatenhierarchie', p. 50. The more elaborate and
solemn *formula* also mentioned a golden bull whereas the
simpler one for the *rex Saxonias* etc. omitted it but this may
be due to careless compilation.

73   *Die Briefe des Bischofs Rather von Verona*, ed. F. Weigle, *MGH,
Die Briefe der deutschen Kaiserzeit*, I (Weimar 1949) no. 7,
p. 41, Hiestand, p. 206 and H. Keller, 'Das Kaisertum Ottos
des Grossen im Verständnis seiner Zeit', *Deutsches Archiv
für Erforschung des Mittelalters*, XX (1964) p. 339.

74   On Byzantine relations with Anglo-Saxon England see R. S.
Lopez, 'Le Problème des relations anglo-byzantines du
septième au dixième siècle', *Byz.*, XVIII (1948) pp. 139ff. On
tenth-century English works of art that owed something to
Byzantine prototypes see D. Talbot Rice, 'Britain and the
Byzantine World in the Middle Ages' in *Byzantine Art – An
European Art*, Lectures given on the occasion of the 9th Exhibition
of the Council of Europe (Athens 1966) pp. 33ff.

75   *Die Briefsammlung Gerberts von Reims*, ed. F. Weigle, *MGH,
Die Briefe der deutschen Kaiserzeit*, II (Berlin, Zürich, Dublin
1966) no. III, pp. 139ff, and A. Vasiliev, 'Hugh Capet of France
and Byzantium', *DOP*, VI (1951) pp. 229ff whose genea-
logies however do not convince. Cf. Dölger, *BZ*, XLV (1952),
pp. 467ff.

76   For Robert's marriage to Rozala-Susanna, the daughter of
Berengar II of Italy and Willa, see R. Köpke and E. Dümmler, *Kaiser Otto der Grosse* (Leipzig 1876) p. 380 and n. 2, and

[Ch.] Pfister, *[Études sur le règne de Robert le Pieux (996–1031)]*, B[*ibliothèque de l']É[cole des]* H[*autes]* É[*tudes]*, LXIV (Paris 1885) pp. 43ff.

77 On Bishop Odalric's pilgrimage (between 1025–8) see Rodulf Glaber, *Historiarum Libri Quinque*, IV, c. 6, ed. cit., pp. 107ff, and Pfister, pp. 349, 353.

78 *Willelmi Malmesbiriensis Monachi de gestis regum Anglorum*, II, 135, ed. W. Stubbs, *RS* (1887) I, pp. 149ff. For Hugh the Great's marriage see P. Lauer, *Robert Ier et Raoul de Bourgogne (923–936)*, BÉ HÉ, CLXXXVIII (Paris 1910) p. 45 and C. N. L. Brooke, *The Saxon and Norman Kings* (London 1963), pp. 135ff, where however Baldwin count of Flanders (*ob.* 918) is wrongly named as Hugh's ambassador instead of his son Adelolf. For the poem see [L. H.] Loomis, ['The Holy Relics of Charlemagne and King Athelstan: The Lances of Longinus and St. Mauricius'], *Speculum*, XXV (1950) pp. 437ff.

79 On the relics and their dispersal see Loomis, and 'The Athelstan gift story and its influence on English Chronicles and Carolingian Romances', *Publications of the Modern Languages Association*, LXVII (1952) pp. 521ff. For a commentary on Hugh the Great's presents and on royal treasures in the early Middle Ages see especially P. E. Schramm and F. Mütherich, *Denkmale der deutschen Könige und Kaiser* (Munich 1962) pp. 26ff, 55, 57, 69, 95ff.

80 Bishop Odalric of Orléans received a large particle of the cross and many cloths of silk for King Robert from the emperor Constantine VIII (*supra* n. 77). Henry II had a relic of St Andrew from Basil II. See Ohnsorge, 'Die Legation des Kaisers Basileios II. an Heinrich II.', *Abendland und Byzanz*, p. 301.

81 G. Henderson, *Early Medieval Style and Civilization* (ed. London 1972) pp. 115 ff. In a late twelfth-century Abingdon notice William of Malmesbury's *vas quoddam ex onichino* (*Gesta Regum*, p. 150) has become an *antiquum vas quoddam ex onichino*, *Chronicon Monasterii de Abingdon*, ed. J. Stevenson, *RS* (1858) II, p. 276, n. 7. For the onyx cup sent to King Hugh of Italy see *De Cerimoniis*, II, c. 44, p. 661. The 32 onyx chalices in the treasury of St Marks, Venice, are listed, described and illustrated in A. Pasini, *Il Tesoro di San Marco* (Venice 1886) pp. 54ff.

82 Glass-ware and perfumes figure on Epiphanios's list of gifts for King Hugh and on Widukind's (cf. *supra* p. 40 and n. 61 and Widukind, III, c. 56, p. 135) though it must be remembered that the Saxon writer lumped together presents from Byzantium, Córdoba and Rome. The theme of exotic animals *Saxonibus antea invisa* (loc. cit.) or perfumes *qualia nunquam antea in Anglia visa fuerant* (William of Malmesbury, loc. cit.) presented by envoys from afar, was common ground for writers who wanted to proclaim the rising renown and authority of their rulers.

83 *Ruodlieb*, v, l. 314 and esp. ll. 321ff, ed. K. Langosch, *Waltharius. Ruodlieb. Märchenepen*, 3 ed., Wissenschaftliche Buchgesellschaft (Darmstadt 1967) pp. 132ff. The jewellery is described in v, ll. 351ff, and on p. 373, no. 144 and pp. 168ff in Schramm-Mütherich, op. cit.

84 A.Boeckler, 'Ottonische Kunst in Deutschland', *I problemi comuni dell'Europa post-Carolinga*, Settimane di Studio del Centro Italiano di Studi sull'Alto Medioevo, 11 (Spoleto 1955) p.351.

85 That the *loros* (latin *trabea*) became part of Ottonian imperial dress is shown convincingly by J.Déer, 'Byzanz und die Herrschaftszeichen des Abendlandes', *BZ*, L (1957) pp. 405ff. A fine example is the Cluny ivory showing Otto II and Theophanu crowned by Christ (Schramm-Mütherich, no. 73 and cf. no. 74), another the great image of Otto III in the Reichenau Gospels at Munich (op. cit., no. 108). Whether the golden stole Henry II is shown wearing in the Gospels he gave to Monte Cassino (MS Vat. Ottob. lat. 74) belongs to this genre, is less certain (Schramm-Mütherich, no. 141) but the circumscription '. . . caesar et augustus trabeali munere dignus', suggests that it was some kind of *loros*. Monte Cassino lay in a contested sphere of influence between the two empires and here above all the western emperor wanted to be seen as the *basileus's* peer who saw to it that justice was done. For a different view see K.Hoffmann, *Taufsymbolik im mittelalterlichen Herrscherbild, Bonner Beiträge zur Kunstwissenschaft*, IX (Düsseldorf 1968) pp. 77ff who thought that the emperor is shown wearing a deacon's stole as *rex et sacerdos*. See also H.Bloch, 'Monte Cassino, Byzantium and the West in the earlier Middle Ages', *DOP*, III (1946) pp. 166ff. For a full-page illumination of an emperor, again Henry II, crowned by Christ see H. Jantzen, *Ottonische Kunst* (Munich 1947) p. 103 and pl. 89, the sacramentary he gave to Bamberg.

86 Thietmar of Merseburg, *Chronicon*, II, c. 15, p. 56. The debate about Theophanu's origins and parentage has not yet ended. It is difficult to discredit Thietmar's statement that she was John Tsimiskes's niece and not the bride the Ottonians really wanted. It is corroborated by her dower diploma (*MGH, Urkunden*, II, I, no. 21, p. 29) and Thietmar whose father served the empress had no reason to belittle her. For him she was all the same *immensa nobilitate* (IV, c. 14, p. 148).

87 H. Wentzel, 'Das byzantinische Erbe der ottonischen Kaiser. Hypotesen über den Brautschatz der Theophano', *Aachener Kunstblätter*, XL (1971) pp. 15ff would lead the whole complex of Byzantine objects and works of art associated with Henry II back to Theophanu's bridal treasure. I owe this reference to Dr J.O.Alexander.

88 For brief general surveys see Boeckler, op. cit. (n. 84 *supra*), W.Messerer, 'Zur byzantinischen Frage in der ottonischen Kunst', *BZ*, LII (1959) pp. 32ff, K.Weitzmann, 'Various Aspects of Byzantine Influence on the Latin Countries from the sixth to the twelfth Century', *DOP*, XX (1966) pp. 14–19, O.Demus, 'The Role of Byzantine Art in Europe', *Byzantine Art – An European Art*, pp. 89ff.

89 For example the full-face seals of Otto I after 962 (Messerer, op. cit., pp. 41ff) and Liudprand of Cremona's clandestine efforts to buy purple *pallia* for Otto at Constantinople in 968 (*Legatio*, cc. 53, 54, p. 204). Some of the lessons were older. However much the East-Frankish kings, Louis the German,

his sons and their historian Meginhard frowned on Charles the Bald's emperorship they had taken careful note of his new Greek ways as did Hincmar. See *Annales Fuldenses*, 876 ed. F. Kurze, *MGH, SRG* (Hanover 1891) p. 86 and *Annales Bertiniani*, ed. G. Waitz, *MGH, SRG* (Hanover 1883) pp. 130ff. Regensburg, the workshop of Henry II's sacramentary, in the tenth century possessed the *Codex Aureus* of *c.* 870 with its full-page picture of the enthroned Charles, one of the most splendid creations of his court school. Of the two representations of Henry in the sacramentary, one followed this model (Schramm-Mütherich, cf. nos 52 and 111). If Dr J. M. Wallace-Hadrill is right and Charles's 'interest in Late Antiquity was markedly stronger than his alleged interest in Byzantium', *Early Germanic Kingship in England and on the Continent* (Oxford 1971) p. 132, this source too could strengthen the hand of an Ottonian emperor against his Byzantine peers.

90 W. Ohnsorge, 'Das nach Goslar gelangte Auslandsschreiben des Konstantinos IX. Monomachos für Kaiser Heinrich III von 1049', *Abendland und Byzanz*, pp. 319ff.

91 For a survey of these titles and offices in Otto III's entourage see Schramm's article in *Kaiser, Könige und Päpste*, III, pp. 277ff and C. Erdmann, *Forschungen zur politischen Ideenwelt des Frühmittelalters* (Berlin 1951) pp. 105ff. Both wanted to diminish their Byzantine echoes. In the case of Otto III's *logothetes* Fleckenstein, *Hofkapelle*, pp. 107ff has shown that the young emperor borrowed more than a mere word.

92 The sources are quoted and discussed in M. Uhlirz, *Jahrbücher des Deutschen Reiches unter Otto II. und Otto III*, II, pp. 549ff.

93 Thietmar of Merseburg, IV, c. 47, p. 184 and Schramm, *Kaiser, Rom und Renovatio*, pp. 110ff.

94 Thietmar, IV, c. 44, p. 182 : '... comitantibus secum Ziazone tunc patricio et Roberto oblacionario.' On his identity which has been much disputed I hope to say something in another place.

95 Preserved amongst Gerbert's letters. See *Briefsammlung*, no. 186, p. 222.

96 K. Holl, *Enthusiasmus und Bussgewalt beim griechischen Mönchtum* (Leipzig 1898). I owe this reference to Mr P. Brown.

97 Perhaps the Calabrian monk Gregory, abbot of Burtscheid, should be added to this list but see A. Hofmeister's critique of Gregory's two *vitae* in 'Studien zu Theophano', *Festschrift Edmund E. Stengel* (Münster/Cologne 1952) pp. 238ff.

98 Otto III's quest for spiritual advice and his penances are described in, for example, Peter Damian's *Vita Beati Romualdi*, c. 25, ed. G. Tabacco, *Fonti per la storia d'Italia* (Rome 1957) pp. 53ff, in the *Vita* of bishop Burchard of Worms, c. 3 (*MGH, SS*, IV, p. 833) and in that of St Nilus, cc. 91, 92, 93, excerpted in op. cit., pp. 617ff. See also Brun of Querfurt's *Vita Quinque Fratrum*, c. 7, *MGH, SS*, XV, II, p. 724 : 'vigiliae tamen, saccus et ieiunium, quibus pollebat'. Some of Otto's friends shared these experiences. For his relations with Odilo of Cluny see E. Sackur, *Die Cluniazenser* (Halle 1892) I, pp. 334ff. That they lacked warmth may be inferred

from a passage in Jotsaldus's *Epitaphium* of the abbot, Bk i,
c. 6 : '. . . Principibus et potestatibus christianis . . . ita amica-
bilem et officiosum se reddidit, ut tamquam alter Ioseph ab
omnibus mirabiliter amaretur . . . Concurrat in hunc amorem
Rotbertus rex Francorum; accedat Adheleida mater Ottonum;
veniat etiam Heinricus imperator Romanorum . . .' Otto III
is missing. (*MGH, SS*, xv, p. 813.)

99   Otto's ascetic pursuits were reproved in Brun, op. cit., c. 7,
p. 724. Thietmar wrote : 'multa faciebat, quae diversi diverse
sentiebant' (iv, c. 47, p. 184).

100 Widukind, iii, c. 71, p. 148 and cf. p. 103.

101 *Die Briefsammlung Gerberts von Reims*, no. 26, p. 49.

102 Alpertus, *De Episcopis Mettensibus Libellus*, c. i, *MGH, SS*,
iv, p. 698.

103 Otloh, *Liber Visionum*, 17, *MGH, SS*, xi, p. 385 and the
same story in a codex once belonging to St Michael's,
Hildesheim, *MGH, SS*, iv, p. 888. Whether the passage in
Adam of Bremen's *Gesta Hammaburgensis Ecclesiae Pontificum*,
iii, c. 32, ed. B. Schmeidler, *MGH, SRG* (Hanover/Leipzig
1917) p. 174 : 'Ideoque nec mirum esse, si Grecos diligeret,
quos vellet etiam habitu et moribus imitari; quod et fecit'
really refers to Henry iii rather than to Archbishop Adalbert
must remain a little uncertain.

104 A South-Italian Greek bishop, Leo, who was expelled for
abetting Otto ii's invasion in 982, found a refuge in Liège.
See Rupert's *Chronicon Sancti Laurentii Leodiensis*, c. 10, *MGH,
SS*, viii, p. 266. In general see J. M. McNulty and B. Hamil-
ton, 'Orientale Lumen et Magistra Latinitas : Greek influences on Western Monasticism (900–1100)', *Le Millénaire
du Mont Athos, 963–1963, Études et Mélanges* (Chevetogne
1963) i, pp. 181ff. For want of concrete evidence the authors
are forced to conclude that these influences were 'imponder-
able' (p. 215). B. Bischoff's indispensable paper 'Das grie-
chische Element in der abendländischen Bildung des Mittelalters,' now in *Mittelalterliche Studien* (Stuttgart 1967) ii,
pp. 246ff prompts caution.

105 William of Malmesbury, *Gesta Regum*, ii, 148, ed. cit., i, p.
165. For the Greek bishop see the *Liber Eliensis*, ed. E. O.
Blake, Camden Society, 3rd series, xcii (London 1962)
p. 73. I am indebted to Mr James Campbell for this reference.

106 Archbishop Brun's Greek *eloquentia* was praised not only by
his biographer Routger but also in the *Vita Iohannis Gorziensis*, c. 116, *MGH, SS*, iv, p. 370.

107 On the spirit of the eleventh-century pilgrimage to Jerusalem : R. W. Southern, *The Making of the Middle Ages*
(London 1953) pp. 51ff. Also E. R. Labande, 'Recherches sur
les pèlerins dans l'Europe des xie et xiie siècles', *Cahiers de
Civilisation Médiévale*, i (1958) pp. 159ff, 339ff.

108 There are some useful pages on French pilgrimages in the
eleventh century in R. Pfister, op. cit., pp. 344ff. Cf. also J.
Ebersolt, *Orient et Occident, Recherches sur les influences byzantines et orientales en France avant les Croisades* (Paris/Bruxelles
1928) pp. 71ff and H. Dauphin, *Le Bienheureux Richard Abbé
de Saint-Vanne de Verdun, Bibliothèque de la Revue d'Histoire
Ecclésiastique*, xxiv (Paris/Louvain 1946) pp. 278ff. Abbot

Richard was said to have headed 700 pilgrims. Duke Robert
of Normandy went : 'ingenti multitudine.' Rodulf Glaber,
IV, c.7, p.108.

109 *Das Register Gregors VII*, I, 46; 49; II, 37, ed. E.Caspar,
MGH, Epistolae Selectae (2 ed. Berlin 1955) I, pp.69ff, 75ff,
172ff.

110 Cf. *supra* p.1 and Rodulf Glaber, IV, c.6, p.106: 'Per idem
tempus ex universo orbe tam innumerabilis multitudo cepit
confluere ad Sepulchrum Salvatoris Iherosolimis quantam
nullus hominum prius sperare poterat.'

111 Ibid.

112 Among the pilgrims from Germany it is easier to find women
making the journey in the tenth century than in the eleventh.
Cf. R.Röhricht, *Die Deutschen im Heiligen Lande* (Innsbruck
1894).

113 *Ekkeberti Vita Sancti Haimeradi Presbiteri*, c.4, *MGH, SS*,
x, p.600.

114 See J.Becker's introduction to ed. cit., pp.xxxiiff.

115 He may have gone to Byzantium again on a more festive
mission only three years later in 971. Cf. n.24 *supra*.

116 Ohnsorge, 'Die Anerkennung des Kaisertums Ottos I. durch
Byzanz', *Konstantinopel und der Okzident*, pp.189ff.

117 Liudprand, *Legatio*, p.175 for the *inscriptio*, c.5, p.178; c.41,
p.197; c.52, p.203; cc.60–2, pp.208–10.

118 Op. cit., c.3, p.177; c.10, p.181; c.41, pp.197ff; c.52, p.203.

119 Op. cit., c.46, p.200, l.11; and c.55, p.205, l.25 and c.65,
p.212, ll.6ff. Once Liudprand eluded his guards in a church
and received messages from his clandestine connections. In
Saxon historiography Nikephoras's downfall in December
969 was linked with his failure against Otto I.

120 Op. cit., cc.29, 30, pp.190ff. Cf. also c.37, p.194.

121 *Notkeri Balbuli Gesta Karoli Magni Imperatoris*, II, cc.5, 6, ed.
H.F.Haefele, *MGH, SRG*, new series, XII (Berlin 1959)
pp.52ff.

122 *Annales Altahenses Maiores*, ed. E.L.B. von Oefele, *MGH,
SRG* (Hanover 1891) p.67. Bishop Gunther of Bamberg
wrote home : 'Experti enim sumus Ungros sine fide famul-
antes, Vulgarios occulte rapientes, fugimus Uzos aperte
debachantes, Constantinopolitanos vidimus graece et im-
perialiter arrogantes.'

William of Tyre

R.H.C.DAVIS

William of Tyre's *Historia Rerum in Partibus Transmarinis Gestarum* (henceforth referred to as *The Overseas History*) recounts the history of the Latin kingdom of Jerusalem from 1094 to 1184, the earlier part being compiled from previous chronicles and the later (particularly from 1167) being written as contemporary history while William was at the very centre of affairs. Its value for the history of the crusades has long been recognised; indeed it is not too much to say that almost all western histories of the crusades stem directly from his work. It is therefore curious that the most recent edition of it (in the *Recueil des Historiens des Croisades*) dates from as long ago as 1844,[1] and sad that it is physically so cumbersome (a folio volume of 1134 pages) that it is difficult to read it for any length of time 'at a sitting'. In this latter respect relief comes from the very effective English translation by E.A. Babcock and A.C.Krey in Columbia University's *Records of Civilization* series, but because it was published in 1944 it is extremely rare in England.[2] A new edition of the Latin text, complete with the twelfth chapter of Book XIX which was previously thought missing, has now been promised by R.B.C. Huygens,[3] and if that fulfils expectations and identifies all William's sources, the study of the *Overseas History* will enter a new and happier era. For the present we will content ourselves with some general, and rather elementary, remarks about the work as a monument of cultural history and its effectiveness as a contact between East and West.

On the face of it, William of Tyre was the perfect 'contact man'. Born in Jerusalem (*c.* 1130), probably of Italian parents, he had a good working knowledge of both Greek and Arabic. To this he added a full western education, studying Arts and Theology at Paris for sixteen years (*c.* 1145–61) and Civil Law at Bologna for another four (1161–5).[4] He visited the papal curia at least twice, in 1169 and 1178, the second occasion being for the third Lateran council of which he wrote a history which is now lost. He went to Byzantium on embassies in 1167–8 and 1179. He was supplied with Arabic histories by Amaury I, king of Jerusalem, who knew him well, and who commissioned him to write the history of his own reign, of the kingdom since 1094, and of the neighbouring oriental princes. Thanks mainly to royal patronage, he received a prebend in Tyre Cathedral in 1165, was made archdeacon in 1167, tutor to the king's son Baldwin (IV) in 1170, chancellor of the kingdom in 1174, and archbishop of Tyre in 1175. It was his ambition to end his life as patriarch of Jerusalem, but when the vacancy occurred he had lost his former influence at court, and he was disappointed. He continued writing his history, which he brought down to the end of 1184, till within a month or two of his death, but its tone was decidedly pessimistic:

> Up to the present time, in the preceding books, we have described to the best of our ability the remarkable deeds of the brave men who for eighty years and more have held the ruling power in our part of the Orient, and particularly at Jerusalem. Now, in utter detestation of the present, amazed at the material which is presented before our eyes and ears, things unfit to be told even in the songs of a Codrus or the recitals of a Maevius, whatever they may be, we lack courage to continue.[5]...

This pessimism is not a thing which should be overlooked, for it has a bearing on William's impartiality which, though remarkable by medieval standards, was certainly not absolute. If we read the history straight through from 1095 to 1184 (two volumes in English translation) we cannot help getting the impression that the author is consciously writing a tragedy, which might well have been entitled 'The Rise and Fall of the Kingdom of Jerusalem'. When we get to the end, it is with surprise that we discover that the history does not reach its seemingly appointed end, but stops abruptly almost three years before the battle of Hattin, and the fall of Jerusalem. This, of course, was because the author had died in 1184. But how did he know that the kingdom was going to fall? In fact, of course, he was only prophesying, but people who prophesy do so because they have a Message. What was his?

To discover this we will do best to start with what he tells us about himself. First, he was a patriot. When he came to write a prologue to his whole history, he admitted freely that it was 'the command of King Amaury I' which had induced him to start the work. But the reason why he had kept on with it, he says, was 'an insistent love of my country'.

> She spurs me on, I repeat, and with that authority which belongs to her imperiously commands that those things which have been accomplished by her during the course of almost a century be not buried in silence and allowed to fall into undeserved oblivion.[6]

This patriotism was the more intense because William, unlike most crusaders, had actually been born in the kingdom, Jerusalem being (as we now know from the recently discovered chapter XIX. 12) his native city. This is important because the crusaders who were born in the Holy Land formed a distinct party known as *pullani* who were constantly at odds with those who came out from the West;[7] and the reason why William himself was not elected patriarch of Jerusalem in 1180 was that at that time the *pullani* were out of favour, all things being ordered by their arch-enemy Agnes de Courtenay, the queen-mother.

William of Tyre, though he wrote in a very dispassionate manner, was undoubtedly a party man. In his *Overseas History* he quietly but consistently praised the *pullani*, notably Raymond of Tripoli, and showed how failure after failure was due to the blundering of those crusaders who came out from the West and insisted on deciding the military strategy of the kingdom before they had begun to understand the realities of the situation. It is a view which, thanks to William, has received very wide support from modern historians, but, as might be expected, it was not general in the Middle Ages. Most western chroniclers thought that it was the *pullani* who were responsible for the collapse of the kingdom, accusing them of having put their private interests before those of the kingdom, and of having misled, deserted and betrayed King Guy at the battle of Hattin (1187). As William of Newburgh put it:

> The new natives of that land, whom they call *pullani*, have been infected by the neighbourhood of the Saracens, and as between Christians and Saracens seem to be neither one thing nor the other.[8]

Jacques de Vitry put it more strongly:

> They make treaties with the Saracens and are glad to be at peace with Christ's enemies; they are quick to quarrel with one another, and skirmish and levy civil war against one another; they often call upon the enemies of the faith to help them against Christians, and are not ashamed to waste the forces and treasure, which they ought to use against the infidels to God's glory, in fighting against one another to the injury of Christendom.[9]

It is an interesting fact that though western chroniclers were almost unanimous in their condemnation of the *pullani*, they never seem to have identified William of Tyre as being one of them – and this in spite of the fact that they knew his *Overseas History* well. Captivated by his picturesque narrative and self-evident devotion to the kingdom, they assumed he was 'one of themselves', and proceeded to read their own thoughts into what he had written. Jacques de Vitry, for example, obviously thought that in attacking the *pullani* he was merely echoing the opinions of William of Tyre. But though we can tell which chapter of William's work he was following, because he repeats many of its words and phrases, it is clear that he missed the point completely.

In this chapter (xxi. 7) William is trying to explain why it was that though the earlier crusaders had often succeeded in defeating Muslim forces which were superior in number, the later crusaders were often defeated by inferior forces. He offers three reasons. First (conventionally) 'that our forefathers were religious men and feared God'. Second (and perhaps as a consequence of the first), that whereas the original crusaders were accustomed to military discipline, the people of the East had now become 'unused to the art of war and unfamiliar with the rules of battle, and gloried in their state of inactivity'. This, of course, was the passage which attracted the attention of Jacques de Vitry and furnished him with the material for his diatribe on the debility and moral turpitude of the *pullani*, but in William of Tyre's chapter it served merely as a prologue for the third reason, which was the one which really mattered, and to which he gave more space than both the others together. This was the fact that whereas in the time of the First Crusade the Muslims were disunited, almost every city having its own ruler, 'now, since God has so willed it, all the Kingdoms adjacent to us have been brought under the power of one man'.[10] To him the fact that mattered was the steady progress of Muslim unity from Zangi and Nur-ed-Din to Saladin. But this was a point which went over the heads of most westerners. They preferred the sermon about the decline of martial valour, and failed to notice that the general theme of William's *History* amounted, not to an attack, but to a defence of the general strategy of the native-born barons or *pullani*.

William never states in so many words what that strategy was, but it is not difficult to divine. Since the Muslims gained strength as they became united, the Christians had to ensure that they were kept disunited; and since the Christians were few and the Muslims many, it was in the interest of the Christians to maintain a balance of power by allying with one Muslim against another. Thus William thought it sensible of King Fulk to join forces with the Muslim ruler of Damascus against the rising power of Zangi, and he was careful to explain that the alliance was worthwhile since the Muslim fulfilled his part of the bargain and helped the crusaders to capture Banyas (1140).

> Then might be witnessed a strange and novel sight : a hostile people [Damascenes] encouraging an enemy [Crusaders] to the fiercest warfare, and as an ally actually in arms for the destruction of the common foe [Zangi]. Nor could it be readily discerned which of the allied armies battled more valiantly against the common enemy or urged on the attack more bitterly or persevered the longer in the burden of battle. Christians and Damascenes were equal in courage and united in purpose. (xv. 9)

That was an example of *pullani* policy at its best.

In sharp contrast was King Amaury's invasion of Egypt. It was undertaken in order to stiffen the resistance of the Fatimids to Nur-ed-Din but, as William pointed out, it had exactly the opposite effect. Instead of keeping Nur-ed-Din out of Egypt it merely brought his armies in, and enabled him to control the policy of Egypt as well as of Syria (1169).

> But now, on the contrary, all things have been changed for the worse. 'How is the most fine gold changed' and 'my harp also is turned into mourning'. Wherever I turn I find only reasons for fear and uneasiness. The sea refuses to give us a peaceful passage, all the regions round about are subject to the enemy, and the neighbouring Kingdoms are making preparations to destroy us. (XX. 10)

From this time on, the hope was that Nur-ed-Din's generals in Egypt, Shirkuh and his nephew Saladin, would fall out with their master and make themselves independent. This hope was not realised, but when Nur-ed-Din died (1174), Saladin set about seizing the whole kingdom for himself. He won Damascus quickly, but was opposed by Nur-ed-Din's son, Es-Salih, who established himself at Aleppo. In William of Tyre's view the crusaders should then have done everything possible to perpetuate this division, bolstering up Es-Salih with well-timed diversionary attacks on Saladin. But, in fact, they did little or nothing, and in 1182 Aleppo fell to Saladin.

> Redoubled fear took hold of our people on hearing this news, for the result most dreaded had come to pass. From the first it had been apparent to the Christians that if Saladin should succeed in adding Aleppo to his principality, our territory would be as completely encompassed by his power and strength as if it were in a state of siege. (XXII. 24)

The general point is illustrated by some of William's remarks about Humphrey de Toron II (d. 1179), who belonged to the inner circle of the *pullani* and was constable of the kingdom. He tells us how in 1152 the Christian army was harassed by Nur-ed-Din on its march from Tell Beshir to Antioch, and how Humphrey received vital information from an enemy soldier 'who belonged to the household of a very powerful Turkish noble who was bound to the constable in fraternal alliance', and that very closely (*qui eidem constabulario fraterno foedere junctus erat, et in eo tenacissimus*). He reported that Nur-ed-Din intended to return with his army to his own land that very night, for all the provisions in his camp were exhausted and he could not pursue the Christians further' (XVII. 17). It should be noticed that William of Tyre does not criticise Humphrey for having friends among the Muslims. On the contrary, he accepts such alliances as the simplest and most economical way of trying to reduce the power of Nur-ed-Din. The only trouble was that after Nur-ed-Din's death the power which had to be reduced was not that of his son, Es-Salih, but of his rival Saladin, and then Humphrey was liable to find himself with the 'wrong' friends. In theory he should have dropped his former allies among the Muslims and made new ones to suit the changed political circumstances, but in fact he remained (as William of Tyre complained) 'too closely associated in the bonds of friendship with Saladin', and negotiated a truce with him.

> His action was decidedly detrimental to our interests, for thus this prince [Saladin], who should have been resisted to the utmost lest his insolence towards us increase with his power, won our good will, and he whose ever-increasing strength was to the disadvantage of the Christians dared to count upon us (XXI. 8).

William of Tyre and his *pullani* friends believed in maintaining a balance of power in the 'Eastern parts', and consequently thought it desirable to know Arabic and maintain contacts with the Muslims, so that they could understand the political situation as it really was, and exploit every possible division in Islam. They did not object to the idea of alliances with the Muslims, but insisted that such alliances should be made with those Muslims who were on the decline. As part of the same policy they believed that they should work for the greatest possible unity amongst the Christian states, and be prepared in particular to collaborate with the Byzantine Empire. If Damascus and Cairo could be kept in a state of mutual hostility, and Constantinople and Jerusalem be united in a common purpose, the future of the Latin kingdom would be assured.

It was true that the Byzantines and crusaders had a long tradition of mutual ill-will, but by the third quarter of the twelfth century both were in such peril from the Muslims that they were prepared to sink their differences. The emperor Manuel I (1143–80), whose mother was a Hungarian, and whose two successive wives were both Westerners, was particularly well disposed, and in 1167 proposed an alliance with the crusaders against Egypt. King Amaury responded favourably and sent William of Tyre as one of his envoys to Constantinople to conclude a treaty. The mission was accomplished successfully, and as a result a considerable Byzantine fleet (consisting of 150 well-armed galleys, 60 vessels for transporting horses, and 10–20 supply-ships) assisted the crusaders in their attack on Damietta in 1169. The attack proved a failure, but in 1171 King Amaury went to Constantinople himself to convince the emperor of the feasibility of further projects.

> In frequent intimate talks with the emperor, sometimes privately and sometimes in the presence of the illustrious

F

nobles of the imperial court, the King explained the reasons
that had led to his visit and set forth at length the needs of
his Kingdom. He dwelt upon the immortal fame which the
emperor might win by undertaking the subjugation of Egypt,
and demonstrated by positive proofs how easily the project
might be accomplished. Persuaded by his words, the emperor
lent a favourable ear to the King's proposition and promised
to carry out his wishes in full. (xx. 23)

This is a far cry from the usual run of crusader chronicles which
lashed themselves into a fury over the 'vanity', 'plausibility' and
'treachery' of the Greeks, but in his *Overseas History* William of
Tyre was continuing the diplomatic work which he had begun as
King Amaury's ambassador. He was trying to persuade his fellow
Latins that though they might not like the Greeks they could not
afford to be enemies.

Whenever he touches on the subject of Byzantium, William
shows himself to be a master of 'public relations'. He does not deny
unpleasant facts. He makes it quite clear that he is aware of them
and casually drops remarks such as 'like all Greeks, he was extremely effeminate and given over to the sins of the flesh';[11] but he
takes them in his stride as facts which have to be faced and lived
with. Even when circumstances were particularly difficult, as after
the great massacre of the Latins in Constantinople in 1182, he did
his best to quieten emotions by reporting dispassionately the under-
lying causes of the tragedy. As for the actual events, he followed
his account of the massacre with an equally long report of the
counter-massacres by the Latins – they sacked all the towns and
monasteries they could find on the Sea of Marmara – and com-
mented favourably on those Latins who 'shrank from these deeds
of slaughter and rapine' but simply embarked with their wives,
children and 'came down to us in Syria' (xxii. 13). They were
sensible because they realized that further bitterness between
Latins and Greeks could only weaken the position of both *vis-à-vis*
the Muslims.

William of Tyre's 'message' was that the kingdom of Jerusalem
could only be saved if the Muslims were divided and the Greek and
Latin Christians united. One does not have to read very far in
modern histories to see how persuasive he has been in our own
times; Guy of Lusignan and his Poitevins have hardly a defender,
the *pullani* are generally approved and their policy applauded as
realistic common sense. In part this is because modern historians,
with all the advantages of hindsight, can see that William's
prophecy came true : that the Poitevins did oust the *pullani*, and
that Jerusalem did fall to the Muslims. But in the century following
William's death these events were not generally linked as cause and

effect in the way that William would have liked. So far from being convinced, the Latin West hardly comprehended what the message of William of Tyre was. Ordinary chroniclers like Jacques de Vitry continued to assume that Jerusalem had been lost because of the lassitude, non-cooperation and treachery of the *pullani*, and ordinary laymen did in fact turn against Constantinople, to capture it and overthrow the Byzantine Empire in 1204. For all the effect that William of Tyre had on the next generation of crusaders, he might never have written his *Overseas History*.

This is a puzzling fact indeed, for as Babcock and Krey have put it, 'the number of manuscripts of the various continuations still extant would imply that William's history must have been known in nearly every castle and considerable town in Europe'.[12] The Latin text survives in nine manuscripts, and the Old French translation of it in at least seventy-one. The speed with which it was disseminated must have been very rapid, for a Latin continuation, with an account of the battle of Hattin, seems to have been written in England as early as 1192, and everything goes to suggest that almost every European chronicler who touched on the history of the crusades after that date was indebted in some measure or other to William of Tyre. Why was it that hardly anyone understood his message?

The first clue is to be found in the fate of William's companion work, the *Historia Orientalium Principum*. We have no text of it, but we know about it from several references in William's main history. In the prologue he writes:

> Moreover at the order of the King [Amaury] who himself furnished the necessary Arabic documents, we have also written another history. As the principal source for this we have used the work of the venerable patriarch of Alexandria, Seith son of Patrick [Said ibn Batrick]. This history begins from the time of the false prophet Mohammad and extends through five hundred and seventy years even to the present year, which is the 1184th of the Incarnation of the Lord.[13]

We know that Jacques de Vitry found a copy of this book at Damietta in 1218 and used it for his own *Historia Orientalium*, that it was used by William of Tripoli in his *Tractatus de Statu Sarracenorum*, and that in 1231 Peter des Roches, bishop of Winchester, brought back a copy from the Holy Land and presented it to the abbey of St Albans.[14] But though we can reconstruct fragments of its text, it is clear that it was a book which was not appreciated.[15] Not only have all manuscripts of it been lost, but Matthew Paris, who tells us about the copy at St Albans, does not give any sign of having read it; crusades were interesting, but Muslims were not.

None the less there was a good deal that had to be explained

about the Muslims even in a history of the crusades, and William
has a number of interesting digressions about them in his *Overseas
History*. What we would like to know is whether the ordinary
reader enjoyed these digressions or just skipped them. This is
naturally a matter which cannot be decided with certainty, but
some indication can be found by comparing William's Latin text
with the French translation.[16] The translation was obviously intended for the laity and had, as we have already seen, a wide
circulation. The translator did not hesitate to make 'cuts' wherever he found the text tedious, being particularly severe on
passages of purely ecclesiastical interest (for example xiv. 11–14)
and literary-descriptive passages such as the one on the geography
of Egypt with all its classical and Old Testament allusions (xix. 24).
If he had also expected his readers to be bored by purely Muslim
affairs, he would surely have cut passages such as the description
and history of Cairo (xix. 15), and the explanation of the origin of
the Shī'a and the Fatimid caliphate (xix. 21). In fact he does not
do so. The general impression – and we have not attempted to gain
anything more than that – is that on Muslim affairs the French
version is as complete as the Latin, and sometimes even better
informed.

A small example of superior knowledge occurs in the account
of the battle of Mont Gisard (1177). William says that the Arabs
waited to see whether the Turks or Christians were winning before
rushing off to break the news to the Turkish rearguard at El Arish;
Arabes is what William calls them, but his translator renders this
li Turc d' Arrabe que l'on apele Bedoins – a small matter, but one which
shows that he was both knowledgeable and anxious to explain
(xix. 24). More significant, perhaps, are the differences in the Latin
and French versions of the account of the origins of the Shī'a
(xix. 21). In a picturesque and one-sided account of the fifth
caliph Ali (Mohammed's son-in-law), William alleges that Ali 're-
viled Mohammed and spread among the people a story to the effect
that the Angel Gabriel, the propounder of the Law [*legislator*],
had actually been sent to him from on High but by mistake had
conferred the supreme honour on Mohammed'. This, of course, is
nothing more than a scurrilous story, though it seems to derive
from Muslim rather than Christian folk-lore, since there are several
popular tales in Arabic about pseudo-prophets who pretended to
be inspired by the angel Gabriel. But the French version is interesting because it clarifies *angelus legislator Gabriel* by rendering it as
*Gabriel lie anges que Dame Diex avait envoié pour enseigner la foit des
Sarrazins* ('Gabriel, the angel whom the Lord God had sent to
teach the faith of the Saracens'), thus making it clear that the
reference is to Gabriel dictating the Koran to Mohammed.

Later in the same chapter William had to refer to Ubaydullah el Mahdi the first Fatimid caliph (909–34). He said that 'after conquering all the lands of that region he called himself the Leveller [*complanans*] as one who directs all things to calm'.[17] In fact he had mistaken the Arabic word *Mahdi* ('the Guided one') for *mahada* ('to level'). This mistake was not repeated in the French version which says that 'he called himself *Mehedi* which means a man of worth [*vaillanz*], because he did not like the mouths of the proud or the stories his enemies told about him'.[18] It is a brave attempt to put the record straight, and even though it is not completely successful, it shows that the translator was anxious to explain the Arabic word correctly.

The French translation of William of Tyre's *Overseas History*, therefore, did nothing to diminish the interest or accuracy of those chapters which were concerned with the Muslims. Nor did it abridge what William had to say about Byzantium. It preserved the general sense of his book intact, and even accentuated it;[19] and (if we may repeat the fact) it had a very large circulation. If we are to explain why William failed to 'get his message across', therefore, it is no use trying to put the blame on the translation. Even though William knew Greek and Arabic, had had a full education at the schools of Paris and Bologna, and had lived at the centre of the events he described, there must have been some fault either in him or in the book which he wrote. What was it?

I think the answer is that though William was very anxious to explain, his understanding was not sufficiently deep; and that though his readers revelled in his descriptions of the East, he won their interest only by being picturesque. When one asks what William understood by the East, one cannot avoid answering that it was the countries surrounding the Holy Land. He did not consider himself as part of the East but rather as a Western bishop in the East. The very title of *The Overseas History* (*Historia Rerum in Partibus Transmarinis Gestarum*) shows that even though he was himself born in Jerusalem, he really thought of the Holy Land as an extension, or colony, of the West. He was not interested in the history of Islam for its own sake but only for its practical use; and one suspects that the reason why he stopped to explain the Shī'a was that it was a heresy which might be exploited by the Christians in order to keep Islam divided.[20] He does not stop to ask what Muslims thought, let alone to ask what they thought about Christians, and as a result his book was undemanding. It confronted the western reader not with the realities of the East, but with a picture of places and circumstances where westerners could have adventures.

That was why the *Overseas History* was so popular. What William of Tyre's readers wanted was the literary equivalent of *chinoiserie*, descriptions like that which William collected from eye-witnesses of the crusaders' introduction to the caliph's palace in Cairo (1167).

> After passing through many winding passages and devious ways, whose wonders might well detain even the busiest of men in contemplation they reached the palace itself. Here still larger groups of armed men and throngs of attending satellites testified by their appearance and numbers to the incomparable glory of their lord. The very aspect of the place gave indisputable proof of the opulence and extraordinary riches of the monarch. They approached and were admitted to the inner part of the palace. Here the sultan showed the usual reverence to his lord, according to custom; twice he prostrated himself on the ground and humbly offered as to a divinity due worship and a kind of abject adoration. Then for a third time bowing to the ground, he laid down the sword which he wore suspended from his neck. Thereupon the curtains embroidered with pearls and gold which hung down and hid the throne, were drawn aside with marvellous rapidity, and the caliph was revealed with face unveiled. Seated on a throne of gold, surrounded by some of his privy counsellors and eunuchs he presented an appearance more than regal. (XIX. 19)

In fact the description is not without interest, particularly if the ceremonial is compared with that of the Byzantine emperor as described in XX. 23, but so far as medieval readers were concerned, one suspects that it was the *chinoiserie* that mattered. What they wanted was wonders, and in the *Overseas History* they found plenty of them.

The tragedy was that that was not William of Tyre's purpose at all. He had written his book out of love for his country, to explain how it could be saved, and to persuade men to come and save it. He would have been horrified to find that his book was treated as escapist literature, and would have found little consolation in the old saying that 'you can take a horse to the water, but you can't make him drink'. William of Tyre wrote about the East *per se* in his *Historia Orientalium Principum* and hardly anyone read it. He wrote a popular *Overseas History* about the crusades and became one of the best known but least understood authors in Christendom. It was the same sort of experience, perhaps, as that of those idealists who, in recent times, have fostered foreign tours for the sake of international understanding. For just as the majority of tourists think that the point of travelling is to take photographs and buy knick-knacks, so the medieval readers of William of Tyre admired his descriptions and enjoyed his stories, without realising that there was a point to them.

Perhaps the root of the trouble was the same then as it is now. William of Tyre's *Overseas History* is a very long book, and it cannot have been any easier to read in manuscript than it is now in the folio volumes of the *Recueil*. We know that at least seventy-one copies of the French translation were made, and that they were intended for the laity. But how many kings, princes, barons or knights would have had the time to read it from beginning to end? 'Tell me another story from William of Tyre' – is that not what they would have said? To them it was probably more like *The Blue Story Book* than a genuine contact between East and West by a man who really did – and this is the tragedy – know both. William himself may have had his failings, but his readers had more. They did not want to be instructed, but only to be excited and amused. They turned a deaf ear to the message he was trying to convey; and he, if he had lived, would have realised that it was no use trying to be a contact-man if nobody wanted the contact to be made.[21]

NOTES

1   *Historia Rerum in Partibus Transmarinis Gestis*, ed. A. Beugnot and A. Le Prévost, in *RHC; Historiens Occidentaux*, 1 (2 parts 1844).

2   [E.A.] B[abcock] and [A.C.] K[rey], *A History of the deeds done beyond the sea, by William of Tyre, Records of Civilization series*, 2 vols (Columbia 1944). How grateful we would all be if Columbia would reprint it!

3   [R.B.C.] Huygens, ['Guillaume de Tyr étudiant: un chapitre (XIX. 12) de son "Histoire" retrouvé'], in *Latomus* XXI (1962) pp. 811–28.

4   These facts emerge from the 'missing chapter' printed by Huygens with a full discussion of its implications. At Paris William went to most of the same teachers as John of Salisbury, though he was too late to hear Abelard.

5   W[illiam] of T[yre], XXIII, preface (B and K, II, p. 505).

6   *WT*, prologue (B and K, I, p. 55).

7   Mrs M.R. Morgan has shown in her unpublished Oxford D.Phil. thesis on 'The Old French Continuations of the Chronicle of William Archbishop of Tyre to 1232' that the word *pullanus* or (Old French *polain*) was derived from *pullus* (the young of an animal), and that 'the implication is that the *Polains* were at least second generation colonials, not at all that they were of mixed blood'.

8   William of Newburgh, in *Chronicles of the Reigns of Stephen, Henry II and Richard I*, ed. Richard Howlett, *RS* (1884–9) I, p. 254.

9   Trans. Aubrey Stewart, *The History of Jerusalem. A.D. 1180, by Jacques de Vitry*, Palestine Pilgrims' Text Soc., XXXI (1896) pp. 64–5.

10   B and K, ii, p. 407.

11   Ibid., p. 462.

12   Ibid., i, p. 43.

13   Ibid., i, p. 56. For Said ibn Batrik (877–93), otherwise known as Eutychius, see *S. Eutychii Patriarchae Alexandrini Annales, Lat. et arab.*, ed. Pococke (Oxford 1658).

14   *Matthei Parisiensis . . . Historia Minor*, ed. F. Madden, R*S* (1866) i, p. 183.

15   Hans Prutz, 'Studien über Wilhelm von Tyrus', *Neues Archiv*, vii (1883) pp. 93–132, esp. pp. 107–14.

16   In fact there are several French versions. I am told that a thesis on them is being prepared by Mr Oliver Goulden of University College London. The text which I have used is the main text printed in *RHC*.

17   'Vocavit se Mehedi quod interpretatur Complanans, quasi qui universa ad quietum dirigit; et sine offendiculo vias populo effecit planiores' (xix. 21).

18   'Lors se fist apeler Mehedi qui sonne autant comme vaillanz, parce qu'il n'amoit pas les boches des orgueilleuses et les contanz de ceuls qui contre lui estoient, et fesoit les voies pleines, parce que la seue gent poissent aller sanz contredit et estre à repox' (xix. 21).

19   In recounting the counter-massacres by the Latins in the Sea of Marmara (1182), the French version adds that the reason why some Latins did not want to join in the slaughter (p. 70, above) was because the Greeks were Christian. 'Aucuns i ot de ces Latins qui ne voudrent plus entendre a genz occire n'à peçoier les viles, *porce que Crestiens estoient*' (xxii. 13).

20   The chapter-heading (xix. 21) reads 'Subjungitur quare idem ipse [princeps Aegypticus] dicatur Calipha; et quo modo sit adversarius Baldacensi caliphae'.

21   I wish to express my thanks to Messrs C. A. Robson and D. S. Richards for help with Old French and Arabic respectively; and to members of the conference, especially Drs N. Daniel and J. S. G. Riley-Smith, for many useful comments and suggestions.

Cultural Relations between East and West
in the Twelfth Century*

ANTHONY BRYER

During the twelfth century the Byzantine and western worlds met
each other in all spheres and at all levels more closely than ever
before. It is natural to expect and seek results of the encounter. In
the field of art, to begin with, the question has been debated ever
since Vasari. But the scope and need for further research remains
considerable.[1] In the field of learning the question is a much more
recent one. Here the obvious enquiry is whether links between the
twelfth-century 'renaissance' in western Europe and equivalent
movements – philosophical, theological and literary – in Comnene
Byzantium can be established and defined.[2]

On the face of it, these questions seem large and important. But
it must be said at once that the extent of the Frankish encounter
with Byzantium and the Levant is out of all proportion to what we
know of its effects in the fields of art and learning, among others,
in the West. Byzantium absorbed even less from the experience.
To begin with, one will not get very far looking for Byzantine
works of art which are known to have been in the West in the
twelfth century. They are largely confined in Italy to the sumptu-
ary work for which Byzantium was famed – reliquaries, great
bronze doors and the astonishing *Pala d'Oro*.[3] The empire exported
glassware and, of course, silk; Byzantium may even have initiated
the western craft of stained glass.[4] But no more than a handful of
illuminated manuscripts is known to have reached the West in the
twelfth century and only one authentic Byzantine icon – a *Panagia*
which Frederick I Barbarossa gave Spoleto cathedral in 1185.[5]
Clearly there were more items than now survive in cathedral
treasuries and libraries, but not, one may speculate, very much
more or of a different nature. As transmitters, the western artists
who travelled in the East with their copy books were obviously
more important than the Byzantine objects which found their way
to the West. Examples of such artists' work have been identified
and examined, but in the twelfth century they are rare, isolated
and undeniably freakish.[6] Similarly the evidence for Byzantine
artists working in Italy (outside Sicily and, perhaps, Venice), let
alone elsewhere, is meagre. This makes the powerful hold of the
maniera greca, the distinguishing mark of the Italian *ducento*, all the

more difficult to explain. The point, I think, is that it was a manner, a style, and little more. Except for special cases, like those Ottonian artists who had attempted to adapt to the requirements of their emperors a certain type of Byzantine picture which expressed a ceremonial dignity, it was the Byzantine style which travelled, rather than its iconography, the meaning of a picture. This was not for the first time; the separation of manner from meaning is surely the clue to the earlier problem paintings of Castelseprio.[7] It is certainly true of the *ducento*. In the rare cases where both style and iconography were transplanted in the West, the iconography was often misinterpreted. Now the characteristic stylistic feature of the *ducento* was the clinging drapery, the damp folds which give bodies substance beneath the robes and 'humanise' them.[8] This is an undoubtedly Byzantine inspiration, but not only Byzantine of the twelfth century. What western artists were evidently seeking in Byzantium was not necessarily the refinements of contemporary Comnene art but a repository of what westerners and Byzantines believed was the genuine and lively classical tradition. Through Byzantium, Italian artists were looking for Rome; what in fact they found was the Byzantine style, and little else. A parallel might be the vogue for *chinoiserie* in eighteenth-century Europe; one cannot expect to convey an ancient, complex and alien culture by mannerisms alone, and yet its appeal rests upon the delusion that one can. The influence of Byzantine art in Italy obviously went deeper than that and the fashionable *maniera greca* gave the *ducento* its peculiar quality. But beyond Italy the style was usually interpreted at third, rather than second, hand. This does not mean that some examples of the second, or even third, hand (such as at Berzé-la-Ville or Canterbury, or in the St Albans or Henry of Blois psalters) could not be more or less close to the original. But, whatever western medieval scholars may sometimes wish to believe, such examples never ring true and create only a fleeting atmosphere of Byzantinism.[9]

   In the fields of learning and piety the situation is somewhat the same. I suppose that a Byzantine parallel to Anselm (1033–1109) comes a century earlier in Symeon the New Theologian (949–1022).[10] The fervour and near-lyricism of their writings are perhaps comparable, but the gulf between them is much wider than that of three generations. For Symeon, the demons who tormented the athletes of God of the desert are totally real; so is the aim to reach an essentially corporeal unity of Man with Christ. Symeon surely belongs to a peculiarly Byzantine mystical tradition, with very practical undertones, which was to find its fullest expression in the fourteenth century. A closer contemporary to Anselm would be Theophylact of Ochrida, archbishop of Bulgaria from before

1088 / 9 until after 1107 / 8. At Pope Urban II's council of 1098, held at Bari to integrate the Greek and Latin Churches of southern Italy, Anselm argued for an intelligent and reasonable charity in considering outward distinctions of worship.[11] Here Theophylact would have been in complete agreement – except that he had now seen western Christians in numbers for the first time, unhappily at their worst in a splinter of the First Crusade which had rampaged through his archdiocese. Like his emperor, Alexius I Comnenus, he had kept his tact, but to Theophylact it was an eye-opener.[12] Even so, there was a formidable gulf between an essentially Greek prelate, such as Theophylact, and Anselm in everything save a determination to maintain a sympathetic and open mind on the superficial differences between the two Churches.

One of Theophylact's most interesting writings points to a more fundamental difference of outlook and tradition. It is an appeal to his emperor to support education in the art of rhetoric, 'to restore a custom which has fallen into decay in the course of time and to reintroduce the tradition of delivering speeches in the imperial presence'.[13] Rhetoric! What sort of world was this? No westerner could really begin to get to grips with the living classicism – or antiquarianism – of Byzantium. Theophylact was a pupil of Michael Psellus and of the group of scholars who refounded the university of Constantinople in 1045. And, with characteristic immodesty, Psellus described how he had not only mastered and interpreted the philosophy of the pagan Hellenes, Aristotle and Plato, but had proceeded, via Plotinus and Proclus, to the Fathers and 'also made some contribution to the body of divine teaching on my own account'.[14] By contrast, Dr Southern has put the stage at which western scholars began to feel comfortable about their command of the achievement of the past in the second generation of the twelfth century.[15] The point is that not only Psellus, but most Byzantine scholars who had worked through their standard collections of classical texts, would have felt uncomfortable outside the achievement of the past.

To eleventh- and twelfth-century Byzantine intellectuals, the long Christianised distinctions between Plato and Aristotle were very live issues; in the writings of Bessarion and of George of Trebizond the argument was to survive the fall of Constantinople itself. They may have boasted more than they knew, but summaries of classical learning were their everyday intellectual currency. Now it is true that there are important examples of the transmission of classical texts from East to West during the twelfth century. For example, Henry Aristippus of Sicily translated part of the *Timaeus* and James of Venice Aristotle's *Ethics*.[16] But both translators were probably Greek and both were representatives of the overlap world between Byzantium and the West. Their translations got no further. Westerners seemed positively to prefer their Aristotle through the Arabic, rather than the Greek, tradition. Similarly Manuel I Comnenus may have sent a copy of Ptolemy's *Almagest* (the *Megale Syntaxis*) to Roger II of Sicily, but the real impact of this work was delayed in the West for almost two centuries.[17]

The common twelfth-century eastern and western concern for Aristotle was, I suspect, no more than a happy coincidence of quite separate processes of intellectual evolution and rediscovery. In the same way, Barbarossa's lawyers' interest in Roman law has little to do with twelfth-century Byzantium. Maybe, as is often claimed, the preservation of Roman law is among Byzantium's chief practical legacies to the West, but as a matter of practice the Justinianic and Theodosian codes which the Bolognese lawyers were studying had comparatively little relevance to twelfth-century Byzantine civil law (and even less to those of contemporary Italy).[18]

It does, however, seem likely that the renewed twelfth-century Byzantine interest in canon law, and the works of Theodore Balsamon, patriarch of Antioch in the last decades of the century, are not unconnected with contemporary western concerns in the subject. People were beginning to realise that the question of authority lay at the root of what was to be called the 'Eastern schism'. Here twelfth-century Byzantine views on the source of authority and the position of the emperor had, through the works of Neilos Doxopatres, a direct connection with Roger II's relations with his Church.[19] To be one's own papal legate is not a bad interpretation of the Byzantine imperial position. But also at the root of the eastern question lay something more intangible: the growing eastern understanding that, while to westerners the question of Reunion seemed to be a matter of discipline, to Byzantines it touched their very identity. As early as the reign of Manuel I Comnenus, Patriarch Michael III of Anchialus (1169–77) was wondering if the turban of the Turk was not, even then, preferable to the tiara of the pope: 'Let the Muslim be my master in outward things rather than the Latin dominate me in matters of the spirit. For if I am subject to the Muslim, at least he will not force me to share his faith. But if I have to be under the Frankish rule and united with the Roman Church, I may have to separate myself from God.'[20] Byzantine experience with both Latins and Turks in the twelfth century revealed that the patriarch's prognosis was largely correct.[21]

How can one characterise this situation? The Byzantine near-contemporary of Peter Lombard (d. 1160) would have been Eustathius, archbishop of Thessalonica (d. *c.* 1193), author of a massive commentary on the *Iliad* which remains a starting point of modern Homeric scholarship and, incidentally, witness of a much more frightful Frankish outrage than Theophylact had to bear with in Bulgaria: the Norman sack of his city in 1185.[22] For Eustathius, the learning of the past, conveyed in the living (albeit written, rather than spoken) language of the past, was directly applicable to contemporary problems. Their outlook was so different: the view of Nicetas Choniates, another contemporary, on the Latins was that 'We are poles apart; we have not a thought in common.'[23]

Like artists, there are a few isolated examples of scholars crossing the boundaries: John Italus, Psellus's successor, or Barlaam in the fourteenth century. But both came from the special region of Byzantine Italy, an area of cultural overlap, and it must not be forgotten that both were condemned in Byzantium. If we are looking for a direct transmission of thought, or even for informed mutual understanding, we must move into the fourteenth and fifteenth centuries, perhaps to the small but distinguished group of Byzantine intellectuals who submitted, through reasoned conviction, to the Latin Church. But by then Byzantine intellectuals seem to have been better informed of the traditions of western scholasticism than ever the humanists of Italy, dilettantes like Pico della Mirandola who struggled to learn Greek because it was fashionable, knew of the Byzantine classical heritage. By the fourteenth century Aquinas was available in Greek in Constantinople, but one wonders if Gregory Palamas, the last great Father of Orthodoxy, was much heard of, let alone read, in the West.[24]

As in the field of art, it is true that there are a few significant examples of Byzantine literary and theological works passing into the West in the twelfth century, but, as in the field of art, their impact does not seem to have been particularly great. Peter Lombard had the earliest Latin translation (made in the second quarter of the century) of John of Damascus's great summary of Orthodox thought. But it was not until Aquinas that the version was used seriously. What seems more interesting is the circumstance of this translation: it was made by a Byzantine-educated Venetian in Hungary, one of the twelfth-century areas of overlap between the two cultures which are, potentially, a much more fruitful source of enquiry.

In the fields of art and learning I have tried to show that style, rather than substance, and some common sources, rather than contemporary intellectual developments, could be transmitted from Byzantium to the West in the twelfth century – sometimes in the guise of a western 'rediscovery' of the common classical past.

But on the other hand I have tried to hint that, if one is to look for tangible results of the meeting, the only real thresholds are the geographical ones, not only the traditional Byzantine-Western meeting-grounds in southern Italy and Venice, but also those which the events of the twelfth century created, from Hungary in the north to Mount Sinai in the south. Hungary is an excellent example of an area of overlap. Byzantine-Hungarian relations begin with the first appearance of the Magyars in Europe. Their Arpad kings from St Stephen (997–1038) adopted a Byzantine style of rule, but not the Byzantine Church. They were crowned with the coronet which Michael VII had sent to the 'kral of Tourkia' in 1074. Relations remained more or less close until Manuel I Comnenus, frustrated in his Italian ambitions by an intervening Serbo-Hungarian alliance, was forced into obtaining a complete Byzantine military victory over Hungary and establishing a sort of protectorate over the country after 1161. But by then a new situation had developed in Italy and Manuel had Barbarossa to face. Hungary also bedevilled Byzantine relations with Venice in Dalmatia. Nevertheless twelfth-century connections between the two countries were remarkably intimate. Now that the Pechenegs had been destroyed, the two states met along the Danube border. Byzantine-Hungarian relations were at two levels. First there were formal alliances. Manuel was the grandson of St Ladislas; his mother was the Hungarian empress Irene, foundress of the great Comnene monastery of the Pantocrator in Constantinople; and his daughter was originally designated for the future Bela III. By naming Bela as his successor, Manuel even seems to have entertained the hope of uniting the two states. On his accession to the Hungarian throne in 1172, Bela made certain undertakings to Byzantium, which held good until his death and the final separation of the two states in 1176; he married his daughter to Isaac II Angelus.

These relations were more than dynastic and there were more than simply Byzantine jewels at Esztergom. The second level of contact lay, for example, in the Byzantine liturgical books and the Orthodox calendar which strongly influenced Hungarian church practice. There are good examples of a hybrid Byzantine and local art in the eleventh century, from when at least four Greek monasteries flourished in Hungary. It is not clear how far these monasteries, and the Greek bishop in Hungary, served a Greek minority or were representatives of a genuinely composite culture. Certainly there was a sizeable Greek minority in Hungary, visited by Cardinal Isidore in the fifteenth century, when Pope Pius II significantly advised the Hungarian king to learn Greek for the sake of his Greek subjects. Pannonhalma, one of these Greek monasteries, was the scene of the twelfth-century translation into

Latin of parts of the works of John of Damascus and of Maximus the Confessor.[25]

I suggest that if one is looking for serious links, of substance as well as style, they can only really be found where there are Greeks on Latin soil and Latins on Greek. But such minorities, immensely extended during the twelfth century, tended to create sub-cultures of their own, with their own self-generated momentum, which hardly influenced the primary cultures of either participant. Professor Davis's contribution on William of Tyre exempts me from a discussion of Jerusalem and crusader Mount Sinai, but in the field of icon painting, at least, Outremer offers a very good example of how a genuinely common art, in manner as well as iconography, can be a growth of itself, hardly touching western or Byzantine traditions. Indeed, only one crusader icon seems to have reached the West.[26]

The new Serbian rulers, from *c.* 1168, like the Hungarians adopted a style of rule from the Comnenes. But Serbia lay much closer to Byzantium. There was a substantial Greek minority, later to be recognised in the title of Stephen Urosh iv Dushan (1331–55). Here there was also Latin influence, in style if not substance. Some of the decoration of the church of Stephen Nemanja (*c.* 1168–96) at Studenica (the arcaded cornices, receding columns and foliated capitals) have long been recognised as belonging to a western tradition – but which? One reminder is the tomb chapel of Bohemund of Antioch, built outside the cathedral of S. Sabinus at Canosa, near Bari, after 1111. This singular mausoleum sums up the cultural confusions of the earlier part of the century. It is in the form of a domed eastern church, with some remarkable bronze doors with Arab niello ornament. What reminds one of Studenica is the fine marble sheeting, recessed arcading and proportions of the building.[27] If, however, a connection could be established, it would be to a common source, a Latin style developed, like that of the crusader icons, in the Levant and not extending much further than its area of origin.

It is surprising that the major successful Serbian and Bulgarian risings against Byzantium were postponed until the last decades of the twelfth century. An explanation for the relative peacefulness of the twelfth-century Balkans seems to lie in their substantial Greek minorities and in the network of Greek landowners, officials and ecclesiastics. By the end of the century, patriarchal service was beginning to offer a more influential and extensive career to ambitious Greeks than could the empire itself; it was such men who held the Byzantine world together after the thirteenth century and after the empire of Constantinople itself ceased to count for very much. They are among a floating educated population and are

matched by a number of Byzantine dynasties which managed to
maintain a foothold in another area of overlap which must be considered: that between the Greek, Seljuk and Turkoman spheres of
influence in Anatolia. In the years between the collapse of Byzantine control in the East, before 1071, and the substitution of an
effective Seljuk alternative in the first decades of the twelfth
century, there were opportunities here for Frankish adventurers,
like Roussel de Bailleul or the Italian Crispin, and Armenian war-
lords such as Philaretos Vahrām.[28] How far this encounter affected
Seljuk art and architecture of the period is debatable.[29] In popular
religion, innumerable local cults bridged the gulf between the
official theologies of patriarchate and caliphate. The Comnene
emperors and Seljuk sultans Mas'ūd I and Kilij Arslan II were far
from being basically antagonistic. They were jointly opposed to
the Turkoman peoples who dominated the area of overlap between
their two states. As always, there were adventurers. Some Comnene princes turned Turk and at least one Turk turned, quite
literally, Comnene. Axouch, a Turkish prisoner of John II Comnenus, fought for the Byzantines. His son, Alexius Axouchos, was
protostrator under Manuel I and married Maria, grand-daughter
of John II. Their son, the Grand Domestic John Comnenus
Axouchos, was a pretender to the throne in 1201. In Trebizond,
John I Axouchos was Grand Comnenus in 1235-8. Similarly the
Athonite monastery of Koutloumousiou appears, as its name suggests, to have been founded by a Christian member of the Turkish
princely family.[30]

Some Byzantine families with strong local ties were torn between the two major powers. The best example is the Gabrades,
semi-autonomous dukes of Chaldia between the 1060s and 1140s.
Theodore Gabras, who died fighting the Turks in 1098, was
canonised as a Christian martyr, but in Turkoman heroic poetry
his amazonian daughter fought for Islam. In all probability St
Theodore Gabras's estates passed within a century, through
normal family inheritance, to a Mangujakid emir of Erzinjan
(whose dynasty issued coins bearing their Greek titles and the
figures of Orthodox saints) and to Hasan ibn Gabras, Kilij Arslan
II's vizir, who disputed them in 1192. Of the twelfth and thirteenth-
century Gabrades, four seem to have maintained a foothold in their
old estates in the Pontos, between the two cultures; two or three
served the Comnene emperors; and five or six held posts under the
Seljuk sultans. When Kaykubad sent an envoy to Pope Gregory
IX and the emperor Frederick II in 1234-6 he chose, of course, a
Seljuk Christian Gabras. The family seems to have ended up as
princes of Greek Gotthia, in the Crimea – but that is a different
hybrid culture.[31]

Families such as the Gabrades entered the twilight world between the Seljuk and Byzantine cultures. Another area of overlap was created by a few Frankish families in Byzantium, such as the Petraliphas (who were to produce an Orthodox saint) from about 1099,[32] and the Raoul or Rallis (who became equally Byzantinised) from about 1080.[33] Manuel I Comnenus, for whom the easy chivalry of the West was particularly appealing and whose happy personal relationship with the emperor Conrad is well known, employed a number of Latins, such as Alexander, count of Gravina and Roggero Sclavo, duke of Dalmatia.[34]

Comparable Byzantines in the West would be Christodoulos (Abdul-Rahman al-Nasrani), George of Antioch and Eugenius, Greek emirs of Norman Sicily. But we must be careful here: the presence of what one might call international Greeks, such as George of Antioch, in high places in Sicily, or of the Raouls in Byzantium, may not mean very much. There is a great difference between the Martorana, the Greek nunnery church which George of Antioch built in Palermo in 1143 in the most up-to-date 'international Byzantine' style of the time, and the humble and mundane contemporary churches of the local Greek communities of Sicily and Calabria. The Norman counts and kings endowed or founded up to seventy Greek religious houses before 1139, after which Roger II increasingly favoured the Latin foundations – the Greek chancery seems to have been abandoned by 1166. But the surviving buildings of these Greek monasteries are very homely affairs, reminiscent of local eighteenth-century Aegean architecture. It was not to this indigenous Byzantinism of Sicily and southern Italy that the Norman kings turned for their style of rule and major monuments, but to the international Byzantinism of men like George of Antioch, which on Sicilian soil became a new and hybrid tradition. But splendid as is the appearance of the great monuments of Norman Sicily, it is no more than a Byzantinism, a style. In essentials, the liturgical requirements which dictate the architectural plans and decorative programmes of such monuments as Cefalu (1131) and Monreale (1174), are unequivocally western.[35]

There were three possibilities open to Latins in Byzantium and the Levant, largely depending upon the circumstances of their arrival there. They could go native, like the Raoul family. This sometimes puzzled westerners. The fourth crusaders expected, but did not receive, a welcome from Agnes, sister of Philip Augustus, in Constantinople.[36] But she had been the wife of Alexius II, of Andronicus and then of Theodore Branas, and was long Byzantinised. As Choniates wrote of the Greeks who fled Byzantium to settle among the Seljuks: 'Habit, ingrained by the passage of Time, is indeed stronger than race or religion'.[37]

G

Secondly, like most crusaders, they could regard Outremer as a Frankish (or, more particularly, French) province. The Italians were more realistic, but the later internal government and even appearance of such colonies as Caffa, in the Crimea, were an attempt to transplant a north Italian city into the East. Some of the thirteenth-century Frankish building in the Levant is quite as uncompromising as the English mock-Tudor of India. For the background to the cathedrals of Nicosia and Famagusta one must go solely to the Île-de-France and Rheims; for part of the final building in Krak des Chevaliers to the Sainte-Chapelle, and for the Palazzo del Comune in Pera to the Palazzo di San Giorgio in Genoa.³⁸ There is a certain defiance in the legal niceties of the Assizes of Romania and in the gothic purity of the little church of Hagia Sophia at Andravida in the Morea.

The third possibility proved more lasting. It was to create a Levantine sub-culture, a true hybrid. This was largely the work of Latin, principally Italian, merchants in the East. But, until the literary and artistic schools of sixteenth-century Crete (and to a lesser extent Cyprus), it was not culturally very productive. The most notable twelfth-century exceptions are the Pisan brothers Leo Tuscus and Hugo Eterianus, who seem to have had an intelligent and informed interest in Byzantine theology.³⁹

The Pisans and Genoese arrived earliest in the Levant, but the Venetians took advantage of their experience and their long-established connections with Constantinople. Here their special, if ambiguous, relationship with the empire had stood them in good stead with the grant of the bull of 992, and of western powers it was recognised that Venice knew best how to deal with Byzantium. To the Levant came first casual visiting and wintering merchants. then the establishment of small sovereign bases, miniature Hong Kongs, and finally a demand for a say in the government of the host country. The process was slower in Byzantium, but in the Holy Land Venice completed all these stages as early as 1123, with the *Pactum Warmundum*, which made the commune of Tyre a theoretical and practical peer of the kingdom of Jerusalem. In Constantinople the final stage – the take-over of the host country itself – was the devastating conclusion reached in 1204. But the doge's new title of 'lord of a quarter and of half of a quarter of Romania' was in practice little different from his existing position in Tyre and Acre.⁴⁰

We must remember that Venice did not attempt to incorporate an Italian, as opposed to a Levantine, hinterland until after the war of Chioggia and the first years of the fifteenth century. During the twelfth and thirteenth centuries the hinterland of Venice was in practical fact the Levant. In the forty years before 1204 members of

a number of Venetian, including seven dogal, families wound up
their businesses in Italy and established themselves permanently
in the Levant. Regular inhabitants soon outnumbered transient
merchants in the Levantine and Byzantine ports. They became
numerous enough to create a sub-culture with what amounted to a
language of its own, the *lingua franca*. The *lingua franca* reflects the
interests of the sub-culture: many common nautical, commercial
and obscene words in modern Greek and Turkish are derived
from it.[41] There is little else save the impressive size of the Latin
communities. The figures are open to question, but there may have
been as many as 60,000 Italians (including 20,000 Venetians before
1171) in the Latin quarters of late twelfth-century Constantinople,
at a time when the population of Venice itself, large enough, was
about 64,000.[42] It has been claimed that this was the first genuine
European colonial movement of modern times and that some of
the characteristics of twelfth-century Venetian colonisation in the
Levant not only influenced later Italian expansions, but perhaps
even some patterns of colonisation in the Americas.[43]

This is the real threshold of the two cultures in the twelfth
century and, even with the vastly extended Venetian and Genoese
empires of the thirteenth and fourteenth centuries, little 'cultural'
came of it. But three observations can be made on the situation.

First, it is easy enough to assemble the views of Byzantine intellectuals – Theophylact of Ochrida, Anna Comnena, Eustathius of
Thessalonica or Nicetas Choniates – to show a mounting realisation for a distaste for the West and all its works throughout the
twelfth century. Byzantine aristocratic and intellectual prejudices
are typified in the consolation, helpfully offered in 1149 by Theodore Prodromus, to the mother of Manuel's niece Theodora when
she married Henry Babenberger, duke of Austria – or rather, was
'immolated to the Beast of the West'.[44] But I am not so sure how far
down the social scale this sort of feeling went. In the eleventh
century Crispin had been popular enough with the peasantry of
Colonia (Shebinkarahisar)[45] and Renier of Montferrat, Manuel's
son-in-law, seems later to have been well-liked in Macedonia.[46]
But ordinary Byzantines had other problems to contend with by
the last two decades of the twelfth century, for the main burden of
taxation was now being passed to them during a period of mounting local insecurity.[47] Some of Theodore Prodromus's other works
reveal that the real Byzantine dissensions were now between the
abbots and the great holders of land in *pronoia* and what were beginning to look like their serfs. From the Byzantine point of view,
1204 is only the culmination of an internal social, geographical and
political disintegration which, with the loss to local rulers of much

of the Balkans, Anatolia and Cyprus, had so far advanced that one wonders, if the Fourth Crusade had not come, the Greeks would not have had to invent it. In reality the crusaders conquered not an empire, initially, but a city, and the people of Thrace only jeered when they saw the archons of Constantinople fleeing it in 1204.[48]

It may be argued that the anti-Latin antagonism, shown in the Venetian expulsion from Constantinople in 1171 and the wave of anti-Latin feeling which brought Andronicus I Comnenus to the throne in 1182, express a resentment which is more than that of the intellectuals. But this was the urban mob of Constantinople, the ochlocrats who just as gleefully lynched Andronicus in 1185. Even the intellectuals could say one thing and do another. John Cinnamus, the historian and secretary to Manuel, sheltered and helped Venetians in their crisis of 1171[49]; Nicetas Choniates may have inveighed righteously against the Latins, but it was a Latin family that saved his life in 1204.[50] What can perhaps be traced is a growing awareness of a Greek, as opposed to Frankish, identity which was more specific than the old concepts of Orthodoxy and Romania. One of the earliest apparent uses of the term 'Hellene' in an ethnic, as opposed to a more or less pejorative pagan sense, comes in a letter of George Tornikes, later metropolitan of Ephesus, in about 1153.[51] This sort of distinction was largely confined to intellectuals until the fifteenth century, but it is a pointer. An argument can be made that the restored empire of 1261, or even that of 1205, was the first consciously Greek national state.

Lastly there is the question of the development of a 'Frankish', as opposed to Byzantine, identity. Part of the pride felt by the Normans of Sicily grew out of their encounters with the empire. It has been argued that the *Chanson de Roland* owes its origin as an encouragement of the morale of Robert Guiscard's troops in their campaigns against the Byzantines in the 1080s. But Franks rarely needed encouragement. As the first crusaders found, Byzantines were especially touchy about protocol and ceremony, always the targets of Frankish ridicule. The incident at Corfu in 1149, when Manuel's Venetian allies staged a mock coronation of an Ethiopian slave, dressed up as the emperor, and Manuel's reaction to the outrage, is particularly instructive.[52] By the mid-twelfth century the Frankish superiority complex was just as well developed as the Byzantine.

A second consideration is that, far from draining the life-blood of the empire's commerce, the Venetians in fact gave Byzantium trade on a scale that it had never enjoyed before. The feeding of the great population of Constantinople had always been a major imperial economic problem; now the city became an emporium and transit port such as it had never really been before, as well as an insatiable consumer. Commercially, the Italians created rather than supplanted. It is true that there was still the prohibitive 10 per cent *kommerkion* on Byzantine shipping while the Italians became near-exempt. But for Byzantine merchants the real problems were inadequate credit facilities and a failure to consider investment in large-scale commercial ventures; the Byzantine merchant marine was in fact almost entirely composed of local coastal shipping. The Venetians were certainly aggressive, but they were hardly competing against the Greeks and they brought them nothing but profit – albeit indirect. For example, the very first Comnene bull in favour of Venice of 1084 (with which I tentatively propose that the making of the Torcello apse mosaic and of the central bronze door of San Marco might perhaps be associated) gave the empire the use of the Venetian fleet in certain circumstances. Manuel revived and made substantial use of this clause. Nor is it true that the twelfth-century Byzantine economy was wrecked by either the Italians or the Seljuks – another unexpectedly profitable trading partner. After Alexius I Comnenus's monetary reforms, the Byzantine economy proved remarkably stable for most of the century. Some prices and salaries remained more or less static and gold coin of a fair standard was more abundant during most of the century than it had been for a very long time. It is true that there were devaluations, especially in the baser denominations, but it was not until the 1250s that the Italian cites had to replace Byzantine with their own gold as a reserve currency.[53] All this makes Manuel's blunder with the Venetians – particularly in the riots of 1171 and in the years of indemnity that followed – all the more impressive. It is comparable with the military and diplomatic blunder of Basil II in his treatment of the Armenian states, which helped lead the Seljuks into Byzantium.

Finally, I have narrowed down twelfth-century East-West cultural relations to a Levantine sub-culture, whose artistic and literary pretensions hardly existed. There were, in practice, no real papal restrictions on intermarriage in the twelfth century,[54] but the popular risings against the Latins in 1171 and 1182 suggest that, in certain circumstances and places, the Frankish communities had grown apart. In such situations prejudice, envy and suspicion get the upper hand, born of an ignorance which is never dispelled. But more often, Greek, Frankish and other communities lived side by side, apathetic of the true backgrounds to each others' cultures, borrowing only a style or an *argot* and feeding on rumours of the others' dangerous habits – like sinister azymite or prozymite practices. Anyone who knows modern Anatolia or the Lebanon will understand how two cultures can not so much co-exist as exist independently for centuries without serious contact or necessarily coming into conflict. One knows of adjacent villages and, in towns, even parallel streets, whose inhabitants are drawn from not very different ethnic, linguistic or religious traditions, but which hardly recognise each others' existence. Unconcerned by their immediate neighbours, they look to a wider world of related communities elsewhere. The Byzantine Jews, whose small communities were scattered over the empire and described by Benjamin of Tudela in the 1160s,[55] were one such example and the twelfth-century Franks fell quite naturally into the pattern. This attitude arises not from antagonism, but rather a simple lack of curiosity. When both sides were obliged to meet, they did so on limited and severely practical terms, charmingly exemplified in a Greco-Latin conversation manual which survives.[56] Reminiscent of the *aperçu linguistique* of a *Guide Bleu*, the manual lists phrases which would enable a Frank to obtain an hotel room and other conveniences in Constantinople. But then, what did one expect – a Socratic dialogue?

So the original aim of identifying serious East-West cultural contacts in the twelfth century has proved unreasonable. Unless they felt threatened, Greeks and Latins were still basically incurious of each other. The only practical results of the encounters of the century were the hybrid societies they created, the quays where the *lingua franca* was spoken, the international Greeks, the Greco-Hungarians, Greco-Turks and Greco-Latins. There is little high culture among them and their influence was always local, but that is where the enquiry must eventually take one.

NOTES

*   I am grateful to members of the Department of History Colloquium on 'East-West contacts in the Middle Ages' at the Institute for Advanced Studies in the Humanities, University of Edinburgh, and to Mr Michael Hendy and Mr David Winfield, for criticism of this paper.

1   [Ernst] Kitzinger, ['The Byzantine Contribution to Western Art of the Twelfth and Thirteenth Centuries'], *DOP*, xx (1966) p. 47 : 'Here lies a vast field of further enquiry'.

2   Robert Browning, 'Byzantine scholarship', *Past & Present*, 28 (July 1964) p. 16 : 'The question which springs to the mind is what sort of connection there is between this renewal of philosophy in Constantinople and the so-called twelfth-century Renaissance in western Europe'.

3   See *Il Tesoro di San Marco, La Pala d'Oro*, ed. H. R. Hahnloser (Florence 1965) and J. Déer, 'Die Pala d'Oro in neuer Sicht', *BZ*, LXII (1969) pp. 308–44.

4   One of the most interesting examples of twelfth- or thirteenth-century silkwork is the painted silk icon of St Justus in the

cathedral of San Giusto, Trieste. On the discovery of stained glass of *c.* 1126, evidently antedating the Augsburg examples, in the Comnene church of the Pantocrator in Constantinople, see Arthur H. S. Megaw, 'Notes on Recent Work of the Byzantine Institute in Istanbul', *D O P*, xvii (1963) pp. 349–364 and figs F–L.

5   S. G. Mercati, 'Sulla Santissima Icone nel duomo di Spoleto', *Spoletium*, iii (1956) pp. 3ff.

6   See Hans R. Hahnloser, *Das Musterbuch von Wolfenbüttel, Mitteilungen der Gesellschaft für Vervielfältigende Kunst* (Vienna 1929) and Kurt Weitzmann, 'Zur byzantinischen Quelle des Wolfenbüttler Musterbuches', *Festschrift Hans R. Hahnloser* (Basel 1961) pp. 223ff.

7   There is now a substantial literature on Castelseprio; see especially Kurt Weitzmann, *The Fresco Cycle of S. Maria di Castelseprio* (Princeton 1951).

8   Cf. Wilhelm Koehler, 'Byzantine Art in the West', *D O P*, i (1941) pp. 61–87, an important paper which initiated current discussion on the subject.

9   See Kitzinger; David Talbot Rice, *Byzantine Painting, The Last Phase* (London 1968) pp. 73–103; Kurt Weitzmann, 'Various Aspects of Byzantine Influence on the Latin Countries from the Sixth to the Twelfth Century', *D O P*, xx (1966) pp. 20–4; and J. Wettstein, 'Les Fresques bourguignonnes de Berzé-la-Ville et la question byzantine', *Byz*, xxxviii (1968) pp. 243–66. In Christopher Brooke, *The Twelfth Century Renaissance* (London 1969) illustrations 115–118 (of St Paul in Canterbury cathedral and in the Palatine chapel, Palermo, and of the Dormition of the Mother of God in the Henry of Blois psalter and in the Martorana, Palermo) clearly demonstrate how wide was the gulf between eastern and western models, although the author apparently chose them to prove the opposite. This failure to more than approximate Byzantine models is seen again in the nineteenth century before the use of photography, in, for example, the restoration of a number of mosaics in Ravenna, the copy of the Galla Placidia mosaic of the Good Shepherd in Holt church, Worcestershire and, even, in the copies of the sub-Byzantine mosaics of San Marco which John Ruskin commissioned.

10   See [J. M.] Hussey, *Church and Learning in the [Byzantine Empire, 867–1185]* (London 1937) pp. 201–25.

11   Cf. [Steven] Runciman, *[The Eastern] Schism* (Oxford 1955) pp. 72–7 and Martin Jugie, *Le Schisme byzantin* (Paris 1941) pp. 243–6. Theophylact's treatise on the Latins is in *P G*, cxxvi, cols 222–50.

12   See Theophylact's peevish letter in *P G*, cxxvi, cols 324–5.

13   Oration in *P G*, cxxvi, col. 306; cf. Ernest Barker, *Social and Political Thought in Byzantium* (Oxford 1957) p. 149; and, on the academic background of Theophylact, Karl Prachter, 'Antike Quellen des Theophylaktos von Bulgarien', *BZ*, i (1892) pp. 399–414.

14   *The Chronographia of Michael Psellus*, tr. E. R. A. Sewter (London 1953) pp. 127–30; cf. Hussey, *Church and Learning*, pp. 73–88.

15 R.W. Southern, *The Making of the Middle Ages* (London 1953) pp. 210, 220.

16 See K. Setton, 'The Byzantine Background to the Italian Renaissance', *Proceedings of the American Philosophical Society*, c (1956) p. 19; L. Minio-Paluello, 'Jacobus Veneticus Grecus', *Traditio*, VIII (1952) pp. 265–304; and C. H. Haskins, *Studies in the History of Medieval Science* (Cambridge 1924) pp. 227–32.

17 See C. H. Haskins, *The Renaissance of the Twelfth Century* (Cleveland-New York 1968) pp. 292–3.

18 Cf. Peter Munz, *Frederick Barbarossa* (London 1969) p. 168 n. 1; and H. J. Scheltema in [*The*] *C* [*ambridge*] *M* [*edieval*] *H* [*istory*], IV, 2 (Cambridge 1967) pp. 71–3.

19 Deno J. Geanakoplos, *Byzantine East and Latin West: Two Worlds of Christendom in the Middle Ages and Renaissance* (Oxford 1966) pp. 33–4; and John Julius Norwich, *The Kingdom in the Sun* (London 1970) p. 91.

20 Runciman, *Schism*, p. 122; Manouel I. Gedeon, *Patriarchikoi Pinakes* (Constantinople n.d.) pp. 365–8.

21 Cf. Osman Turan, 'Les Souverains seljoukides et leurs sujets non-musulmans', *S* [*tudia*] *I* [*slamica*], I (1953) pp. 65–100; Halil Inalcik, 'Ottoman methods of conquest', *SI*, II (1954) pp. 103–30; Claude Cahen, *Pre-Ottoman Turkey* (London 1968) pp. 202–15; and, for the experience of Edessa (Urfa) in and before 1146, J. B. Segal, *Edessa, 'The Blessed City'* (Oxford 1970) pp. 241–54.

22 Eustathius of Thessalonica, *De capta Thessalonica narratio*, in *CSHB* (1842) pp. 365–512; cf. [Charles M.] Brand, *Byzantium confronts the West*, [*1180–1204*] (Cambridge, Mass., 1968) pp. 166–9.

23 Nicetas Choniates, *Historia*, in *CSHB* (1835) p. 391; cf. Donald M. Nicol, 'The Byzantine View of Western Europe', *Greek, Roman and Byzantine Studies*, VIII, 4 (1967) p. 330.

24 See, for example, Démétrius Cydonès, *Correspondance*, ed. Giuseppe Cammelli (Paris 1930) pp. v–xxxiv; Steven Runciman, *The Last Byzantine Renaissance* (Cambridge 1970) pp. 42, 74–5; and John Meyendorff, *A Study of Gregory Palamas* (London 1964).

25 See Andrew B. Urbansky, *Byzantium and the Danube Frontier* (New York 1968); G. Moravcsik in *CMH*, IV, 1 (1966) pp. 567–92; and the same's *Byzantium and the Magyars* (Amsterdam 1970).

26 In Grottaferrata: Kurt Weitzmann, 'Icon Painting in the Crusader Kingdom', *DOP*, XX (1966) p. 75; see also Hugo Buchthal, *Miniature Painting in the Latin Kingdom of Jerusalem* (Oxford 1957).

27 See *Studenica*, ed. M. Maletić (Belgrade 1968); and, on Bohemund's tomb, Pietro Toesca, *Storia dell'arte italiana*, I (Turin 1927) pp. 605–7, 1107, 1115; Émile Bertaux (who observes that it looks more like a Muslim *türbe* than a Christian tomb), *L'Art dans l'Italie méridionale*, I (Paris 1904) pp. 313–15 and figs 121–3; and R. B. Yewdale, *Bohemund I, Prince of Antioch* (Princeton 1924 / Amsterdam 1970) pp. 133–4. I am grateful to Professor E. K. Waterhouse for originally drawing my attention to this monument.

28 The best work on the subject remains [J.] Laurent, *Byzance et les Turcs [seldjoucides dans l'Asie Occidentale jusqu'en 1081]* (Nancy 1913).

29 For a survey, incorporating a review of Cahen, *Pre-Ottoman Turkey*, see J.M.Rogers, 'Recent Work on Seljuk Anatolia', *Kunst des Orients*, VI, 2 (1970) pp.134–69.

30 On the Axouchos family, see [Ferdinand] Chalandon, *Les Comnène*, II (Paris 1912/New York, n.d.) *passim*; and William Miller, *Trebizond, The last Greek Empire (of the Byzantine Era)* (London 1926/Chicago 1969) ed. Anastasius C.Bandy, pp.19, 24, 26. On the Athonite monastery, see Paul Lemerle, *Actes de Kutlumus, Archives de l'Athos*, II (Paris 1946) pp.3–5; the notions of L.L.Lousides in 'Koutlomoussion-Koutlomousi', *Byzantinisch-neugriechische Jahrbücher*, XVI (1939–43) pp.53–60, are too tortuous to be convincing.

31 See Anthony Bryer, 'A Byzantine family: the Gabrades, *c.* 979–*c.*1653', in the 'Byzantina-Metabyzantina' issue of the *U[niversity of] B[irmingham] H[istorical] J[ournal]*, XII, 2 (1970) pp.164–87.

32 Donald M.Nicol, *The Despotate of Epiros* (Oxford 1957) pp. 215–16.

33 Antonios Ch. Chatzes, *Hoi Rhaoul, Rhal, Rhalai (1080–1800)* (Kirchhain N.-L. 1909) pp.9–13. The family ended up by founding the Raleigh Bicycle Company.

34 Chalandon, *Les Comnène*, II, 1, p.363. On Manuel's relations with the West, see the magisterial work of Paolo Lamma, *Comneni e Staufer*, II (Rome 1957).

35 See Giuseppe Agnello, *I monumenti bizantini della Sicilia* (Florence n.d.); Mario Scaduto, *Il monachismo basiliano nella Sicilia Medievale* (Rome 1947); Otto Demus, *The Mosaics of Norman Sicily* (London 1950); F.Chalandon, *Histoire de la domination normande en Italie et en Sicile* (Paris 1907)); E. Jamison, *Admiral Eugenius of Sicily* (London 1957); Denis Mack Smith, *A History of Sicily: Medieval Sicily, 800–1713* (London 1968); and Henry Gally Knight, *The Normans in Sicily* (London 1838), which describes some now deteriorated monuments.

36 Robert de Clary, 'La Prise de Constantinople' in Charles Hopf, *Chroniques gréco-romanes* (Berlin 1873/Athens 1961) p. 45.

37 Nicetas Choniates in *CSHB*, p.50; cf. p.657 and John Cinnamus, '*Epitome rerum ab Ioanne et Alexio Comnenis gestarum*', in *CSHB* (1836) p.22.

38 Now hardly recognisable; see Semavi Eyice, *Galata ve kulesi – Galata and its Tower* (Istanbul 1969) pp.16, 52–3.

39 See M.Anastos, 'Some aspects of Byzantine influence on Latin Thought, *Twelfth Century Europe and the Foundations of Modern Society* (Madison 1961) pp.138–49.

40 Joshua Prawer, *The Venetians and the Venetian colonies in the Latin kingdom of Jerusalem*, cyclostyled paper given at the conference on 'Venice and the Levant', Cini Foundation (Venice 1968); cf. the same's *Histoire du royaume latin de Jérusalem*, I (Paris 1969) pp.500–3; Freddy Thiriet, *La Romanie vénitienne au Moyen-âge*, I (Leipzig 1885/Amsterdam 1967) pp.129–264.

41 Henry and Renée Kahane and Andreas Tietze, *The Lingua*

Franca in the Levant (Urbana 1958) is a study of Turkish
nautical terms of Italian and Greek origin; see also Phaidon
Koukoules, *Byzantinon Bios kai Politismos*, vi (Athens 1955)
pp. 536–9.

42   See Brand, *Byzantium confronts the West*, pp. 202–6; and
Horatio F. Brown, 'The Venetians and the Venetian Quarter
in Constantinople to the Close of the Twelfth Century',
Journal of Hellenic Studies, xl (1920) pp. 68–88.

43   See Prawer, in p. 93, n. 40.

44   Cited by Steven Runciman in *A History of the Crusades*, ii
(Cambridge 1952) p. 285.

45   Laurent, *Byzance et les Turcs*, pp. 65–6.

46   Chalandon, *Les Comnène*, ii, pp. 212, 600; R. L. Wolff, 'The
Fourth Crusade' in *A History of the Crusades*, ed. K. M. Setton
and others, ii (Philadelphia 1962) p. 165.

47   See Judith Herrin, 'The collapse of the Byzantine Empire in
the twelfth century : a study of a medieval economy',
UBHJ, xii, 2 (1970) pp. 188–203.

48   Nicetas Choniates in *CSHB*, p. 785; see also Anthony Bryer,
'The First Encounter with the West' in *Byzantium. An Introduction*, ed. P. D. Whitting (Oxford 1970) pp. 104–9.

49   John Cinnamus in *CSHB*, pp. 280–6.

50   Nicetas Choniates in *CSHB*, pp. 776–85.

51   Robert Browning, *Greece – Ancient and Mediaeval* (London,
Birkbeck College, 1966) p. 16 and n. 56.

52   Dj. Sp. Radojičić, 'Un Poème épique yougoslave du XIᵉ
siècle : les *gesta* ou exploits de Vladimir, prince de Dioclée',
Byz, xxxv (1965) p. 532; Chalandon, *Les Comnène*, ii, p. 329.

53   The twelfth-century Byzantine economy is still open to
differing interpretations. For recent discussions, see Herrin,
UBHJ, xii, 2, (1970) pp. 188–203; H. Antoniadis-Bibicou, 'Problèmes d'histoire économique de Byzance au XIᵉ
siècle : démographie, salaires et prix', *Byzantinoslavica*, xxviii
(1967) pp. 255–61 and E. Frances, 'Alexis Comnène et les
privilèges octroyés à Venise', *Byzantinoslavica*, xxix (1968)
pp. 17–23; on the monetary economy, see Michael F. Hendy,
Coinage and Money in the Byzantine Empire, 1081–1267, Dumbarton Oaks Studies, xii (1969); on shipping, see Hélène
Ahrweiler, *Byzance et la mer* (Paris 1966) pp. 256–7; on Constantinople, see Dean A. Miller, *Imperial Constantinople* (n.p.
1969) pp. 43–78; and on credit facilities, see Steven Runciman,
The Emperor Romanus Lecapenus and his reign (Cambridge
1963) pp. 252–3 (appendix iii).

54   Cf. D. M. Nicol, 'Mixed Marriages in Byzantium in the Thirteenth Century', *Studies in Church History*, i (London 1964),
pp. 160–74.

55   Joshua Starr, *The Jews in the Byzantine Empire, 641–1204*
(Athens 1939 / Farnborough 1969) pp. 228–35.

56   M. A. Triantaphyllides, *Neoellenike grammatike : Historike
eisagoge* (Athens 1938) p. 195; cf. George Thomson, *The
Greek Language* (Cambridge 1960) pp. 51–2.

Innocent III and the Greeks : Aggressor or Apostle?

JOSEPH GILL, S.J.

Walter Norden, author of the deservedly well-known book, *Das Papsttum und Byzanz*, freely admits that Pope Innocent after the conquest of Constantinople in 1204 did not try to impose upon the Greeks conformity with the Latins in faith and rite. He then asks why and answers in these words.

> The Curia employed this restraint simply and solely for political ends. It appears here obviously that the papacy, as a purely ecclesiastical power and also in spheres where she entered not as a directly political power whether in Italy or in the world at large, aimed in the main at a political goal, in so far, that is, as for her it all came to this – to govern and to wield influence. Since Innocent III in respect of the Greek Church let the spiritual drive fall back into the second place and declared himself satisfied with obedience from the Greek clergy in respect of Rome, he disclosed the basic characteristic of the Roman Church as being one of spiritual politics; he revealed it as the continuation, admittedly rooted in the consciousness of a religious mission, of the *Imperium Romanum*. The transformation of Greek priests, who hitherto had stood outside the Roman organism, into pliant tools of Roman domination, as if in government offices, was the chief objective of the Curia in latinised Byzantium; on the other hand, she considered the conversion of the Greeks to the Roman faith – which [conversion], by the way, as we saw, she by no means lost sight of and which she regarded, owing to the predominantly Latin character of Romania [i.e. the Empire], merely as a question of time – as an affair of a less pressing nature, as one of second-rate importance. She left, however, the Greek rite definitely free.[1]

Norden's judgement of Pope Innocent's actions is shared by many other historians.[2] The papal letters, especially those directed to countries and Churches outside the Latin Church – but not only those – seem *prima facie* to endorse that judgement fully. They abound in assertions of the primacy of the see of Rome, of the exalted position of its bishop as successor of St Peter and vicar of Christ and of his consequent universal jurisdiction. In his first letters to the Greek emperor Alexius III and the patriarch John Camaterus (August 1198) Innocent reminds them both that the Greek Church should return as daughter to the Church which is

mother and mistress of all the faithful.[3] A year later, replying at
length to the patriarch's rebuttal of his claims, he gives argument
after argument in their favour, that 'the Roman Church, not by
the decision of some council, but by divine ordinance is head and
mother of all the Churches'.[4] When an occasion offered for these
convictions to be given practical effect he did not let it slip. After
the first capture of Constantinople in 1203 by Alexius IV and the
crusaders, Innocent wrote to them all urging that a proof of the
sincerity of their promises and excuses would be if they prevailed
on the patriarch 'to recognise the primacy and the supreme teaching office of the Roman Church, to promise reverence and obedience to Us, and to request from the Apostolic See the pallium taken
from the body of St Peter, without which he cannot validly [*rite*]
exercise the patriarchal office'.[5]

What the pallium signified is described in the formula used at
its bestowal on the Bulgarian archbishop of Tirnovo. It was 'the
mark of the fulness of the pontifical office', and was to be worn by
metropolitans only in churches subject to them and on certain
feastdays and occasions. There was this limitation because 'only
the Roman Pontiff uses the pallium in the Mass always and everywhere, since he has been invested with the fulness of ecclesiastical
power, which is symbolised by the pallium. Others should wear
it neither always nor everywhere but on certain days and in their
own Church in which they have received ecclesiastical jurisdiction,
for they are called to a part of the solicitude [of the Churches] not
to the plenitude of power'.[6]

Let these few quotations suffice to illustrate the way Innocent
insisted on the claims of the see of Rome and of its occupant. They
could be supplemented by dozens and dozens of others from his
sermons and letters to Bulgaria, Armenia and other countries, to
Greeks and Latins in the Eastern Empire, to prelates and kings in
the West. They witness to his absolute conviction and belief that
as pope he was head of all Christians, vicar of Christ, successor of
St Peter, heir to the universal jurisdiction accorded by Christ to the
prince of the Apostles, and holder of a teaching office that others
should honour. If his endless repetition of statements to this effect
strikes us as utterly extravagant and almost nauseating, yet we
should not forget that the substance of them was, and is, the belief
of the Roman Church, usually expressed, may be, in more sober
terms but not less firmly.

In 1439 the Council of Florence with the approval of the numerous Greek members present, in words almost reminiscent of
Innocent III, defined:

> Also in the same way we define that the holy, apostolic See
> and the Roman Pontiff hold the primacy over the whole

world and that the Roman Pontiff himself is the successor of St Peter, prince of the Apostles, and that he is the true vicar of Christ, head of the whole Church and father and teacher of all Christians, and that to the same in St Peter was given plenary power of feeding, ruling and governing the whole Church, as is contained also in the Acts of the ecumenical councils and the sacred canons.[7]

The first Vatican Council in 1870 repeated verbatim the definition of Florence and continued:

In consequence we teach and declare that the] Roman Church possesses by dominical ordinance a primacy of ordinary power and that this power of jurisdiction of the Roman pontiff is truly episcopal and immediate. Pastors of all ranks and rites and the faithful, each one separately and all together, are held to the duty of hierarchical subordination and of true obedience, not only in questions of faith and morals but also in those that pertain to the discipline and the government of the Church spread over all the world.[8]

The second Vatican Council in various places in chapter III of the dogmatic constitution *Lumen gentium* repeated the teaching of Vatican I. 'This holy council, following in the footsteps of Vatican I', teaches that Christ founded a Church with bishops. 'In order that the episcopate should be one and undivided, He set St Peter over the other Apostles and in him established a perpetual and visible principle and foundation of unity of faith and communion.[9] This doctrine about the institution, permanence, validity and reason of the sacred primacy of the Roman pontiff and of his infallible authority and office, the Holy Synod again proposes to be firmly believed by all the faithful.' 'In virtue of his office, that is, as Vicar of Christ and Pastor of the whole Church, the Roman Pontiff has full, supreme and universal power over the Church, which he may always exercise freely'.[10]

This fact that the universality of the jurisdiction of the bishop of Rome was for Innocent and the western Church a doctrine, and not merely an aim, has been forgotten by many. In consequence they can affirm or imply that Innocent's insistence on the oath of obedience in, for example, his dealings with the Greeks was to put faith in the second place or in no place at all, and to pursue a policy of purely political domination. That is not so. The oath of obedience was the external sign of acceptance of the Roman teaching on the primacy and, while it may also have tended towards – and, if you like, have been meant by Innocent to tend towards – political domination, its primary purpose was to insist on the point of doctrine that it asserted.

Innocent, however, is blamed for harping on this one point

and ignoring whatever other dogmatic questions divided the
Churches. In his letters he often stated that the Greek Church had
left the universal Church by embracing error. He specified only
two forms of that error; the one, their denial of the primacy of
Rome; the other, their rejection of the *Filioque* doctrine. He never,
it is true, personally[11] exhorted the Greeks to recant their trinitarian aberration, whereas he never ceased to insist on their
acceptance of obedience. But the reason is not far to seek. The one
included the other. The full idea of Roman supremacy implied also
a superior teaching authority. Whoever sincerely accepted that
Peter and his successors were the rock on which the Church was
founded and the principal receivers of the keys accepted a papal
primacy of teaching as well as of jurisdiction, for the rock meant
inerrancy in faith and the keys a supremacy of jurisdiction. Innocent wrote to the patriarch of Constantinople and the emperor in
identical terms on this point.

> Seeing then . . . that the Roman Church is the head and mother
> of all Churches not by the decision of some council but by
> divine ordinance, so, because of difference neither of rite nor
> of dogma, should you hesitate to obey Us as your head
> generously and devotedly in accordance with ancient custom
> and the canons, since what is certain is not to be abandoned
> in favour of what is doubtful.[12]

For Innocent what was certain was the primacy of faith and jurisdiction of the successor of St Peter. What in another Church did
not harmonise with that was at the least doubtful.

An example, typical in many ways, of Innocent's expression of
this conviction is contained in the long letter that he wrote on
13 November 1204 'To the Bishops, Abbots, and other Clerics
with the Army of the Crusaders in Constantinople'. It consists of
an intricate exegesis of the visits of Mary Magdalen and the
apostles Peter and John to the tomb of the risen Lord. St Peter and
the Latin Church are the New Testament; St John and the Greek
Church, the Old Testament.[13] St Peter entered the tomb; St John
remained outside. So the Latins had the fulness of the teaching of
the New Testament; the Greeks enmeshed in the Old Testament
fell short of that, being in error in their trinitarian doctrine.

> If this mystery had been understood by the Greeks, they
> would already have entered with the Latins into the sepulchre,
> knowing that God is not a God of dissension but of peace. But,
> because John did not yet know the scriptures, namely, that
> Christ must rise again from the dead, it is nothing to be
> surprised at if the Greeks still do not know that, where the
> Spirit of Christ lives, the letter is dead. But they will soon
> know; such is Our belief and hope. They will know; yes, they

will know; and the rest of them will be converted with all their hearts . . . For [John] will see what Peter had seen and will believe what the Church of the Latins believes, so that henceforward they will walk in the house of the Lord in harmony.[14]

Though he never doubted about the supremacy of the Church of which he was the head, Innocent did not employ or permit repressive measures to impose the Latin Church on the Greeks. He recognised as valid the orders of bishops, priests and deacons of the oriental Church. It is true that he thought the ordination rites defective because they contained no anointings. In the more pliant Bulgarian Church he ordered that the missing unctions should be supplied to those already consecrated and ordained, but in the Greek Church he allowed bishops and abbots already in office to remain unmolested, even though new bishops and abbots were to have the anointings. When the Latin archbishop of Athens deposed Theodore of Negroponte because he would not submit to supplementary anointings, Innocent on the appeal of the victim appointed a commission to reinstate him; and this was done. Otherwise he changed nothing of the Greek rite, though there were many differences of detail between it and the Roman rite. He encouraged monks to abide in their monasteries, for which he cherished an admiration : 'But, because to the Greek people was given St John, who was the source of the religious life of perfect monks, the Greek Church well portrays the character of the Spirit, who seeks and loves spiritual men'.[15] The monasteries of Mount Athos and others he took under his protection. He sent legates to meet the Greeks in theological conversations to draw them to unity. Benedict, cardinal of S. Susanna, was well known for his gentleness of manner and geniality of character. Pelagius, bishop of Albano, has a reputation for being harsh and brusque, but Nicholas Mesarites in his account of the discussions held with him in 1214 portrays him (not quite fairly) as proud, but not as overbearing.

But, of course, Innocent did insist on all prelates taking an oath of obedience to himself and to the Latin patriarch. Yet even this insistence was to be tempered as much as possible with moderation. The reluctant were to be given three canonical warnings before excommunication. If they persisted in their contumacy the cardinal legate (but not Morosini) should remove them from the administration of their bishoprics and replace them, but not even he should promulgate the sentence of degradation, so as to leave the door open to a possible change of heart.[16] Few Greek bishops did, however, take the oath and among them no one of high importance. They preferred to leave their sees for Nicaea or Epirus and the hope of a final Greek triumph. The oath of obedience was, in fact, a form of pressure from which many suffered.

What might have been the alternative? To leave the Greek patriarch and hierarchy in their sees and the whole Greek Church in the same schismatical relationship with the Latin as before, though by then the Latins were the kings and princes of the country and established in every part? The mentality of today would approve of this solution. But I wonder if it was possible for the men of yesterday. Innocent would not tolerate two bishops in any one diocese. Such would have been a monster, a body with two heads.[17] Would it have been conceivable in the thirteenth century that Latins of pure faith (as they believed) and unassailable rite should be under Greeks whose faith was defective and whose rite and customs strange and in part distressing?

For Innocent there was no problem seeking a solution. The new situation had simplified the issue. In his eyes the military conquest of the Greek Empire involved automatically the union of the eastern and the western Churches. He declared this time and again in his letters after the capture, and offered no explanation. He only drew practical conclusions that he hoped would follow. In his letter to the ecclesiastics of Constantinople of 13 November 1204 he wrote : God 'transferred the Empire of Constantinople from the proud to the humble, from the disobedient to the devoted, from schismatics to Catholics, that is, from the Greeks to the Latins . . . the right hand of the Lord has done acts of valour to exalt the holy Roman Church, as it brings back the daughter to the mother, the part to the whole, and the member to the head'.[18] In his next letter to them he comes back to the idea more than once. Commenting on the incident of Our Lord preaching from Peter's boat and of the miraculous draught of fishes, he wrote :

> The other ship was the Greek Church . . . [which] We summoned to come to help Us, that is, that returning they should take up again part of Our solicitude as helpers in the providential task allotted to Us. But by God's grace they came because, after the Empire of Constantinople was transferred in these days to the Latins, the Church also of Constantinople came back to obedience to the Apostolic See as a daughter to her mother and a member to the head, so that for the future there might reign between Us and them an undivided partnership. Truly We proclaim them brethren, partners, and friends, because, though We have over them the office of government, it is a government that leads not to domination but to service . . . See, then, our partners come to help us, because the Church of the Greeks returns to obedience of the Apostolic see.[19]

These quotations express Innocent's conviction clearly, a conviction he did not change. He reiterated it time and again as the years passed. It figured even in the Acts of the Council of the Lateran, which preceded his death by only a little over a year. The fourth *capitulum* of that council, entitled 'On the Pride of the Greeks against the Latins', opens with the words : 'Whereas we wish to cherish and honour the Greeks, who in our day return to obedience to the Holy See, by maintaining as far as we can in the Lord their customs and rites, nevertheless . . .'[20]

This equating of political conquest with ecclesiastical union as being almost axiomatic is strange. The explanation may lie in historical precedent. Allegiance to Constantinople or Rome of the Greek churches and monasteries of Sicily and South Italy tended to come and go according as Greek or Norman held the reins of government. On the whole the popes had defended the Greek rite and been not a little responsible for its survival despite the determination of Normans like Roger of Sicily to latinize everything. It showed that the Greek rite could flourish under Roman jurisdiction, and, in point of fact, it was flourishing in Innocent's day and with his support. The interpreter of both Cardinal Benedict and Cardinal Pelagius was the Greek abbot of Otranto, Nicholas. Then, too, the will of monarchs, particularly of oriental monarchs, counted for much. Leo the Isaurian, as a retaliation for opposition to his iconoclastic policy, had punished Rome by transferring Illyricum and Sicily to the jurisdiction of Constantinople. Innocent believed that the Greek emperors of his day could command obedience from the patriarch and the Church. He told Alexius III : 'Strive – nay! seeing that you can do it, bring it about – that the Church of the Greeks return to the unity of the Apostolic See and that the daughter come back to the mother'.[21] Alexius IV, too, was expected to direct both patriarch and Church towards Rome.[22] The princes, not the Churches, of Serbia, Bulgaria and Armenia had all solicited his protection, and the Churches had enthusiastically concurred. In Jerusalem, Antioch and Alexandria Latin patriarchs had been appointed. In Jerusalem the see was vacant when the Latins arrived ; in the other two cities it was a question of Latin or Greek influence and in Antioch an irate prince manipulated the patriarchate to further his own interests. In Cyprus also, with the political domination of western power, the main sees of the local Church were put into Latin hands and the indigenous Greek Church was made subordinate. In other words, it had been the custom and it was the custom. Innocent did no more than follow the custom in the conviction that he was conferring the benefit of the truth on the misguided.

For, after all, the victory of the pilgrim army was an act of God.

H

Emperor Baldwin in his letter announcing the capture of the eastern capital had no doubt of it : 'God's wonders follow ever one on another in our regard, so that even the infidel should not doubt that the hand of God is bringing all this to pass, since nothing of what we had previously hoped for and forecast succeeded and then in the end the Lord provided new aids when nothing of human counsel remained'.[23] Pope Innocent was equally convinced. He opened his letter to the Latin ecclesiastics of Constantinople with these words :

> We read in the prophet Daniel that it is God in heaven who reveals mysteries; He changes times and transfers kingdoms. This we see fulfilled in our day in the kingdom of the Greeks and we rejoice, since He who holds power in the kingdom of men and who will give it to whomso He wills, has transferred the Empire of Constantinople from the proud to the humble, from the disobedient to the devoted, from schismatics to Catholics, that is, from the Greeks to the Latins. Indeed, that was done by the Lord and it is marvellous in our sight. This is verily the change of the right hand of the Most High in which the right hand of the Lord performs acts of valour'.[24]

Not only was the victory the act of the right hand of the Lord to favour the Latins and their faith. It was at the same time a punishment of the Greeks for their sin of schism. The emperor Baldwin in the same letter recorded his belief. 'These and other ravings [i.e. the Greek errors and their treatment of Latins] which the limits of a letter cannot narrate at length, when the cup of their iniquities had been filled full (iniquities which moved even God to nausea), divine Justice by our means visited with a worthy vengeance and, driving out men who hate God and love only themselves, has given to us a land flowing with abundance of every good'.[25] This is a theme that Innocent only touched on in his communications to the crusaders, but he agreed with it and in a letter to Theodore Lascaris himself he propounded his belief though with moderation. Lascaris had written to the pope accusing the Latins of apostasy for turning Christian arms against Christians, of sacrilege for sacking holy places in Constantinople, of perjury for breaking treaties. Innocent replied : 'We do not excuse the Latins whom often We have reproved for their excesses, but We have thought good to put before you in this letter the excuses they make for themselves', whereupon he repeats almost verbatim the explanation offered him in August 1205 by Montferrat.[26] He continued :

> But allowing that they are not altogether without blame, still We believe that through them the Greeks were punished by a just judgement of God, because they acted to rend the seam-

less garment of Jesus Christ. For since God's judgements are
so hidden that they are called a vast abyss by the prophet, it
often occurs that by His hidden, but ever most just judgement,
the evil are punished by the agency of the evil.

He ended by counselling Theodore to accept that judgement and
to submit to the Latin emperor Henry, to whom divine power had
given the empire.[27]

When Constantinople was taken by the crusade that Innocent
had set in motion and promoted, he could and, I think, did expect
that the conquered territories would become a fief of sorts of the
Holy See, even though he had never approved of the diversion
of the army to the Bosphorus. His letter answering Baldwin's
announcement of the victory suggests such a hope and it was in
harmony with the trend in the West. Whether this supposition is
true or not, once he had received the terms of the pact entered into
by French and Venetians before the final assault on the city, he could
no longer harbour any such hopes. The pact eliminated as far as it
could papal interference in the new empire. The victors allotted
territories and within them ecclesiastical administration. They set
up canons of the cathedral of S. Sophia and elected a new patriarch.
They appropriated all church property, allowing to the ecclesiastics – diocesan clergy and monasteries – what they judged should
suffice for their needs. Innocent, of course, did not accept these
conditions, but there was little he could do about it immediately
and in fact the problem of church property was not satisfactorily
settled within his lifetime.

A consequence was that, as he had no rights as a sovereign and
since the Church, whether Latin or Greek, in the empire was on
the whole without estates and poor (some dioceses could support
not more than two canons), he could exercise little influence on
the progress of political events. Further, most of the magnates of
the empire from the emperor downwards were at loggerheads with
the Holy See because of their depredations of ecclesiastical property, their refusal to pay tenths, and their forbidding of legacies
for pious purposes. Moreover, they alternately supported the
Greek clergy against their Latin superiors and exploited the same
Greeks contrary to the protective measures taken by their Latin
superiors. The princes of Athens and Achaia were frequent
offenders and the utmost sanction of the Church, interdict, had to
be threatened and applied in order to force amendment. The means
used to achieve order in the Latin Church and obedience from the
Greek Church were canonical, the application of the canons, and
that, as has been noted, not harshly but with a certain moderation.

Innocent III was a canonist who had studied at Bologna under
the famous Uguccio, whose teaching he followed closely.[28] One

thinks that he had the canonist's mind, that is, a tendency to adhere somewhat narrowly to the law; that having established the legal principle he applied it exactly. That is what he seems to have done in his relations with the Greeks. In theory the conquest of their empire brought with it the subjection of their Church. Hence, after 1204, it was reunited with the Latin Church and under the authority of the pope. That was to be acknowledged by individuals through the oath of obedience. Once a man had taken the oath he was legally the equal of the Latins, and submissive Greek bishops 'should enjoy in their dioceses the same liberty as the Latins enjoy in theirs'.[29] Conversely, till they took the oath, they were schismatics and out of the Church of God. Hence, when the Lateran Council was convoked, Innocent summoned to it all the western bishops and many other western clerics whose reform or help was to be gained by the council. From the East he invited those who were canonically members of the Church, those who had taken the oath of obedience. Such action was canonical; it was logical; and so it was done.[30]

When in that Lateran Council of 1215 Innocent approved the fourth *capitulum* with its introductory phrase, 'The Greeks return to obedience to the Holy See,'[31] it was obvious to everybody that in fact they did not. No Greek metropolitan or archbishop had made his submission. There was a Greek patriarch in Nicaea on whom the Greeks centred their Church loyalties. Most bishops and many monks had gone either to Nicaea or to Epirus to escape from the oath. On the other hand a fair number of suffragan bishops, the great bulk of the parochial clergy and a generous proportion of monks remained within the old diocesan organisation of Greece, where now, however, all the larger dioceses had Latin incumbents. But even so, it cannot be said that the Greek clergy who remained within the empire had in their hearts abandoned their allegiance to the Greek patriarch no matter where he resided.

In view of this should Innocent have dropped the pretence that there was a union and have changed his tactics in respect of the Greeks? Perhaps one should rather ask, not 'Should Innocent have changed his tactics?', but 'Could he?'. Having once begun insisting on the oath of obedience, which for him and for the Greeks implied a point of doctrine, he could hardly have openly ceased to demand it without seeming himself to call that doctrine in question. That would have been true of any pope. It was doubly impossible for Innocent with his legal mind and legal methods. And it would not have helped. At that time just after the capture of Constantinople and the pillaging, in the knowledge of what had happened in the patriarchates of Jerusalem, Antioch and Alexandria and in Cyprus, where the Latins had latinised the Greek

Church as far as they could, and aware of the Latin encroachment on the Churches of Serbia and Bulgaria, the Greeks would not have combined with the Latins on any terms. The usurper Murtzuphlus, who deposed Isaac II and Alexius IV, opened sincere or feigned negotiations with the crusaders, which the emperor Baldwin reported to the pope. On one point he was adamant. 'But he so firmly refused the obedience to the Roman Church and the aid for the Holy Land that Alexius had guaranteed by oath and an imperial rescript, that he would prefer to lose life itself and that Greece should be ruined rather than that the Oriental Church should be made subordinate to Latin prelates'.[32] Murtzuphlus's words most probably reflected the sentiments also of the leading Greeks.

Nevertheless, fifty years later, in 1254, an emperor of Nicaea with the backing of the patriarch of Nicaea offered to Innocent III's third successor union of the Churches on conditions almost identical with those that Innocent had stipulated. The Greek Church and clergy would commemorate the pope in the liturgy, show him canonical obedience, accept him as a court of appeal, obey his decision if not against the canons, acknowledge his right to preside at general councils and accept his judgements there if not against scripture or the canons, and they would approve his verdicts in all other ecclesiastical business if not against the canons. The *Filioque* dispute, it is true, should be settled by free discussion in a general council, but at that time there was a fair prospect of agreement even on that thorny question: Nicephorus Blemmydes, whose reputation for learning brought him great respect and influence—he was selected as patriarch to succeed Manuel II in 1255 but refused the office on grounds of ill health – was then multiplying treatises to disprove 'from the Father only' in favour of 'from the Father through the Son'. There was a price, of course, set for this acquiescence : the restoration to their respective thrones in Constantinople of Emperor Vatatzes and Patriarch Manuel, with the ejection of their Latin rivals.[33] What would have been the result if these proposals had been implemented there is no knowing – whether or not the Greek Church at large would have followed the lead given by their emperor and their patriarch. What actually happened was that all the three protagonists, pope, emperor and patriarch, died in 1254. The new emperor of Nicaea, Theodore II Lascaris, finding the political situation easier, was less interested, and the negotiations though renewed came to nothing. The whole incident, however, suggests that Innocent III was less extravagant in his expectations and demands than is sometimes supposed.

The personages of the past were men as we are, with the same basic qualities, virtues and vices. They, like us, could rise to heights of heroism. They, as we, could be victims to the lust for power, for riches, for pleasures of all kinds. Innocent III was a man, and a man in a position where he wielded power and could have striven, consciously or unconsciously, continually for more. Exalting the Holy See and ruling the Church, he could have been seeking his own satisfaction in the name of religion.

But the people of earlier centuries, though basically like us, were conditioned very differently. They thought largely in other categories; their scale of values was different; their outlook was simpler, more direct. Religion made a greater impact on them than it normally does on men of today. It entered into the very fabric of their lives. The Church was world-wide, supranational, divine. Faith was God-given; heresy the greatest of evils. The Holy Land and Jerusalem were worth fighting for. Religion added its sanction to the daily relations of man with his fellowmen; of villeins with their lords; of lords with their feudal masters. Oaths and excommunications might for a time be lightly regarded, but in the end they usually prevailed. The one essential for every man was to ensure his eternal salvation.

Innocent was also subject to these religious influences and that to an unusually high degree because of his upbringing and training. For him the Church was indeed divine, founded by Christ, constructed hierarchically, endowed with supreme authority. That authority, though it was by no means confined to him, was conferred in its fulness on St Peter and then on his successors in the see of Rome. Innocent was such a successor. He did not have to seek authority. He possessed it. His task was to apply it to the highest good of man and the benefit of the Church as the ark of salvation. Was that his ultimate purpose and intention in his dealings with the Greeks? To judge him one must force oneself back to his day and clothe oneself with its mentality. A difficult task.

NOTES

1   W. Norden, *Papsttum und Byzanz* (Berlin 1903) pp. 195–6.
2   For example A. Luchaire, *Innocent III. La question de l'Orient* (Paris 1907) pp. 235–6; H. Tillmann, *Papst Innocenz III* (Bonn 1954) p. 219, blames him for subordinating Church union to politics.
3   *PL*, CCXIV, cols 326C, 328C.
4   12 Nov. 1199, *PL*, CCXIV, col. 764C.
5   7 Feb. 1204, *PL*, CCXV, cols 260D, 262A.
6   *PL*, CCXV, cols 294CD.
7   *Acta graeca Concilii Florentini*, ed. J. Gill (Rome 1953) p. 464.
8   *Conciliorum oecumenicorum decreta*, edd. J. Alberigo, P.-P. Ioannou, C. Leonardi, P. Prodi (Freiburg im B., 2 ed. 1962) pp. 789–90.

9 Cf. Innocent III, 'Christ entrusted the Church to Peter for ruling, that unity might exclude division', *PL*, ccxv, col. 512D.

10 *Constitutiones, Decreta, Declarationes* (Vatican City State 1966) para. 18, pp. 124–5, para. 22, p. 132.

11 He commissioned his legates to persuade the Greeks on the *Filioque* and other questions.

12 *PL*, ccxiv, cols 764C, 771B.

13 Innocent considered Constantinople Joannine because St John lived at Ephesus.

14 *Reg[esta Innocentii III]*, vii.154, esp. *PL*, ccxv, cols 459CD.

15 *PL*, ccxv, cols 458D.

16 Letter to Morosini of 2 Aug. 1206, *Reg.* ix.140, esp. *PL*, ccxv, col. 963.

17 Lateran Council, *capitulum* 9, Mansi, xxii, col. 998.

18 13 Nov. 1204, *Reg.* vii, 154.

19 20 Jan. 1205, *Reg.* vii.203 esp. *PL*, ccxv, cols 513D, 514AD.

20 Mansi xxii, col. 989.

21 *PL*, ccxiv, col. 327A

22 *Reg.* v.229.

23 *Reg.* vii.152, *PL*, ccxv, col. 447B.

24 *Reg.* vii.154, *PL*, ccxv, cols 456A.

25 *Reg.* vii.152, *PL*, ccxv, col. 452C.

26 *Reg.* viii.133.

27 *Reg.* xi.47. A similar thought was expressed by a group of 'Bishops, priests, deacons and other clergy and faithful of Constantinople', admittedly in a letter to the pope seeking leave to elect a patriarch for themselves (1206): 'For our sins we have been given over to this Christian people by a judgement of God more kindly than just' – their misfortunes continued without ceasing because they had not yet sincerely repented. A. Heisenberg, *Neue Quellen zur Geschichte des lateinischen Kaisertums und der Kirchenunion. 1: Der Epitaphios des Nikolaos Mesarites auf seinen Bruder Johannes* (Munich 1922) p. 63.

Two and a half centuries later, when Mahomet the Conqueror reigned in the Byzantine capital, Patriarch Gennadius would believe that it was a punishment for sin. *On the Fall of Constantinople*, in Petit, Sidéridès, Jugie, *Œuvres complètes de Gennadios-Scholarios*, iv (Paris 1931) pp. 215–23.

28 Cf. M. Maccarrone, *Chiesa e Stato nella dottrina di papa Innocenzo III, Lateranum*, nova serie., an. vi.3–4 (Rome 1940).

29 *Reg.* xv.134.

30 Innocent did not propose as matter for the council the doctrines of the primacy and the *Filioque*: it was a practical council for reform and the crusade. But even if he had, it is most unlikely that he would have altered his mode of action to invite 'schismatics'.

At Lyons in 1274, agreement (of a sort) on the Trinitarian doctrine was a preliminary condition for the presence of the Greeks. It needed the Great Schism of the West to open the way for a Council of Florence where there was no previous agreement, genuine debate and (I personally am convinced) a real, though short-lived, union.

31 Mansi XXII, col. 989.
32 *PL*, CCXV, col. 450A.
33 *Acta Alexandri P.P. IV (1254–1261)*, edd. T. T. Haluscyn-
    skyj and M. M. Wojnar, Pontificia commissio . . . iuris canon-
    ici orientalis, Fontes, 3 ser., IV, 11 (Città del Vaticano 1966)
    no. 28, pp. 39–44.
    Vatatzes had already put out a feeler in this direction when
    he asked the Roman envoys to Nicaea in 1233 whether, if
    the patriarch agreed to obey him, the pope would give him
    back his right [to the patriarchal throne in Constantinople] –
    restituet ei Dominus Papa ius suum? P. G. Golubovich, 'Dispu-
    tatio Latinorum et Graecorum', in *Archivum Franciscanum
    Historicum*, XII (1919) p. 445. This suggests that patriarch
    Germanus, like his successor Manuel, would not have
    repudiated the proposal.
    W. Norden, *Das Papsttum und Byzanz* (Berlin 1903) p. 372
    n. 3 and App. XII, attributes to patriarch Manuel II a
    treatise on the Holy Spirit found in Bibl. Bodl. Oxford. cod.
    Barocc. 131, fols 361^v–3^v. But the *incipit* and *desinit* show that
    it is identical with Blemmydes's *Oratio II ad Theodorum
    Lascarin*, *PG*, CXLII, cols 565–84.

Government in Latin Syria and the Commercial Privileges of Foreign Merchants

JONATHAN RILEY-SMITH

Historians of the crusades have described, with varying degrees of emphasis, the communities of European merchants in the Latin East as over-endowed bodies, benefiting from the short-sighted policies of successive rulers, who granted massive privileges to them at the expense of their own long-term interests.[1] Historians of Mediterranean trade have been more circumspect,[2] but nevertheless the weight of academic opinion sees the merchants exercising their great jurisdictional and commercial rights to the detriment of Latin Syria in the late twelfth and thirteenth centuries. The privileges granted to them can be summarised as being territorial, or the gifts of quarters in the cities, including churches, ovens and baths; jurisdictional, or the rights of judging not only their own nationals, but also in some cases those living in their quarters; and commercial, or the rights of entering, remaining in and leaving specified ports, the reduction or removal of entry, exit and sales dues payable to the lords and sometimes the possession of their own markets. It is the commercial exemptions with which this paper will be concerned, and it will be argued that in the context of local conditions and administrative practice they are not so outrageous as they appear to be at first sight.

In the first place the frailty of the Latin colonies has been exaggerated. There is some evidence, especially for the first half of the thirteenth century, before the arrival of the Mongols and the consequent disruption of the trade routes to the East, that the cities on the Levantine sea-board were rich.[3] On them the Muslim hinterland depended for its prosperity, a fact that discouraged Arab rulers from attacking them;[4] and their wealth may have contributed to what must otherwise appear to be the absurdly romantic interest in them of the emperor Frederick II, Charles I of Naples and the kings of Cyprus. In the early 1240s Richard of Cornwall was told by the Military Orders that Acre alone was worth 50,000 pounds of silver each year to its lord;[5] and it is possible that revenues from trade went some way to compensate for the territorial losses suffered by the kingdom of Jerusalem in 1187, because the surviving grants of money-fiefs from the returns of Acre, Tyre and the smaller towns[6] lead one to suppose that the impressive feudal host put into the field by the kingdom at the battle of Gaza in 1244 was financed largely out of the profits of the ports.[7]

The possessors of the coastal towns, moreover, seem to have enjoyed a large proportion of their revenues in spite of the partial or complete exemptions from tolls and dues gained by many merchant communities. This may partly explain the paradox that while there was a continuing aggressiveness on the part of the government of Latin Jerusalem towards the merchants' jurisdictional and territorial rights,[8] there is little evidence for a similar concern about their commercial exemptions, save in a few fields that will be discussed below.[9] And kings and lords continued well into the thirteenth century to make grants to European merchants or to reduce the dues they had to pay. In 1202 Plebanus of Botrun gave privileges to Pisa[10] and in 1203 Bohemond IV of Tripoli made a grant to Genoa.[11] In 1217 Guy of Jubail gave rights to the Venetians;[12] and in the early 1220s John of Ibelin issued an important series of charters to the Genoese, Venetians and Marseillais in a clear attempt to encourage commerce in his town of Beirut.[13] Charters were also granted by Frederick II of Jerusalem and Bohemond V of Tripoli for Montpellier in 1229 and 1243 respectively;[14] by Rohard of Haifa for Genoa in 1234,[15] by the High Court of Jerusalem for Ancona in 1257[16] and by Bohemond VII of Tripoli for Venice in 1277.[17] One also finds tolls being progressively reduced: for the Pisans in Jaffa[18] and for the Venetians, Pisans and Amalfitans in Antioch.[19] The care, however, with which grants were usually made is shown by the way certain commodities were specifically excluded from them. In 1183 the Venetians in Antioch had to pay dues on the merchandise they bought in the markets;[20] in 1190 the Marseillais in Palestine were exempted only from port taxes and not from sales dues;[21] in 1202 the Pisans in Botrun were to pay a tax on every ship of theirs bringing in corn for sale;[22] when in 1223 John of Beirut confirmed a charter of 1221 exempting the Genoese from port entry, and part of the exit dues, he specified that pottery, wine, oil and corn were taxable;[23] and the charter granted to the Venetians by Bohemond VII of Tripoli in 1277 was hedged about by limitations.[24] There seem always to have been certain commodities on which rulers were reluctant to lose customs duties. In 1190 Guy of Lusignan envisaged bans on the export of corn from Palestine.[25] In 1244 the Venetian *bailli*, Marsiglio Giorgio complained that his compatriots had been forced to pay a tax on horses and slaves that they imported to sell in Acre and this is paralleled by what seems to have been an unsuccessful attempt by Frederick II's officers to impose a tax on horses brought in by the Pisans before 1229.[26] In Acre and elsewhere duty was taken on the export of coins and precious metal for use in minting, although the Genoese in Tripoli were exempted in 1203.[27] A tax on merchants engaged in the pilgrim traffic always seems to have been imposed[28] and most rulers were keen to take dues from Italian merchants who tried to deal directly with the Muslim hinterland. It will be suggested that this was because the goods involved would normally have passed through their own markets and that they would have lost revenues if the merchandise had been taken by the Italians straight to their privileged quarters.[29]

While there is, therefore, nothing to suggest that rulers carelessly or unconsciously lost control over trade, the continuing granting of privileges to European merchants suggests that they knew that it was in their interest that these merchants be encouraged to visit their ports. In 1243 Bohemond v of Tripoli made a grant to Montpellier, 'regarding the good renown of the commune and the profit that can come to me and my lordship through their visits to the land'. The rights contained in the charter were to be enjoyed for ten years, during which time the men of Montpellier would guarantee to send each year at least one ship of a specified size to Tripoli. If in any year the ship should not arrive, Bohemond was thenceforward to be released from his obligations.[30] In 1257 the *bailli* of Jerusalem and the High Court made a grant, admittedly political in that they needed support in the War of St Sabas, to the merchants of Ancona, having regard for 'the greater utility and manifest profit for the kingdom'.[31] In 1261 the Master of the Temple was complaining of the shortage of exchange and therefore of ready cash that resulted from the absence of the Genoese and their allies from Acre in the wake of the War of St Sabas.[32] In 1277 Bohemond vii of Tripoli granted rights to the Venetians that were to last only as long as he and his heirs pleased. The privileges could be revoked at will.[33] The reasoning of the leaders of Latin Syria seems to have been realistic. The geographical advantages of the Levantine ports as the termini of the Asiatic trade routes would mean nothing if they were not visited by those capable of carrying to Europe the goods that had reached them. The wealth of the Latins in the East depended on a through-traffic of commodities that could not flow without the regular arrival of fleets to take the goods away. This is obvious, as are the benefits accruing to the European merchants. What have in the past been ignored are the benefits for the rulers themselves.

In every port there were several administrative or judicial offices involved in the organisation and the levying of dues on commerce. Two of these, the *secrete*, which may have had some sort of overall control, and the *Cour des Bourgeois*, which seems to have laid taxes on the retail shopkeepers, need not concern us directly, but the others must be considered. They were the *chaine*, the city gates, the *fonde* and the markets of the European merchants.

The *chaine* or *cathena* was a chain stretched across the harbour entrance that could be raised in time of danger. But its name was also given to the port, or one of the ports,[34] to the area of the town bordering on this port,[35] and to an office, in Acre in a *khan*-like building,[36] which combined several functions, being at least from the reign of Amalric a maritime court,[37] but also the body responsible for the running and upkeep of the port,[38] a department accounting revenues and paying out a proportion of them in rents and money-fiefs,[39] and a customs house. It is the last of these that is relevant to this study. We know very little about how it was run. In the thirteenth century it was supervised by *baillis*,[40] who were perhaps the same officers as the *custodes* of the port mentioned in an early document,[41] and it also employed scribes.[42] It is possible that its administration had been inherited from the Muslims and it might be best to compare its practices with what we know of the system in Egyptian ports at about the same time.[43]

In Egypt the cargo of a merchant ship entering a port was involved in four processes: disembarkation, registration, storage and sale. On arrival the vessel was usually moored in the centre of the harbour, not at the quayside, and lighters ferried its cargo to the quays, while the captain paid a tax for the right to remain at anchor. The same sort of procedure seems to have been followed in the major Latin Syrian ports. The arrival of ships outside Acre was signalled by the tolling of a bell and each was met by a small boat,[44] doubtless a pilot boat, that may have directed it either to a berth in the centre of the harbour – it seems that boats did not tie up alongside the *Port de la Chaine*[45] and one must assume that barges carried cargo from them to the shore – or to the second port of Acre, the *Mer de la Riviere*, which seems to have had facilities for the mooring of *ligna* along its wharves.[46] As in Egypt, a port tax was levied on each ship, known as *anchoragia*, but unlike Egypt it does not seem to have varied according to the size of vessel involved.[47]

In Egypt the goods, once disembarked, were inspected and registered for taxation on an *ad valorem* basis, that is a tax that varied according to the estimated value of the commodity, usually expressed in a percentage, although no tax was levied until after the sale in the market. Between registration and sale the cargo might be stored in warehouses at the port side. Registration of goods seems also to have taken place in the Latin Syrian ports. In the late 1120s King Baldwin II of Jerusalem freed pilgrims from dues on their personal belongings. In future they would pay no tax on luggage or other things valued at less than 40 besants and none on any excess if they could persuade the *custodes* of the port that they were not going to sell it. Otherwise they would pay 'what is customary and just in the port'.[48] This is evidence that officers on the quayside checked the goods of, and took declarations from, arrivals to find out if they were bringing in anything dutiable. Unlike Egypt and the Byzantine Empire,[49] it may be that an *ad valorem* tax was taken on entry and before sale by the customs officers themselves, although it must be admitted that the evidence is slightly ambiguous and that probably payment on goods to be sold was postponed, being taken in the market together with the sales tax.[50] The duty itself seems to have varied : in 1231 it was 10 per cent, but a decade later it appears to have been reduced to 8 per cent and later still, it stood at 5¼ per cent.[51] It is possible that some goods were sold on the quayside under the supervision of officials of the *chaine*,[52] but most must have passed out of their jurisdiction on leaving the port area for the markets.[53]

In Egypt an important differentiation was made between imports and exports. Goods on their way out were inspected, taxed and ferried to the ship, which was also taxed; and the captain had to pay for an official authorisation to depart. The export dues were taken on the quayside and unlike the entry taxes were estimated according to quantity, not *ad valorem*, although the bill finally presented might be in a form indistinguishable from the *ad valorem* account, expressed in terms of a percentage of the value, while there were always commodities such as wine, oil and grain that were always regarded as measurable, whichever way they were going.[54] In the Latin East the export tax was certainly taken by the *chaine*,[55] which levied the dues even on re-exports that had not found buyers in the markets.[56] The *chaine* had its own series of weights and measures for estimating the quantity of goods passing through it,[57] but it is not clear that there was a consistent approach to the means of arriving at the dues to be paid : a surviving list of charges made in the *chaine*, at the gates and in the markets of Acre and drawn up possibly in the mid-thirteenth century[58] contains commodities charged by quantity instead of *ad valorem* among both imports and exports, while some exports are taxed on an *ad valorem* basis.[59] An additional harbour tax, known as *terciaria*, was also levied, imposed it seems on the passengers and sailors in a ship.[60]

The privileges to foreign merchants in connection with the *chaine* fall into three groups : general exemptions from all dues owing to the port officials, often including freedom from levies on the re-export of unsold goods, but generally insisting that the privileges be enjoyed only by *bona fide* merchants from the

European city involved and excluding taxes on pilgrim traffic; [61] partial exemptions; [62] and finally a right which seems to have been extended only to the Pisans, who in 1187 were allowed to have their own agents to deal with their nationals in the *chaines* and markets and at the gates of Tyre, Acre and Jaffa. [63] Although the great privileges gained by the Pisans at this time were soon to be annulled [64] and in 1226–8 the *baillis of the chaine* in Acre were certainly trying to enforce authority over them, [65] as late as 1286 the Pisan consul in Acre was believed to be still exercising these powers. [66]

The other means of entering or leaving a city was of course through the land gates and revenues from these were important to the lords. When Bohemond IV gave the Hospitallers a gate in the walls of Tripoli in 1196, he stated that they were not to allow the passage of anything taxable through it. [67] Usually the gates were administered separately from the markets : from the surviving grants of rents and money-fiefs it is apparent that the gates of Jerusalem, Tyre, Beirut, Tripoli and Ascalon were run by their own offices, in much the same way as the ports and markets. [68] The absence of any reference in the documents to the revenues of the gates of Acre is striking and it may be that there the market officials also levied the entry tax imposed on goods that came in by land. [69] It is possible, however, that a famous passage in Ibn Jubair's description of his journey through Palestine in 1184 provides a solution to the problem. Ibn Jubair travelled to Acre from Damascus in company with some merchants. On arrival he and his companions were taken to a *khan* at the gate of which there were Christian scribes who made out their accounts in Arabic. These examined the baggage of those who were not merchants to see whether it contained anything taxable, a procedure that parallels the inspection in the ports of the luggage of arrivals. Ibn Jubair noted that the *dīwān* to which they belonged was held in farm by a man honoured by the title of *ṣāḥib*. All that was taken by the scribes belonged to him and he in turn paid a large sum to the government. [70] Ibn Jubair was certainly not describing the *chaine*, for he had just come into the city by land, while grants made on the revenues of the markets by the king, one of them in the following year, [71] and references in the thirteenth century to the *bailli of the fonde*, a royal official, [72] suggest that the markets were not farmed either. It seems to be most likely that Ibn Jubair was describing the officials at the gates of Acre and that the absence of references to grants made on their revenues by the king can be explained by the fact that they were held in farm. [73]

The gate officials seem to have laid a tax on all imports as well as exports;[74] and it appears that at Acre they would demand from a man who was not exempt an oath that he was bringing in a commodity for his own use. If so he merely paid a passage tax.[75] If the goods imported were to be sold in the town the duty payable at the gates was probably taken at the same time as the sales tax in the markets : this seems to be implied in the wording of some of the grants of exemption and in the clauses of the surviving list of charges on commercial transactions in Acre.[76] Exports were taxed in much the same way as were those passing through the *chaine*, some tolls being estimated according to the quantity of the commodity involved[77] and for some goods an *ad valorem* duty being imposed.[78] In this respect the privileges granted to European merchants meant the same as those accorded to them in the *chaine*, although the loss in revenue by the government may have been less. There were, it is true, strong attempts to force the merchants to make some payment for those goods they had brought in from or were exporting to Islamic countries.[79] The number of Europeans, however, actually engaged in the traffic of merchandise along this section of the trans-Asiatic trade route and organising caravans from Damascus and other Muslim centres to the Levantine sea-board must have been negligible.

Upon entering a town either through the port or by the land gates a merchant and his merchandise would make for the markets. In Acre and some other ports many of these markets seem to have been under the jurisdiction of the officials of the *fonde* or *funda*. The word *fonde* and the linked *fonticum*/*fondicum* were corruptions of the Arabic *funduq*, itself a transliteration of the Greek *pandokeia*.[80] It is to be found in many of the countries bordering on the Mediterranean, but in Latin Syria it had at least four different meanings. It could refer to a building, a *khan*, built round a large open courtyard in which goods were stored and in the upper stories of which there were lodging rooms for visiting merchants. The *funduqs* of the Italians in Alexandria and other Arab centres were of this type.[81] It could also refer to a market in a *khan*-shaped building that at least by the 1140s ought technically to be called a *qayṣārīya*,[82] although markets were often merely held in a square or open space in the town.[83] Market *funduqs* could belong to an individual owner – an Italian commune in Acre for instance[84] – or could be devoted to the sale of a particular commodity,[85] although in Egypt and doubtless also in Latin Syria this rule was by no means strictly kept.

The word *fonde*, moreover, seems to have been applied often not to one but to a group of markets, combined under a single administration. This can be the only explanation of the conglomerate nature of the goods listed in the mid-thirteenth century as being sold in the *fonde* of Acre,[86] and incidentally it may help to make clear a reference in a statute, clumsily inserted into the list, to two *fondes, en amont* and *en aval*.[87] The second of these terms may refer to the 'low' part of Acre that lay by the *Port de la Chaine*,[88] where, we will see, were collected the Italian markets; and the *fonde en aval* may be a collective reference to these. The *fonde en amont*, which was clearly the royal *fonde*,[89] must have been a group of squares and markets in the vicinity of the *Funda Regis* mentioned in a document of 1188 and situated in the south-east part of the town, not far from the eastern line of the walls.[90] Finally *fonde* could refer not to the markets themselves but to their administration : the *bailli* and jurats of the *Cour de la Fonde*, perhaps dating from the reign of Amalric,[91] concerned with minor mercantile matters and, in Acre, with jurisdiction over indigenous residents,[92] and linked to them the office, staffed by sergeants,[93] measurers,[94] scribes[95] and auctioneers,[96] that levied taxes, accounted revenues and granted out money-fiefs and rents.[97] In Acre the *Funda Regis* of 1188, which from the one reference to it was clearly a single building, could simply have been a house situated in the centre of the markets, in which sat the *Cour de la Fonde* and from which they were administered.

There are further complications. It has been suggested that the surviving list of charges made in the *fonde* of Acre is incomplete, because it covers by no means all the goods that are known to have been sold in the city.[98] But it is clear that throughout Latin Syria there were always markets administered separately from the *fondes* : in Antioch the tannery and the wine and fish markets;[99] in Laodicea the tannery and the markets for dyestuffs, *oleum fossimani* and fruit;[100] in Jabala the cloth market;[101] at Margat the market for dyestuffs;[102] in Tripoli the meat market, soapworks, tannery, and the markets for dyestuffs and fish;[103] and in Acre certainly the meat market[104] and probably also the tannery.[105] It is also possible that, whereas in many towns most markets were gathered under one administration, at least in Tyre all the various markets were semi-independent,[106] and the control of commerce may have resembled that of Damascus, with each market under an equivalent of the *'arif*, although probably under the general supervision of a *muḥtasib*. It is noteworthy that the only mention of this Arab official in the documents of Latin Syria is to be found with reference to Tyre between 1210 and 1243, and he is here to be found functioning in much the same way as did the *muḥtasibs* in Damascus – as a commercial judge and a supervisor of the markets.[107]

John of Joinville, describing the capture of Damietta by the crusaders in 1249, wrote that the Christians set fire to 'the *fonde* where were all the merchandise and all the goods that are sold by weight'.[108] In any market many of the commodities involved in commercial transactions were weighed on scales provided by the lord[109] by *mensuratores* appointed by him.[110] In the *fonde* of Acre, and clearly also elsewhere, taxes were levied after the transaction, the tax being estimated *ad valorem* on a percentage basis. Although it can be supplemented by some references to dues by the Venetian *bailli* in 1244,[111] the surviving list of charges made in the market of Acre is a very complicated document, in which the duty payable on goods varies, depending on the commodity, from $4\frac{1}{6}$ per cent[112] to 25 per cent. Of the charges, the most important seem to have been $4\frac{1}{6}$ per cent, almost certainly a transit tax,[113] $8\frac{1}{3}$ per cent, 10 per cent, $11\frac{5}{24}$ per cent, probably the standard tax, since it is called *dreiture enterine*,[114] and 25 per cent, this last laid mainly on local vegetables and fruit.[115] These taxes seem to have been generally lower than the Egyptian *khums* of 20 per cent[116] and often higher than the Byzantine *kommerkion* of 10 per cent.[117]

In Egypt there were two ways of levying the dues in the markets, depending on the kind of business dealings used by the merchants. In the cases of man-to-man bargains struck by the traders together, the Master of the Markets would fix official prices in consultation with the chief merchants. Official price lists, often changed, were not directives – bargains would be struck as usual – but they established the theoretical price of a commodity that was the basis for the *ad valorem* tax on it.[118] The second method was that of the public auction, the *ḥalqa*, which was not popular among the merchants but had by 1200 become the most usual way of transacting business.[119] All the lots of a given commodity would be auctioned together in the market by an official auctioneer. Levying the duty was simple, for the tax was merely taken off the top of the total proceeds of the auction before they were divided among the merchants involved. Both methods seem to have been used in Acre, and there is evidence for the employment of *vendours de la vile*, clearly public auctioneers.[120] But whatever method was used, it seems that, as in Egypt and Constantinople,[121] in most cases the burden of the tax was shared, being divided between the seller and the buyer who each paid half.[122]

Privileges in the *fonde* to European merchants took much the same forms as those they enjoyed in the *chaine* and at the gates, although complete freedom from the market charges was less often granted – there is no evidence, for instance, that the Venetians were ever fully exempted.[123] There was also a general freedom from which certain commodities were excepted;[124] a general reduction of charges, or the reduction of dues on certain goods;[125] and a privilege which applied only to one side of a business transaction :

I

freedom from the charges on sales or on purchases, but not on both.[126] It must, however, be emphasised that whatever form the privilege took it applied to only half the tax levied by the government. If a privileged merchant and a non-privileged had a business dealing – and the majority of the transactions in the markets must have been of this kind – the share of the duty owed by the non-privileged merchant would still have to be paid. Even if total exemption from sales-taxes had been granted to one group of merchants, therefore, they had only to involve themselves in twice as many transactions for the financial break-even point for the government to be reached. The lords of the Syrian ports clearly hoped – and that hope was surely realised – that the presence of European merchants would lead to an increase in business that would more than compensate for any revenue initially lost by encouraging them to come.

In one respect, however, some of the communities of European merchants enjoyed what was a very important privilege. They were allowed to possess their own markets, run by their officials and using their weights and measures.[127] In Acre the Venetian, Genoese and Pisan quarters lay in a semi-circle around the *Port de la Chaine*, although not actually touching the harbour,[128] and goods brought in their ships could be taken straight up to the warehouses of a privileged community[129] for eventual sale. The first of these privileges appears in a grant of 1123 to the Venetians in Acre:

> You may use scales of weight and measures of quantity in the following way. For whenever Venetians have business deals with each other concerning their own goods they ought to use Venetian measures. When indeed Venetians sell their goods to other people they ought to sell them according to their own Venetian measures. But whenever Venetians purchase from foreign peoples other than Venetians, having paid the market tax, they may buy according to royal measures.[130]

It will be noticed that this charter gave the Venetians in Acre the right to use their own weights and measures in business deals among themselves and with others, provided that they were *selling* their goods. If, however, a Venetian wished to *buy* something from a non-Venetian he had to pay tax and use royal measures, in other words visit the royal markets. Although this clause was not repeated in the king's confirmation of the charter in 1125,[131] it seems to have set a standard followed in others, for instance in privileges to the Pisans in Tyre, Jaffa and Acre and to merchants from Provence in Tyre granted by Raymond of Tripoli, Conrad of Monteferrat and Guy of Lusignan. The Pisans were allowed to use weights and measures 'so that they can freely weigh and measure *among them-*

selves and for *strangers buying from them*', the Provençals only for measuring amongst themselves.[132]

It is possible that the same sort of limited right was enjoyed in Tripoli by the Venetians who in 1277 were allowed to establish a market under stringent conditions, among them the obligation for a Venetian to go with a man who had bought from him in his market to register every sale with the count's *fonde* officials.[133] It was also held in Tyre by the Genoese, who were permitted to use their own measures by Conrad of Montferrat in 1190,[134] and by the Venetians, who as owners of a third of the city certainly had their own market.[135] On the other hand, the Genoese seem never to have gained this privilege in Acre. No charter granting them such a right survives and, although Francesco Balducci Pegolotti made reference in his *Pratica* to the measures used in Acre by the Pisans and Venetians, he made no mention of the Genoese.[136] It is interesting to note that not only is there no reference in the source material to a *funduq* in the Genoese quarter, but no foundations of such a building have been discovered. And the Genoese seem to have lost their rights in Tyre by 1264, when they agreed to use the weights and measures of the lord, Philip of Montfort, and to pay him *mensuragium*, a payment on every deal estimated according to the quantity of merchandise involved.[137]

The recipients of the privilege of using their own weights and measures could sell the goods they themselves had imported in their own markets outside royal control, but to load their ships with cargoes for the return to the West, they had to buy the goods coming to the Levant over the Asiatic trade routes in the royal markets where, even if they were freed from the sales tax, the other parties to the deal were probably not.[138] A loophole for them would have been to have gone themselves to the great Muslim centres, conducting caravans from and to the coast, exercising their privilege of free entry and bringing the uncharged goods into a port either for sale in their own markets free of dues or for shipping directly to the West. Alternatively their ships might stop off at a non-Christian port on the way to the Levant and there pick up a cargo which they could dispose of in their own markets, using the Syrian town as a free commercial centre. To combat these it seems that a series of restrictions were imposed on them. Direct trading with the Muslim hinterland was discouraged or at least subjected to tax. In 1192 Henry of Champagne, confirming Genoese rights in Tyre, added that if 'they come by land to Tyre from any Muslim country and sell their merchandise in Tyre they will render the customary taxes. If indeed they do not sell they are held to pay no custom.'[139] In 1244 Marsiglio Giorgio, the Venetian *bailli*, complained: 'If any of the merchants of Venice wishes to go overland to Damascus or to any Muslim city and wishes to take any merchandise with him out of Acre he is forced to pay one carat [$4\frac{1}{6}$ per cent] for each besant of its estimated worth' and that: 'If anyone from Venice wishes to go to Damascus or to any Muslim country and buys merchandise and he wishes to bring it to Acre by land, he must pay $9\frac{7}{24}\%$ if he wants to sell it in Acre', unless he had come to an agreement beforehand with the royal officers.[140] In 1264 the Genoese agreed to pay Philip of Montfort $2\frac{1}{12}$ per cent of all goods exported or imported through the land gates of Tyre. If, however, they took out goods that they could not sell, they were allowed to bring them back into the city without the payment of additional tax.[141]

The complaints of Marsiglio Giorgio also contained a reference to the government's attempts to prevent the Venetians from taking advantage of their privileges by shipping merchandise they themselves had acquired in a Muslim centre directly to Europe. If a Venetian bought goods in Islamic lands and brought them to Acre 'and if he wishes to carry them to Venice, he pays $4\frac{1}{6}\%$ unless he has previously come to an agreement with the royal officer'.[142] Already in 1243, in a charter from Bohemond v which otherwise reduced the dues payable by merchants from Montpellier, there was to be no reduction for those goods brought into Tripoli by land and then exported.[143]

Linked to these restrictions seems to have been one by which the rulers discouraged the merchants from landing merchandise at one Christian port and bringing it overland to another. In 1244 Marsiglio Giorgio grumbled that : 'If any ship comes from Venice and applies at Tyre or any other city and the merchants wish to bring some of their merchandise overland to Acre they are charged $9\frac{1}{3}\%$.'[144] In 1264 Philip of Montfort allowed the Genoese to pay nothing if they had to bring their goods overland to Tyre because their ships had been wrecked or attacked by pirates off his lordship or that of Sidon, provided that they let him or his lieutenant know : a clause that suggests that, as in Acre, a tax would otherwise have been paid.[145] These may have been attempts to prevent the Italians using the ports as free markets : certainly this is what Henry of Champagne seems to have been doing in 1192 when he bound the Genoese in Tyre to pay dues on any goods sold in the markets of Tyre that had been brought in by sea, if the ship in which they were imported had come from Barbary, Egypt or Constantinople by way of some other Islamic country.[146] In 1257 merchants from Ancona had to pay full dues of entry to the *baillis of the chaine* in Acre if they imported for sale in the city taxable goods they had bought in Islamic lands. If these were not sold but re-exported, they would, moreover, have to pay the full export tax.[147] And in 1277 the Venetians were allowed to establish a market in Tripoli on condition that this right was limited only to Venetians and not to representatives appointed by them and that if a Venetian sold to one of his compatriots or established a retail shop or bought corn, vegetables and probably oil in order to resell them he would pay the full market dues.[148]

Finally, the rulers of Latin Syria seem to have tried to discourage their own subjects from buying goods in the exempt markets. They appear to have had no objection to foreign merchants from Damascus and elsewhere, once they had sold their merchandise in the royal markets, going down to the European *funduqs* to acquire commodities to load their camels for their return home – the gate officials would of course tax what they took out of the city.[149] But in Tripoli in 1277 the Venetians were allowed to establish a market provided that if they sold to 'humble people' anything that owed 'two rights' to the officials of the *fonde* or the fishmarket they would register the sale in the *Cour de la Fonde* and pay the tax owed by the buyer.[150] If the *fonde en amont* and the *fonde en aval* in Acre referred to above were the royal and Italian markets respectively, then the significance of the statute inserted into the list of dues to be taken in the city becomes clear. This commanded that all the indigenous inhabitants of Acre, those who were answerable to the *Cour de la Fonde*, should live around the *fonde en amont* and not near the *fonde en aval*, 'because otherwise the lord could not enjoy those rights it is established he should take from them'. The rights mentioned were the levying of dues, ranging from $4\frac{1}{6}$ per cent to $12\frac{1}{2}$ per cent, *de passage au canton de la fonde en amont* on those purchases made in the *fonde en aval* by the natives, whether shopkeepers or others, and by all villagers in the royal domain around Acre. Clearly if locals went to buy in the Italian markets, government officers would take a tax on their purchases on their way back to that part of the city where lay the royal markets.[151] The date of this statute has been much debated,[152] but there is evidence for similar royal activity elsewhere. Between 1210 and 1225 King John of Brienne exempted native Syrians in Tyre from royal *chaine* dues, thus encouraging them to live in the royal rather than in the Venetian part of the city where they were not exempt.[153] The situation in Tyre was not like that in Acre, because the Venetians held one third of the town in lordship, but the king's motives may have been the same as those behind the statute concerning Acre : to discourage the indigenous population from using the Italian markets.

The rights of and limitations upon European merchants and the corresponding advantages for the rulers should now be clear. On arrival with a loaded ship in a Latin Syrian port, a privileged trader passed, with his merchandise untaxed, to the market of his own nationals where he sold it without paying dues on the sale to the town's lord. Merchants from the Muslim interior would come down to buy in the Europeans' markets, but they would be taxed on what they had bought as they left by the gates of the city. Local people in Acre who did the same would be taxed on their purchases as they returned to the part of the town where they lived. A western merchant, however, could not buy goods to fill his ship for the return home in his national market, but would have to go up to the royal or lord's *fonde*, to which were also directed those coming into the city from the hinterland with spices and other commodities. In the town markets a European merchant might well be absolved from the payment of his contribution to the duty on a purchase, but the man from whom he bought would not and the government would generally get at least half the theoretical sales tax. Should the westerners try to get round the obligation to buy in the town markets by involving themselves in the trade between the Muslim cities and the coast, they would find that their privileges of exemption were of no avail and that they were subject to tolls. Having bought in the royal or lord's markets an exempt trader could of course export his purchases to the West without the payment of customs dues. There is no doubt that the privileges he enjoyed were of real benefit to him, but his presence in the Latin East and the increased commercial business that resulted seem to have more than compensated, as far as the rulers were concerned, for the exemptions granted to him.

NOTES

1   For example, see S. Runciman, *A History of the Crusades* (Cambridge 1951–5) III, pp. 354–61; J. L. La Monte, *Feudal Monarchy in the Latin Kingdom of Jerusalem, 1100–1291* (Cambridge, Mass., 1932) pp. 226–42; [J.] Richard, *Le Royaume latin [de Jérusalem]* (Paris 1953) pp. 217–27; J. Prawer, *Histoire du royaume latin de Jérusalem* (Paris 1969ff) I, pp. 502–3.

2   For example, see W. Heyd and F. Raynaud, *Histoire du commerce du Levant au moyen âge* (Leipzig 1885–6) I, pp. 131–90, 310–59; [C.] Cahen, ['Notes sur l'histoire des croisades et de l'Orient latin. 3. Orient latin et commerce du Levant'], *Bulletin de la Faculté des Lettres de l'Université de Strasbourg*, XXIX (Strasbourg 1950–1) pp. 328–46.

3   For most of the twelfth century, as Cahen, pp. 331–3 pointed out, Acre did not rival Constantinople and Alexandria. The real expansion of Levantine trade seems to have begun in the 1180s and continued to the late 1250s. Thereafter there was a steady decline.

4   See the attitude of Sultan Baybars, *Ayyubids, Mamlukes and
     Crusaders. [Selections from the Tārikh al-Duwal wa'l Mulūk of
     Ibn al-Furāt]*, ed. and tr., U. and M.C.Lyons with Hist. Intr.
     and Notes by J.S.C.Riley-Smith (Cambridge 1971), 11, pp.
     43–4. For the Aiyūbids, see H.A.R.Gibb, 'The Aiyūbids',
     A History of the Crusades, ed.-in-chief K.M.Setton (Phila-
     dephia 1955ff) 11, p.694.

5   Matthew Paris, 'Itinéraire de Londres [à Jérusalem (2nd
     redaction)]', ed. H.Michelant and G.Raynaud, *Itinéraires à
     Jérusalem et descriptions de la Terre Sainte rédigés en français aux
     XIᵉ, XIIᵉ & XIIIᵉ siècles* (Geneva 1882) p.137. If this figure
     is accurate – and it should be noted that Matthew Paris (op.
     cit., p.127) gave the sum of 500 pounds of silver, in one
     redaction sterling, for Damascus – then it would seem to be
     roughly equal to Henry 111's total revenues from England.

6   *Tab[ulae] ord[inis] Theut[onici]*. ed. E.Strehlke (Berlin 1869)
     nos 5, 7–9, 13–14, 17, 53, 98; 'Quatre pièces rel[atives à
     l'ordre] teutonique [en Orient]', *Archives de l'Orient latin*, 11
     (Paris 1884) no. 3; *Hist[oria] dipl[omatica] Fred[erici secundi]*,
     ed. J.L.A.de Huillard-Bréholles (Paris 1852–61) 11, pp.
     533–5, 537; 111, pp.122–3, 125; *Cart[ulaire] gén[éral de l'ordre
     des] Hosp[italiers de St.-Jean de Jérusalem (1100–1310)]* ed.
     J.Delaville Le Roulx (Paris 1894–1906) nos 1031–2, 2280.
     I have not included here the large number of rents given to
     ecclesiastical institutions.

7   See *Ayyubids, Mamlukes and Crusaders*, 11, p.xvi.
     One might here take note of the care taken by King Aimery
     in 1197–98 over the distribution of money-fiefs in Acre.
     'L'Estoire d'Eracles [empereur et la conqueste de la Terre
     d'Outremer]', *RHC, Historiens occidentaux*, 11, p.224; *Chro-
     nique d'Ernoul et de Bernard le Trésorier*, ed. L.de Mas Latrie
     (Paris 1871) p.311. For an attempt by the crown in the
     twelfth century to reserve the exploitation of the transit
     trade to itself, see 'Livre au roi', *RHC, Lois*, 1, p.617.

8   See Richard, *Le Royaume latin*, pp.220ff.

9   See below, pp.118–21. The only other case seems to have been
     a strong attempt to make the Genoese pay customs duties in
     the port of Acre in 1231. *Annales Januenses, MGH, SS*,
     XVIII, pp.176–7.

10   *Documenti [sulle relazioni] delle città toscane [coll'Oriente cristiano
     e coi Turchi fino all'anno 1531]*, ed. G.Müller (Florence 1879)
     no.53.

11   [R.] Röhricht, 'Amalrich 1. [König von Jerusalem]',
     Mitteilungen des österreichischen Instituts für Geschichtsforschung,
     XII (Vienna 1891) p.489.

12   *Urkunden [zur älteren Handels- und Staatsgeschichte der Republik]
     Venedig [mit besonderer Beziehung auf Byzanz und die Levante*,
     ed. G.L.F.Tafel and G.M.Thomas] (Vienna 1856–7)
     no. 250.

13   'Liber iurium [rei publicae Ianuensis]', *Historiae patriae
     monumenta* (Turin 1836ff) VII/IX, nos 569, 585; *Urkunden
     Venedig*, nos 261–2; *Histoire [analytique et chronologique] des
     actes[et des délibérations du corps et du conseil de la municipalité]
     de Marseille [depuis le Xᵉ siècle jusqu'à nos jours]*, ed. L.E.Méry
     and F.Guindon (Marseilles 1841–3) 1, pp.287–8.

14   *Acta imperii inedita [saeculi XIII]*, ed. E.Winkelmann (Innsbruck 1880–5) I, no. 302; [A.] Germain, *Histoire de [la commune] de Montpellier [depuis ses origines jusqu'à son incorporation définitive à la monarchie française]* (Montpellier 1851) II, pp.513–15.

15   'Liber iurium', no. 718.

16   *Cod[ice] dipl[omatico del sacro militare ordine] geros[olimitano oggi di Malta]*, ed. S.Pauli (Lucca 1733–7) I, pp.157–61. See an earlier grant made by pope Innocent IV. *Epistolae Saeculi XIII [e regestis pontificum Romanorum selectae]*, *MGH* (Berlin 1893–4) II, no. 125.

17   [E.G.] Rey, *Recherches [géographiques et historiques sur la domination des Latins en Orient]* (Paris 1877) pp.47–50.

18   *Documenti delle città toscane*, no. 6. See also the reduction of dues for the Siennese in Acre, granted by Conradin. *Documenti delle città toscane*, no. 70.

19   *Urkunden Venedig*, nos 46, 55, 61, 68; *Documenti della città toscane*, nos 4, 13, 50, 58; *Memorie [storico-diplomatiche dell'antica città e ducato] di Amalfi*, ed. M.Camera (Naples 1876–1881) I, p.202.

20   *Urkunden Venedig*, no. 68.

21   *Histoire des actes de Marseille*, I, p.195.

22   *Documenti delle città toscane*, no. 53.

23   'Liber iurium', no. 584. See no. 569.

24   Rey, *Recherches*, pp.47–50.

25   *Histoire des actes de Marseille*, I, p.195.

26   *Urkunden Venedig*, no. 300 (p.398); *Documenti delle città toscane*, no. 66.

27   *Urkunden Venedig*, nos 94, 307, 361; Röhricht, 'Amalrich I.', p.489.

28   'Liber iurium', no. 11; *Urkunden Venedig*, nos 40–1, 300 (p.397); *Documenti delle città toscane*, no. 5. See below, pp.113–14.

29   See below pp.119–21.

30   Germain, *Histoire de Montpellier*, II, pp.513–15.

31   *Cod. dipl. geros.*, I, p.157.

32   *Annales monasterii Burtonensis*, ed. H.R.Luard, *Annales monastici*, *RS*, XXXVI (1864) I, p.494.

33   Rey, *Recherches*, pp.49–50.

34   At Acre, for instance, it is clear that there was another main landing place, known as the *Mer de la Rivière*. 'Livre des Assises [de la Cour] des Bourgeois', *RHC, Lois*, II, p.174, §12; *Histoire des actes de Marseille*, I, p.195; *Memorie di Amalfi*, I, p.201; *Documenti delle città toscane*, no. 70. See also *Cod. dipl. geros.*, I, p.159. For various reasons I am inclined to think that this second port lay to the east of the *Port de la Chaine* in the outer harbour and was 'devant la boucherie'. See '[Les] Gestes des Chiprois', *RHC, Documents arméniens*, II, pp.683–4, 813.

35   The street and square of the *Chaine* are mentioned in several documents and appear on the map of Matthew Paris ('Itinéraire de Londres', p.136), although some way to the west of its actual position.

36   The present Khan al-Oumdan in Acre, almost certainly on the site of the *Cour de la Chaine*, is built on the Frankish foundations of a similar building.

37 R.B.Patterson ('The Early Existence of the *Funda* and
Catena in the Twelfth-Century Latin Kingdom of Jerusalem',
Speculum, XXXIX (1964) pp.474–7) has argued that the *Cours
de la Chaine* and *de la Fonde* existed before the reign of
Amalric. But maritime jurisdiction was only one – and in a
sense the least important – of the functions of the *chaine*. It
is clear that some office existed from the first and was probably inherited from the Arabs. By creating a court, the Latins
were merely turning a financial office into a tribunal. They
always tended to do this, for in the West taxation and jurisdiction were linked in a way that they were not in the East.

38 See 'Quatre titres [des propriétés] des Génois [à Acre et à
Tyr]', ed. C.C.Desimoni, *Archives de l'Orient latin*, II (1884)
no. 4 (p.226); also 'Liber iurium', nos 374, 405. In this connection there survives an interesting grant of an indulgence
in 1253 to those in Syria who would help repair the port of
Jaffa. *Le Registre d'Innocent IV*, ed. E.Berger (Paris 1884–
1921) no. 6463.

39 *Tab. ord. Theut.*, nos 5, 17, 63–4; 'Fragment d'un cart[ulaire
de l'ordre de] St. Lazare [en Terre Sainte]', ed. A.de Marsy,
Archives de l'Orient latin, II (1884) no. 28; *Documenti delle
città toscane*, no. 27; 'Quatre pièces rel. teutonique', no. 3;
Cart. gen. Hosp., nos 1031–2, 2280; *Hist. dipl. Fred.*, II, pp.
533–5, 537; III, pp.117–18, 122–3, 125, 130; John of Ibelin,
['Livre'], R*HC, Lois*, I, p.274.

40 *Documenti delle città toscane*, no. 65; *Cod. dipl. geros.*, I, p.158;
'L'Estoire d'Eracles', II, p.475.

41 *Cart[ulaire de l'église du] St.-Sépulcre [de Jérusalem]*, ed. E.de
Rozière (Paris 1849) no. 46. The following seem to have
been officers of the *Chaine*: Menardus in the twelfth century,
and Bernard, Thomas and Simon, the last two father and
son, in the thirteenth. *Cart. gen. Hosp.*, nos 180, 1276, 2166,
2483.

42 'Livre des Assises des Bourgeois', p.220.

43 I have relied on [C.] Cahen, 'Douanes et commerce [dans
les ports méditerranéens de l'Égypte médiévale d'après le
Minhâdj d'al-Makhzûmî]', *Journal of the Economic and Social
History of the Orient*, VII (1964) pp.218–314, and [S.D.]
Goitein, [*A*] *Mediterranean Society* (Berkeley 1967) I, *passim*.

44 See 'L'Estoire d'Eracles', II, pp.75, 76.

45 See the description of the port and also that of Tyre by
Theoderic, *Libellus de locis sanctis*, ed. T.Tobler (St. Gallen
1865) pp.90–1, 111 : also 'L'Estoire d'Eracles', II, p.395.

46 See *Histoire des actes de Marseille*, I, p.195; *Memorie di Amalfi*,
I, p.201. While it is clear that at this time *lignum* was a term
used to describe a particular kind of ship, not merely boats
in general, I have been unable to establish exactly what type
it was.

47 *Documenti delle città toscane*, nos 50, 58; 'Liber iurium', nos
569, 585; *Urkunden Venedig*, nos 261–2; *Histoire des actes de
Marseille*, I, p.195; *Memorie di Amalfi*, I, p.201 (note difference between *anchoragia* and *ancorandum*); Rey, *Recherches*, p.
47. See also *Documenti delle città toscane*, nos 1 B, 5; *Chartes [de
la Terre Sainte provenant de l'abbaye de Notre-Dame] de Josaphat*,
ed. H.F.Delaborde (Paris 1880) nos 18, 28–9, 49; *Analecta*

K

novissima, ed. J.B.Pitra (Paris 1885–8) I, p.556. See
Regesta regni Hierosolymitani, comp. R.Röhricht (Innsbruck
1893–1904) no. 606, in which the charge was 1 silver mark.
See also *Cart. gen. Hosp.,* no. 372. The list of duties in *Hist.
dipl. Fred.,* 11, p.535 is to be found in a charter issued in
Sicily and so may not accurately reflect conditions in the
port of Acre.

48   *Cart. St.-Sépulcre,* no. 46.

49   See [H.] Antoniadis-Bibicou, *Recherches sur les douanes [à
Byzance]* (Paris 1963) pp.107–22.

50   The clearest evidence is to be found in *Cod. dipl. geros.,* I,
p.158; and support is to be found in *Documenti delle città
toscane,* no. 70; *Acta imperii inedita,* I, no. 302; *Cart. gen.
Hosp.,* no. 1372; 'Livre des Assises des Bourgeois', p.174
(§15). See 'Annales Januenses', pp.176–7. On the other
hand, for slight evidence that the combined entry and sales
taxes were taken together in the markets, see 'Livre des
Assises des Bourgeois', pp.173 (rubric), 174 (§12); *Cart.
St.-Sépulcre,* no. 46.

51   'Annales Januenses', pp.176–7; 'Livre des Assises des
Bourgeois', p.174 (§12); Francesco Balducci Pegolotti, *[La
pratica della mercatura],* ed. A.Evans (Cambridge, Mass.,
1936) p.69.

52   See 'Liber iurium', nos 401, 410; Rey, *Recherches,* p.47.

53   Carried presumably by porters, but also by camels. 'L'Estoire
d'Eracles', 11, pp.151–2; 'Livre des Assises des Bourgeois',
p.73.

54   For Latin Jerusalem, see 'Livre des Assises des Bourgeois',
pp.48–9.

55   'Livre des Assises des Bourgeois', p.220; *Cart. St.-Sépulcre,*
no. 155; *Cod. dipl. geros.,* I, p.158; *Epistolae saeculi XIII,* 11,
no. 125. In Egypt the difference between the value of a
merchant's imports and exports was also taxed where the
export was greater than the import. This may be what is
referred to in the charter of 1257 from the High Court of the
kingdom of Jerusalem to Ancona. 'et tout le seurplus que il
solent paier a la chaëne seit quite et absolu perpetuelment'.
Cod. dipl. geros., loc. cit.

56   'Livre des Assises des Bourgeois', p.174 (§12); 'Quatre
titres des Génois', no. 4 (p.226). See 'Liber iurium', no.
569; *Urkunden Venedig,* no. 262; Germain, *Histoire de Montpellier,* 11, p. 513. But see the charter of Guy of Lusignan in
which he promised that the Marseillais would not be forced
against their will to sell what they had brought in, *Histoire
des actes de Marseille,* I, p.195.

57   See Francesco Balducci Pegolotti, pp.63–4; *Documents
inédits sur le commerce de Marseille au moyen âge,* ed. L.Blancard
(Marseilles 1884–85) *passim; Cart. gen. Hosp.,* nos 77, 2298;
'Sankt Samuel auf dem Freudenberge [und sein Besitz nach
einem unbekannten Diplom König Balduins V']', ed. H.E.
Mayer, *Quellen und Forschungen aus Italienischen Archiven und
Bibliotheken,* XLIV (Tübingen 1964) p.68.

58   See [C.] Cahen, 'A propos des coutumes [du marché d'Acre'],
Revue historique de droit français et étranger, sér. 4, XLI (Paris
1963) pp.287–90; [J.] Prawer, 'L'Établissement des cou-

tumes [du marché à St.-Jean d'Acre et la date de la composi-
tion du Livre des Assises des Bourgeois]', *Revue historique de
droit français et étranger*, sér. 4, XXIX (1951) pp.329–51; [J.]
Richard, 'Colonies marchandes [privilégiées et marché sei-
gneurial. La Fonde d'Acre et ses "droitures"]', *Le moyen âge*,
LIX (Paris 1953) pp.325–40.

59 'Livre des Assises des Bourgeois', pp. 173–81. Exit dues are
listed for the following commodities : hazel nuts, carobs,
salted fish, onions, onion bulbs, leather tack and saddles,
merchandise, chickens, glass, wine. There is one transit
charge mentioned – on flax passing through Acre on its way
from Egypt to Damascus. One reference in the 'Assises des
Bourgeois' (p.220) suggests that some dues were paid in
kind; and at Port St.-Simeon one fief in kind was paid out by
the *chaine*; *Tab. ord. Theut.*, no. 9.

60 For pilgrims and passengers : *Urkunden Venedig*, nos 40–1,
300 (p.397). For sailors : Rey, *Recherches*, p.47. See 'Liber
iurium', nos 569, 585; *Urkunden Venedig*, nos 261–2; Germain, *Histoire de Montpellier*, II, p.513. See also *Documenti
delle città toscane*, nos 23–5, 31–2, 50, 58 (no. 39 is not a reference for this tax); *Histoire des actes de Marseille*, I, p.190;
Memorie di Amalfi, I, p.201.

61 'Liber iurium', nos 8, 11, 20, 256, 276, 363, 374–5, 379, 392,
401, 410, 477, 569, 585, 718; *Documenti delle città toscane*,
nos 1, 5, 22–5, 31–2, 37; *Urkunden Venedig*, nos 40–1, 68,
261–2, 369; *Histoire des actes de Marseille*, I, pp.190–1, 195,
287–8; *Memorie di Amalfi*, I, p.201; Rey, *Recherches*, p.47;
'Quatre titres des Génois', no. 4 (pp.225–6); 'Chartae',
Historiae patriae monumenta, I, cols 857–8.

62 *Urkunden Venedig*, nos 46, 61; 'Liber iurium', nos 405, 516,
although the second of these may contain a reference to the
gates; *Documenti delle città toscane*, nos 4, 6, 13, 50, 53, 58, 66,
70; *Memorie di Amalfi*, I, p.202; *Acta imperii inedita*, I, no.
302; *Cod. dipl. geros.* I, p.158; Germain, *Histoire de Montpellier*, II, p.513; *Epistolae saeculi XIII*, II, no. 125; Röhricht,
'Amalrich I.', p.489.

63 *Documenti delle città toscane*, nos 23–5, 31–2.

64 Following his dispute with the Pisans, Henry of Champagne
issued a charter for them in 1193 which merely confirmed
the rights they had held in 1185. *Documenti delle città toscane*,
no. 37.

65 *Documenti delle città toscane*, no. 65, See also no. 66.

66 *Breve* of 1286 from the *Statuti pisani*, printed in *Documenti
delle città toscane*, pp.380–1.

67 *Cart. gen. Hosp.*, no. 990.

68 *Tab. ord. Theut.*, no. 8; *Urkunden Venedig*, nos 63, 299 (p.385);
Cart. gen. Hosp., nos 79, 82; *Cod. dipl. geros.*, I, p.63; 'Fragment
d'un Cart. St.-Lazare', nos 27, 33; 'Un diplôme inédit
d'Amaury I, roi de Jérusalem, en faveur de l'abbaye du
Temple-Notre-Seigneur (1166)', ed. F. Chalandon, *Revue de
l'Orient latin*, VIII (Paris 1900–1) p. 312; [J.] Delaville Le
Roulx, ['L'Ordre de] Montjoye', *Revue de l'Orient latin* I (1893)
p.52.

69 Exit taxes are included in the list of market charges of the
mid thirteenth century, but *chaine* dues are to be found in it

too. 'Livre des Assises des Bourgeois', pp. 173–81. Note that
in 1191, before Acre was retaken, the Hospitallers and the
Templars had promised to take into custody, *redditus fori, et
rerum venalium, et redditus portus Acrae*. There was here no
mention of the gates. *Gesta regis Henrici secundi*, ed. W. Stubbs,
RS, XLIX (1867) II, p. 170.

70   Ibn Jubair, [*Travels*], extr. ed. and tr. *RHC. Historiens
orientaux*, III, p. 449.

71   *Tab. ord. Theut.*, no. 19. See op. cit., nos 5, 7, 13–14; *Documenti delle città toscane*, no. 27; 'Quatre pièces rel. teutonique',
no. 3; 'Fragment d'un cart. St.-Lazare', no. 29.

72   'Livre des Assises des Bourgeois', pp. 171–3; 'L'Estoire
d'Eracles', II, p. 475.

73   See also the farming of the *Chaine* of Limassol in Cyprus by
King Aimery in 1199 for two years for 28,500 white besants.
'Inventaire des pièces de Terre Sainte de l'ordre de l'Hôpital', ed. J. Delaville Le Roulx, *Revue de l'Orient latin*, III
(1895), no. 187. On the other hand Marsiglio Giorgio's
description of the tolls imposed on the Venetians in 1244
(*Urkunden Venedig*, no. 300, p. 398) suggests that perhaps the
gates of Acre were not being farmed then.

74   'Livre des Assises des Bourgeois', pp. 175 (§23 – see note 9),
179 (§12) and perhaps also pp. 177 (§§56, 60), 179 (§15);
Cart. St.-Sépulcre, nos 45, 184; *Urkunden Venedig*, no. 63;
'Quatre titres des Génois', no. 4 (pp. 225–6).

75   'Livre des Assises des Bourgeois', p. 179 (§12).

76   'Livre des Assises des Bourgeois', pp. 177 (§50), 179 (§6),
180 (§22); *Urkunden Venedig*, no. 300 (p. 398); *Tab. ord.
Theut.*, nos 18, 22.

77   'Livre des Assises des Bourgeois', pp. 179 (§§5, 13), 180 (§30).

78   *Urkunden Venedig*, no. 300 (p. 398); 'Livre des Assises des
Bourgeois', pp. 176 (§46), 177 (§§49, 51), 179 (§14), 180
(§§25, 26). See also p. 177 (§53).

79   See below, pp. 119–21.

80   See Cahen, 'Douanes et commerce', p. 238.

81   See S. Y. Labib, *Handelsgeschichte Ägyptens im Spätmittelalter
(1171–1517)* (Wiesbaden 1965) pp. 211ff.

82   See N. Elisséeff, *Nūr ad-Dīn* (Damascus 1967) III, pp. 858–9.

83   See the use of the terms *ius plateatici* and *plateaticum* in *Cart.
gen. Hosp.*, no. 1372; *Hist. dipl. Fred.*, II, p. 535. Also *Documenti delle città toscane*, no. 6: 'Dono . . . Pisanis plateam
unam in Ioppe, ut in ea componant sibi domos et faciant
ibidem forum sibi'.

84   See below, pp. 118–19. A market could be endowed with rights
itself. See the exchange of one at Tyre *cum libertatibus portuum
et portarum. Le Registre d'Urban IV*, ed. J. Guiraud et al. (Paris
1901–58) nos 1019–20.

85   For instance in Acre a *platea* in which onions were sold,
interesting because onions are included in the surviving list
of charges. *Cart. gen. Hosp.*, no. 2919; in Antioch a *funde del
vin. Cart. gen. Hosp.*, no. 2001; in Laodicea a *fondum fructus.
Cart. gen. Hosp.*, no. 437; in Jabala a *platea telarum. Les
Archives, [la bibliothèque et le trésor de l'ordre de St.-Jean de Jérusalem à Malte]*, ed. J. Delaville Le Roulx (Paris 1883) no. 52;
Cart. gen. Hosp., nos 1684, 2143; in the lordship of Margat a

platea tincturia. Cart. gen. Hosp., no. 941; in Tyre, 'item ex alio fontico . . . cum tubis et zallamellis vocinis et tanburis et aliis instrumentis ad ludendum . . . cum uno fontico . . . in quo vendentur mercimonia'. *Urkunden Venedig*, no. 299 (p. 385).

86 'Livre des Assises des Bourgeois', pp. 173–81. See also Francesco Balducci Pegolotti, pp. 63–9.

87 'Livre des Assises des Bourgeois', pp. 178–9. See Prawer, 'L'Établissement des coutumes', pp. 331–44. Richard, 'Colonies marchandes', pp. 335–40, and Cahen, 'A propos des coutumes', pp. 288–9, argue that the phrases should mean 'above' and 'below' the *fonde*. But this is based upon the assumption that there was only one *fonde* in Acre – and one has only to point to references to the Venetian *fonde* to show that this was not the case.

88 See *Tab. ord. Theut.*, nos 73–4; 'Continuation de Guillaume de Tyr de 1229 à 1261, dite du manuscrit de Rothelin', *RHC. Historiens occidentaux*, II, p. 635.

89 See 'Livre des Assises des Bourgeois', p. 178.

90 *Documenti delle città toscane*, no. 27. See also the reference by Frederick II to the *platea publica civitatis* in the same area. *Hist. dipl. Fred.*, III, p. 128.

91 See above, p. 125, n. 37.

92 I have considered this in another article on the lesser officers in the Latin Kingdom which is to be published in the *English Historical Review*, 87 (1972) pp. 6–9.

93 'Livre des Assises des Bourgeois', p. 172.

94 The *mensurator* of Beirut was mentioned in a charter of 1223. 'Liber iurium', no. 585.

95 'Livre des Assises des Bourgeois', p. 220.

96 See below, p. 117.

97 *Tab. ord. Theut.*, nos 5–6, 14, 19, 63–4; *Urkunden Venedig*, no. 299 (p. 367); *Cart. gen. Hosp.*, nos 1215, 2001–2, 2280; *Hist. dipl. Fred.*, III, pp. 117–18, 122–3, 125, 130; 'Fragment d'un cart. St.-Lazare', nos 29–30; 'Sankt Samuel auf dem Freudenberge', pp. 69–70; Delaville Le Roulx, 'Montjoye', p. 52.

98 See Richard, 'Colonies marchandes', p. 330.

99 *Cart. gen. Hosp.*, no. 2001.

100 *Cart. gen. Hosp.*, nos 311, 437.

101 *Les Archives*, no. 52; *Cart. gen. Hosp.*, nos 1684, 2143.

102 *Cart. gen. Hosp.*, no. 941.

103 *Cart. gen. Hosp.*, nos 620, 2002, 2280; Rey, *Recherches*, pp. 47–48, 51. There were also two sources of revenue in Tripoli called *drina* and *paudico* which may in fact have been the *duana* and the *fundico*, i.e. the *chaine* and the *fonde*.

104 *Tab. ord. Theut.*, nos 4–5. See 'Gestes des Chiprois', pp. 683–4, 684, 813.

105 *Cart. gen. Hosp.*, nos 3514–15. See John of Ibelin, p. 274.

106 *Urkunden Venedig*, no. 299 (p. 385). See also no. 63; *Chartes de Josaphat*, no. 46; 'Quatre titres des Génois', no. 4 (p. 228). But see the reference to the *fonde* of Tyre in *Cart. gen. Hosp.*, nos 3346, 3408; *Tab. ord. Theut.*, no. 14.

107 *Urkunden Venedig*, no. 299 (pp. 359–60). For Damascus, see N. A. Ziadeh, *Damascus under the Mamlūks* (Norman 1964) pp. 88–91.

108 John of Joinville, *Histoire de saint Louis*, ed. N. de Wailly
    (Paris 1874) p. 90.

109 For Acre, see Francesco Balducci Pegolotti, p. 64. For Tyre,
    Urkunden Venedig, no. 299 (p. 385): 'cum uno fontico . . .;
    et est in (ibi) statera'. For Beirut, 'Liber iurium', no. 585.
    See also Rey, *Recherches*, p. 48; 'Sankt Samuel auf dem Freu-
    denberge', p. 68.

110 'Liber iurium', no. 585.

111 'Livre des Assises des Bourgeois', pp. 173–81; *Urkunden
    Venedig*, no. 300. That the same system was used in other
    markets is clear from the privileges to the merchants listed
    below, pp. 123–6.

112 An obviously corrupt variant gives the charge on wax ($11\frac{5}{24}$
    per cent) at $2\frac{5}{24}$ per cent.

113 Of the various commodities taxed at this rate, cinnamon is
    listed twice, once obviously as a transit good, while Mar-
    siglio Giorgio, the Venetian *bailli*, reveals that $4\frac{1}{6}$ per cent
    was charged on Venetian goods passing through Acre from
    Islamic countries to the West. It was an easy tax to take,
    being one carouble in the besant. See also Ibn Jubair, p. 447.

114 'Livre des Assises des Bourgeois', pp. 176 (§§ 39–41, 47), 177
    (§ 57), 178 (§ 71).

115 Apples, asparagus, capers, olives, pears, quinces, straw,
    terebinth. Also salt fish from Egypt.

116 Cahen, 'Douanes et commerce', pp. 243ff.

117 Antoniadis-Bibicou, *Recherches sur les douanes, passim*.

118 Cahen, 'Douanes et commerce', pp. 240–1, 251–2; Goitein,
    Mediterranean Society, pp. 192–3, 218–19.

119 Cahen, 'Douanes et commerce', pp. 240–3, 254; Goitein,
    Mediterranean Society, p. 193.

120 See 'Livre des Assises des Bourgeois', pp. 34–5, 191–2.

121 Cahen, 'Douanes et commerce', p. 254; Antoniadis-Bibicou,
    Recherches sur les douanes, p. 112.

122 'nichil plus accipiemus ab illis gentibus, que vobiscum negoci-
    antur, nisi quantum soliti sunt dare, et quanta accipimus ab
    illis, qui cum aliis negociantur gentibus'. *Urkunden Venedig*,
    no. 40. (This does not appear in the confirmation, no. 41.)
    It was to the payment by both parties that Bohemond VII
    of Tripoli seems to have been referring in 1277 when his
    charter mentioned goods owing 'II. dreitures'. Rey, *Re-
    cherches*, pp. 47–8. See also Germain, *Histoire de Montpellier*,
    II, p. 513.

123 The only general exemptions were for the Genoese in
    Antioch, Laodicea, Jabala, Tripoli, Jubail, Tyre, Acre,
    Haifa, Jerusalem, Jaffa and Ascalon: 'Liber iurium', nos
    256, 374, 379, 401, 410, 477, 516, 718; 'Quatre titres des
    Génois', no. 4 (p. 225); 'Chartae', I, cols. 857–8; and for the
    Amalfitans in Acre: *Memorie di Amalfi*, I, p. 201. It is of
    interest that a contemporary charter to the Marseillais did
    not give them this right. *Histoire des actes de Marseille*, p. 195.

124 'Liber iurium', nos 405, 585; Rey, *Recherches*, pp. 47–8. See
    Urkunden Venedig, no. 300 (pp. 397–8).

125 *Documenti delle città toscane*, nos 4, 6, 13, 50; *Urkunden Venedig*,
    nos 61, 250; *Memorie di Amalfi*, I, p. 202; Germain, *Histoire
    de Montpellier*, II, p. 513; Röhricht, 'Amalrich I.', p. 489.

126 Freedom from all tax only on selling : *Histoire des actes de Marseille*, I, pp. 287–8. Freedom from tax only on buying : 'Liber iurium', no. 569; *Urkunden Venedig*, nos 68, 261.

127 See Francesco Balducci Pegolotti, p. 64 and below. Also *Cart. gen. Hosp.*, no. 77; 'Sankt Samuel auf dem Freudenberge', p. 68; J. Richard, 'La Fondation d'une église latine en Orient par S. Louis : Damiette', *Bibliothèque de l'École des Chartes*, CXX (Paris 1962) p. 54.

128 M. Benvenisti, *The Crusaders in the Holy Land* (Jerusalem 1970) pp. 98–104.

129 See *Cod. dipl. geros.*, I, p. 159.

130 *Urkunden Venedig*, no. 40.

131 *Urkunden Venedig*, no. 41.

132 *Documenti delle città toscane*, nos 23–5, 31–2; *Histoire des actes de Marseille*, I, p. 191. The privilege to the Provençals was extended to cover all cities in future taken by the Christians.

133 Rey, *Recherches*, pp. 47–50. See below, p. 121.

134 'Liber iurium', no. 374. Confirmed by Henry of Champagne : no. 405.

135 *Urkunden Venedig*, no. 63, although the profits from *mensuragium* were being withheld from them in 1243, see no. 299 (p. 385).

136 Francesco Balducci Pegolotti, p. 64.

137 'Quatre titres des Génois', no. 4 (pp. 227–8). The Genoese had to pay for measurement – though without holding the *mensuragium* in farm – in Beirut and Cyprus, but they were absolved from it in Haifa, 'Liber iurium', nos 585, 693, 718. The Venetians had to pay for measurement in Tripoli. Rey, *Recherches*, p. 48.

138 See the emphasis on the payment of tolls by visiting Muslim merchants in 'Livre des Assises des Bourgeois', p. 174 (§ 12).

139 'Liber iurium', no. 405.

140 *Urkunden Venedig*, no. 300 (pp. 397–8). The Latin here is very corrupt.

141 'Quatre titres des Génois', no. 4 (p. 226).

142 *Urkunden Venedig*, no. 300 (p. 398).

143 Germain, *Histoire de Montpellier*, II, pp. 513–15. See also the terms of a charter for Provençals from Henry of Cyprus in 1236. *Histoire des actes de Marseille*, I, pp. 419–20.

144 *Urkunden Venedig*, loc. cit.

145 'Quatre titres des Génois', no. 4 (p. 225).

146 'Liber iurium', no. 405. If there was no sale, the Genoese need pay no customs. In 1243, however, Bohemond V of Tripoli reduced by two-thirds the 'passage usé' paid by those Provençals who brought goods from Paynim into Tripoli by sea and loaded their boats with them. Germain, *Histoire de Montpellier*, II, p. 513.

147 *Cod. dipl. geros.*, I, p. 158, although it seems that the cost of entry would be subtracted from it.

148 Rey, *Recherches*, pp. 47–8.

149 See 'Livre des Assises des Bourgeois', p. 174 (§ 12).

150 Rey, *Recherches*, pp. 47–8.

151 'Livre des Assises des Bourgeois', pp. 178–9. Native *estasoniers* probably sold spices, see p. 175 (§ 22); *Urkunden Venedig*,

no. 299 (p. 359). See also Richard, 'Colonies marchandes',
pp. 337–40.
152 Prawer, 'L'Établissement des coutumes', pp. 338–41; Richard,
'Colonies marchandes', p. 333, note 15; Cahen, 'A propos
des coutumes', p. 289.
153 *Urkunden Venedig*, no. 299 (pp. 384–5).

Dante and Islam

R.W. SOUTHERN

The discovery of the influence of Islam on the intellectual development of Europe in the Middle Ages is one which has only slowly
made its full impact in the course of the last hundred years. Yet in
a sense, important though this influence is now seen to have been,
it is only a fragment of a much vaguer and more widespread
penetration of European thought by eastern influences which
earlier scholars had imagined to be possible. It is now well over a
hundred years since Renan showed that philosophy and science
were important areas of Islamic influence.[1] But this was no sooner
shown than the further questions were raised whether western art,
literature and religious life were not affected at least in some degree
by Islam, whether the introduction of the rosary might not have
some connection with Buddhism, and whether the friars might not
represent some strain of oriental influence in western life. It was
also asked whether the troubadours might not have learnt some of
their art from Islam, whether the churches on the pilgrim routes of
southern France might not have been influenced by the architecture of Islamic Spain, and whether the mystics of the later
Middle Ages might not owe something to Muslim mysticism.
Once the hunt was up it was difficult to know where to stop. There
seemed no reason why the surprise of discovering the wide ramifi-
cations of Latin Avicennism and Latin Averroism should not be
followed by similar discoveries in many other areas of activity.
Where cultural influences are concerned it is difficult to know
what symptoms are to be taken seriously and what are to be dismissed as unimportant. Until an instinctive sense of plausibility
has been developed by many trials and much error it is hard to tell
where the line is to be drawn between a possible hypothesis and an
impossible one. The only way to get the experience necessary for
making this distinction is to examine hypothetical contacts and see
what happens. If the hypotheses are right they will gradually
elucidate a widening area of evidence; if they are wrong the area
of elucidation will gradually contract until it has reached vanishing
point.

In the search for cultural contacts between Islam and the West
the name of Miguel Asín Palacios holds a place of special importance. This notable Spanish scholar was born in 1871 and died in
1944. He spent his life examining the literary and religious contacts

between the two races, languages, and religions which have shared the soil of Spain during the greater part of its history, sometimes in fruitful collaboration, more often in bitter hostility and bloodshed. Asin was interested in peaceful penetration, and historians who know what they want to find will generally not look in vain. Asin is no exception to this rule. Everywhere he discovered Islamic influences in the writers of the West – in St John of the Cross, Pascal, and above all in Dante. He expounded these discoveries in a series of books and articles; but of all his publications there can be no question that his *Escatología musulmana en la Divina Commedia*, which appeared in 1919, was the most influential and the most valuable.

The contacts between Islam and the West which Asin claimed to have discovered had both a general and a particular reference. In general, he claimed that Islam exercised much the same kind of influence on the western religious tradition as on its philosophical and scientific tradition. In particular, he claimed that Dante's vision of Heaven and Hell owed a great deal of its structure and many of its details to Muslim sources. And he argued that Dante's receptivity to Muslim influences was conditioned by an unusually knowledgeable and sympathetic attitude to Islamic culture. Asin's work therefore raises three distinct though related issues: Dante's knowledge and attitude to Islam; the influence of Islamic eschatology on the *Divine Comedy*; and the influence of Islam on western culture generally. It will be convenient to deal with them in this order.

With regard to Dante's knowledge of Islam and attitude towards it, this part of the enquiry may seem at first sight a case of making bricks without straw. Whatever Dante may have known or thought on this subject, he is not very expansive about it. In the whole course of the *Divine Comedy* he mentions only five Muslims, mostly very briefly: Avicenna shares a line with Hippocrates and Galen; Averroes and Saladin each have a line to themselves; Mahomet has thirty-eight lines, and his nephew and son-in-law Ali has two. In addition there are some references to the crusade and one or two chance remarks about Muslims and their religion. A study of these details is the first thing that is called for in examining Asin's thesis.

Of the five Muslims mentioned in the *Comedy*, three of them (Averroes, Avicenna and Saladin) are in Limbo among the sages and heroes of Antiquity, and two of them (Mahomet and Ali) are in Hell among the schismatics and sowers of discord.[2] With regard to Averroes and Avicenna very little need be said: they represent branches of learning quite apart from their Islamic background.

These men are not (in this context) Muslims, but simply scholars. They figure among the ancients because, though Averroes died as recently as 1198 and Avicenna less than two centuries earlier, Dante thought of them quite timelessly. It is uncertain whether Dante knew anything about their lives, and if he knew he did not care.

The case of Saladin is much more interesting. All the other inhabitants of Limbo may be regarded as people excluded from baptism by the date or circumstances of their lives : they were pagans by necessity. Saladin however was an active enemy of Christendom, a precursor of Antichrist. He could certainly have become a Christian, but he chose to be a Muslim. In western histories he appeared as the main hammer of the Christians in the Holy Land, the warrior who captured Jerusalem, murdered the Christian hero Reginald of Châtillon, and began the destruction of the Latin kingdom of Jerusalem.[3] Dante must have known at least some of these facts. How then does Saladin come to be among the heroes of Antiquity? It is true he stands apart from the rest – *solo in parte* – but this does not alter the fact that he is among the blameless heroes of the days before Christ. Asin therefore had some excuse for thinking that a notable softness and even sympathy for Islam was necessary to explain Dante's action in condemning Saladin to so mild a fate in so noble a company.

Nevertheless it would be a great mistake to believe Asin's explanation. It is an example of an error into which scholars have often fallen of thinking that the allotted place of minor characters in the *Divine Comedy* represents Dante's judgement on their total character or achievement. There are complications in the placing of major characters which we need not go into here, but it is quite clear that those who achieve no more than a simple mention in the company of others are selected to represent some special characteristic which may be quite remote from the main activities for which they are known to historians. We must ask of these minor characters not 'what light does their place in the *Comedy* throw on Dante's attitude to their character or achievement as a whole?' but only : 'what characteristic, however unimportant or illusory, justifies their being placed where they are?' In Saladin's case there is only one characteristic which would justify his place in Limbo, and it is found not in history but in romance. Gaston Paris long ago investigated the romantic western legends of Saladin, in which he appeared not as the ambitious and treacherous murderer depicted by Latin historians, but as a chivalric hero who toured the camps and courts of the West and would have become a Christian if he had not been deterred by the vices of the clergy.[4] Dante of course never tells us why he places his characters where he does, but it is clear that the legendary Saladin was (as the historical Saladin was not) sufficiently blameless in his paganism to take his place in Limbo among those who through no fault of their own lacked baptism and therefore blessedness. Saladin's place among these heroes is a striking example of Dante's concentration on a single point to the exclusion of all others. It is also an illustration of the popular sources from which much of his information came.

The placing of Saladin in Limbo tells us nothing at all about Dante's attitude to Islam, except in one particular. If the vices of the western clergy were the great obstacle to Saladin's conversion to Christianity, there must be something very wrong with the clergy. The responsibility of a vicious Christian clergy for the rise of Islam was a favourite theme of western critics of the church in the fourteenth century. That Dante shared this point of view is made quite clear in *Paradiso* xv, 142–4, where Cacciaguida speaks of Islam as

> quella legge il cui popolo usurpa
> *per colpa dei pastor* vostra giustizia.

These two lines are an extraordinarily concise and accurate summary of a view of Islam very common in the West after the collapse of the effective crusading movements : the existence of Islam was certainly an injustice to Christendom; but the fault lay within Christendom, and could be corrected only by the reform of the Church. Islam would not have existed if the Christian clergy had been what they ought to be. It was their fault that prevented Saladin's conversion, and made him as blameless as the ancient heroes and sages.

This concentration on Christian vices in viewing the evils of the world explains another small detail which at first sight seems to show that Dante possessed a certain amount of knowledge and appreciation of Islam. In *Purgatorio* xxiii, 103, Forese Donati says that Muslim women are more modest than those of Florence. This remark has been thought to indicate that Dante appreciated the modesty of Muslim women. Certainly this was not an impossible view in the early fourteenth century. More than one western traveller had discovered that the licentiousness of Islam had been greatly overdone in western polemics, and that Muslim women were positively nun-like in their public behaviour. But a very little thought suffices to destroy the illusion that Dante knew or cared anything at all about this. His aim was to show that Florence was worse even than the worst that could be found elsewhere. The drift of Forese's argument is that *even* barbarians and Saracens are more modest than the women of Florence. The words *barbare* and *saracine* are simply vaguely abusive terms, the readiest Dante can lay hands on to describe degraded creatures. They are examples of those 'outsiders', whom more than once Dante used to chastise the vices of Christians. Far from showing either knowledge or appreciation, therefore, this passage discloses a very common state of prejudice and ignorance about Islam, and a passionate hatred of the vices of Florence.

This leaves us only with Mahomet and Ali. Mahomet is placed in the ninth Bolgia of the eighth Circle of Hell among the sowers of discord. This is in keeping with the usual medieval interpretation of Islam as a Christian schism. The role of Mahomet as an agent of schism in the Christian church is emphasised by his punishment : since he had torn apart the body of the Church, his own body from chin to bowels is perpetually cleft in two. So far there is nothing unusual. But a closer scrutiny reveals something very unusual in the scene as a whole.

In the first place, the company in which Mahomet appears is unexpected. We should expect to find him with the other great sowers of discord in the Church, perhaps Nestorius, Pelagius, Manes and some representative patriarch of Constantinople like Photius. But not at all. The company consists of three contemporary sowers of civil war in Italy (Piero della Medicina, Mosca di Lamberti and – prospectively – Fra Dolcino), one ancient Italian trouble-maker (Curio who advised Caesar to cross the Rubicon), and the troubadour Bertram de Born, who caused strife between the English king Henry II and his sons. They are all secular, and most are local enemies of society. Four of the company belong to Italian politics, ancient and modern, and one to the legends of the troubadours. This is a very fair summary of the scope and balance of Dante's political interests. To say the least it indicates a lack of interest in the strictly ecclesiastical nature of Mahomet's offence, and this separates Dante sharply from the anti-Islamic polemical writers of the twelfth and thirteenth centuries. He had no sympathy with Islam, but he already shows the strong drift of the fourteenth century towards secular and anti-ecclesiastical attitudes. Towards Islam he was hostile, indifferent, ignorant; his appearance of sympathy comes from his disillusionment with Christendom.

But we have not yet dealt with the closest of Mahomet's companions. If the companions of Mahomet so far mentioned throw more light on Dante's secular outlook than on his interest in Islam, this companion certainly seems to suggest some degree of special knowledge. Mahomet is preceded in Dante's vision by his son-in-law and third successor, Ali, and their punishments are balanced to show the close relationship between the two men : whereas Mahomet is cleft from chin to bowels, Ali is cleft from forehead to chin. Why? Why, too, does Ali the *successor* of Mahomet *precede* him in Dante's account? Not, we may be sure, by accident.

The mere mention of Ali raises a presumption that Dante knew more about Islam than most of his contemporaries. Those who have seized on this point have generally gone on to explain that Ali's mutilation – less extensive but complementary to that of Mahomet – symbolises his role as the creator of a schism within Islam. Ali was the founder of the Shi'ite schism in the Muslim world, and if this is what Dante intended to symbolise in Ali's punishment then he must indeed have known and cared a great deal about Islamic history. But if this is what he means, why does Ali *precede* Mahomet?

This is an awkward fact that defies explanation until we turn to Benvenuto da Imola, who wrote a Commentary on the *Divine Comedy* about 1375.[5] Here we find it explained that Ali was *parum divisus sed in parte corporis honestiori et principaliori quia Macomethum instruxit et iuvit ad tantum errorem.* Nothing could be simpler. Ali was the mind behind Mahomet, therefore the thinking part of him, his head, is punished; he goes before Mahomet in the hideous procession because thought goes before action, the master before the pupil. But if this is the explanation – and it is the only one I know that fits the facts – Dante has made a very gross blunder. All medieval western accounts of Mahomet's life mention that Mahomet (who was an unlearned man) had a teacher who led him astray, but this teacher is generally given the name of Sergius, a Nestorian monk. It would seem that Dante has simply confused Ali with Sergius. If so, we have another example of his ignorance and indifference to the facts of Islamic history.

A final word must be said about Dante's attitude to the crusade against Islam before we turn to the wider issue of the influence on his imaginative world. Until the last quarter of the thirteenth century most western Europeans believed that the Islamic problem could be solved – that is to say that Islam could be destroyed – by a mixture of force, argument and diplomacy, and the possibility of mounting an effective crusade was the essential element in this threefold policy. After 1291 it became increasingly difficult to believe any longer in this combination. As the difficulties began to grow into impossibilities two distinct points of view began to emerge: the first required an ever greater exertion and dedication to the task; the second recognised the folly of further effort and turned to more domestic issues. There can be no doubt that Dante, despite his outward parade of the values of an earlier age, exemplified the second and more modern of these two attitudes. The great systematic power and universal scope of the *Divine Comedy* must not blind us to the rapid falling off in detailed clarity as soon as we leave Italy. Even in contemporary affairs there is very little clarity of detail outside Italy; and outside the narrowest limits of western Europe all is dark. It is not that Dante is specially hostile to the rest of the world; he just does not see it at all.

But how can this indifference to the outside world be reconciled with the honourable place which the crusade holds in the *Divine Comedy*? There is an easy answer to this question. Dante had two reasons for mentioning the crusade : first, his great ancestor Cacciaguida had died on crusade while following the emperor who knighted him; secondly, his great enemy Boniface VIII had *not* promoted a crusade but had preferred to make war at home. Dante never mentions the crusade except to praise the one or abuse the other, and the way in which he mentions it shows that he had given it no deep thought. Boniface VIII, he tells us, had waged war on his Christian enemies at home instead of attacking Saracens and Jews, the conquerors of Acre and merchants in the sultan's lands.[6] Words such as these show the extent to which the ideal of the crusade had become confused and debased by the first quarter of the fourteenth century. Jews, Saracens, and merchants in the sultan's lands were all lumped together as the enemies of a Christendom which was beginning to experience the first bitter taste of recession. No sane view of the crusade had ever included Jews among the legitimate objects of the Holy War. But Dante, who is generally so precise, has here moved beyond the range of his sharp perceptions. His words about the crusade reflect only his hatred of the enemies of Christendom, and his ignorance of the large indefinite mass of the *gente turpa* who were outside the fold.

I have so far argued that Dante's references to Islam show no special knowledge or sympathy with the Muslim world. They also show little trace of the traditional attitude towards Islam in which Christian polemic and crusading ideals had a prominent place. But we must remember that Dante was a very hospitable, we might almost say haphazard, borrower of impressions, ideas and information from many sources. There was room in the carefully constructed framework of the *Divine Comedy* for many strange associations of facts and fantasies which could only be held together by the force of an imagination as powerful as that of Dante. With this in mind we must now turn to Asin's main contention, that Dante borrowed many details and some main features of his journey through Hell and Heaven from Muslim eschatology. When Asin first made this suggestion in 1919 the initial response was one of outrage; but many things have happened since then to change the climate of opinion. No-one would now be horrified to discover that Dante *had* borrowed eschatological details from Islam, as he borrowed so many other things in his science and philosophy. Nevertheless, if he did so, we should have to extend quite considerably our idea of western receptivity to

Islamic influences. It is one thing to borrow scientific or philo-sophical ideas, which were thought to be the products of natural reason; it is quite another thing to borrow images and incidents which belong to the arcana of Islam.

I do not think that anyone can read Asin's statement of the argu-ments in favour of Dante's widespread borrowing from Muslim eschatology without being half-convinced. Asin produced so many parallels between the *Divine Comedy* and the eschatological litera-ture of Islam that the reader is bludgeoned into submission. There was only one weakness in his original argument : he could not produce any source from which Dante could have learnt about Islamic eschatology. That such a source must have existed was simply an article of faith, and it looked as if the faith would slowly perish for lack of any material evidence. When Asin died in 1944, it seemed likely that his faith would die with him.

By a strange irony what happened was precisely the opposite. In the year of Asin's death the long-sought connection between western Christendom and Islamic eschatology came to light. In Paris, Rome and Oxford, there were discovered two thirteenth century translations into Latin and French of an Arabic work giving a detailed account of Mahomet's journey through Heaven and Hell.[7] This work, which is known as the *Liber de Scala Macho-meti*, appeared to satisfy all the requirements of Asin's thesis and to provide a brilliant vindication of his imaginative insight. The subject-matter was just right. The date and provenance could scarcely have been more apposite. The translation had been made in 1264 by an Italian, Bonaventura of Siena, at the court of Alfonso x of Castile; and, as if this were not enough, Dante's friend Brunetto Latini had been an ambassador at this court in 1260. Moreover the manuscript tradition showed that the translations had had a wide circulation in Italy, France and Spain. Even if they had few readers, they were certainly accessible to a man of Dante's avid curiosity.

In one sense however the discovery of *any* evidence was bound to weaken Asin's case. So long as there was no known docu-mentary source, Asin could build his case on the whole body of Muslim literature. He could pick here and there whatever he wanted, and he could postulate a source containing all the neces-sary details. In the absence of any precise link, all links were possible. But now that a single definite link had been discovered, all hypothetical ones must – unless the discussion was to float for ever in the air – be abandoned. Inevitably therefore the basis of the comparison between Dante and Muslim literature was now drasti-cally narrowed. Some of the best parallels had to be forgotten; many others did not look so good when there was no longer a choice between several versions. What remains when all these deductions have been made?

So far as I can judge, only this. Even on the narrow basis of a single text there are still a number of details which must make a reader pause. In the *Liber de Scala* the role of the angel Gabriel as guide to Mahomet is somewhat similar to the role of Virgil as guide to Dante; the three voices which attempt to deflect Mahomet in his ascent are reminiscent of the three beasts which frighten Dante; the pitiless dry wind of Mahomet's first Hell is not unlike the fierce winds of Dante's second circle; the Great Hell with its walls and seven gates, which Mahomet saw, might be a model for the City of Dis in Dante's sixth circle. These details and a good many others have been analysed by several scholars, but not one of them has yielded any decisive turn of phrase or image which would put the fact of Dante's knowledge beyond reasonable doubt. This is important, because even if Dante did know the text we can say quite certainly that it did not have the kind of influence on his imagination that – for example – some texts of Lucan or Statius (to look no further) can be shown to have had. In other words, even if Dante borrowed some details from Mahomet's journey, none of them excited his poetic imagination to create original images. At the best, the upholders of Asin's thesis are now left with borrowings that are featureless.

Among a handful of possible borrowings, not a single phrase or incident in the *Divine Comedy* cries aloud that it came from the *Scala Mahometi*. It is very significant that most of the suggested parallels consist of tortures, for where tortures are concerned – especially when there are a great many – the human imagination has very distinct limits. Intense heat or cold, frightful mutilations, atrocious contortions, defilements – the list can be prolonged, but in the end there must be a point of exhaustion. Two writers who make a list of tortures cannot fail to have several in common. In this field, general similarities prove nothing at all. Further, it has now been shown that several of the details which Asin referred to Muslim sources, could (if we must have a source) come equally well from Christian visionary literature.[8] This reminder of the common stock of ancient images on which both Christians and Muslims drew is the final blow to Asin's thesis. The discovery of the source which his theory required has turned into a boomerang and administered the *coup de grâce* to his argument in the end.

And yet, we must not be too sure. If the *Liber de Scala* came into Dante's hands he would no doubt have thought it a very poor thing. Yet in its general plan of Heaven and Hell it is a good deal nearer to the plan of the *Divine Comedy* that any existing Christian vision. It has more order, more discussion, more geographical

L

exactitude; and though highly inartistic, it is 'literary' in the sense that no Christian reader would be inclined to take the journey as a genuine revelation. Dante *could* have seen in it some of the emerging order to which he was to give an immensely fuller development in his own poem. Whether he actually *did* see it however has not been, and probably never can be, established. All that we can be sure of is that it was not important in any of the ways in which Asin imagined it to be important.

Nevertheless, even when they are wrong, all hypotheses which have the power to stimulate controversy leave something positive behind them, and this is no exception. It has forced us to think more about the visionary sources, both Christian and Muslim, of Dante's other-world. It has helped forward the task of drawing the limits of Islamic influence in the West in the Middle Ages. And lastly it has given a new turn to some questions about the limitations of Dante's own knowledge and imagination. Let me conclude by saying a few words on each of these subjects.

If we look for the ancestry of the *Divine Comedy* only in Christian sources, we can see that in its general form it is a combination of two main types of literature : on the one hand, visions of the future life which go back in existing texts to the fourth century; on the other, philosophical poems describing allegorical journeys through the heavens in which Reason and Nature hold converse with Grammar, Astronomy, Noys and so on.[9] There can be no doubt that Dante knew more than one example of both these types, and I suppose there can be little doubt that he saw himself as the creator of a new kind of poem which combined the visionary and philosophical qualities of both these well-known literary types. The earlier Christian visions were not works of art but descriptions claiming the authority of first-hand, personal, objective, records of a supernatural experience. Their realism made a powerful appeal to the whole western world, but they presented a chaotic jumble of experiences. They lacked both doctrine and literary form. By contrast, the medieval philosophical poems, with all their doctrine and literary form, were impersonal and remote from human experience. In the *Divine Comedy*, Dante remedied all these contrasting deficiencies in a poem that was intensely personal and visionary, and at the same time orderly, rational, and full of doctrine.

The conflation of these two literary genres was entirely within Dante's powers working on western sources alone. He did not need any Muslim source for his act of creation.

A more important aspect of the discussion is the help it can give in determining the extent of Islamic influence in medieval thought

and experience. The idea that western Christendom was wide open
to outside influences of all kinds now appears even less plausible
than it did in 1919. The accumulating evidence of the reception
of Muslim science and philosophy serves only to underline the
absence of receptivity in other fields. Medieval Europe was extremely resistant to cultural influences except in the single area in
which Islam acted as a link with ancient Greek thought. Nothing
that has a specifically Islamic inspiration took root in the West.

The reason for this is not difficult to find. Western Europe
received Greek science at the hands of Islam because the schools
of the West were ready to receive it. They needed it so badly that
men were prepared to make great efforts to find and translate this
material. By about 1150 the schools and emergent universities were
powerful and necessary organisations within the western ecclesiastical structure, but they were beginning to run out of intellectual
capital. The existing texts had given all that they could, yet it was
not enough. The demand for an organised philosophical and
scientific description of the world was growing stronger every
year. It might be thought that the proper response to this demand
would be to take a new look at the world, to make original
observations and measurements, to start from experience. But the
West was obsessed by the idea that all learning was to be found in
books. Scholars were therefore driven to look for new books – or
rather for old books which had long been lost to the West. This
search took western scholars to the newly reconquered areas of
Spain, as one might now rummage about in an abandoned
country-house or second-hand bookshop. The searchers were not
interested in the previous occupier or owner, but simply in
material for their own researches. They hoped to provide material
for the schools, or exceptionally for religious polemic : they were
not opening their hearts and minds to an alien civilisation.

Philosophy and science were the only areas of thought in
western Europe in which the demand for facts outran the native
supply of material. In all other areas the West had, or thought it had,
enough material to meet all its needs. The stories of the Muslim
world did indeed make a slight penetration in the twelfth century
because a converted Spanish Jew, Peter Alfonsi, gave them a homi-
letic slant; but his work did not start a rush to discover and translate the vast stores of similar stories that Islam possessed. The
theology of Islam became known in the West through the translation of the Koran made for Peter the Venerable, but it had almost
no effect in altering the way men thought about the teachings of
Mahomet. The architecture of Muslim Spain made a marginal
impact on the development of Christian architecture, but it did
not affect the main stream of the transition from romanesque to

gothic. Among these marginal influences where does the *Liber de Scala* stand? Why was it translated at all, and who used it, and how was it used?

The answer to the first of these questions seems to be that the translation was, like Peter Alfonsi's translations of Islamic stories or Peter the Venerable's translations of the Koran, an individual enterprise. It was not made in response to a widely-felt need, like the translations of scientific and philosophic texts. It filled no major gap in western literature. There was already a massive and growing literature of visions and journeys to the other-world which needed no external stimulus. So the journey of Mahomet could never be more than a curiosity, and it stimulated no appetite for more. This lack of interest was not due to anti-Islamic sentiment but simply to satiety. The West had enough of its own. That was all.

It almost always happens in a historical controversy that both sides are wrong, at least to begin with, because no one knows how the question should be handled till it has been much discussed. Asin was wrong to suppose that western Christendom was indiscriminately open to new influences from Islam; he was wrong to think that Dante's mind especially was filled with images drawn from Islamic sources. His critics were wrong in thinking that Dante would reject these images and influences merely because they were Islamic. They were rejected because in the context of western thought they were superfluous. Far from being more knowledgeable or sympathetic to Islam than his contemporaries, Dante's imagination scarcely extended beyond the narrow limits of western Europe. A few western travellers of Dante's day knew Islam at first-hand and brought back a sympathetic understanding of the Muslim way of life, but Dante was not one of them. He was a wholly western man.

NOTES

1   E. Renan, *Averroès et l'averroïsme* (Paris 1852).
2   *Inferno*, IV, 129, 143–4; XXVIII, 22–63.
3   In addition to the unfavourable opinion of Saladin's character among western historians, cf. M. Reeves, *The Influence of Prophecy in the later Middle Ages* (Oxford 1969) pp. 7, 178, 305, for his place in the apocalyptic vision of Joachim of Fiore.
4   G. Paris, 'La Légende de Saladin', *Journal des Savants* (Paris 1893) p. 284.
5   *Benvenuto de Rambaldis de Imola Comentum super Dantis Alighieri Comoediam nunc primum integre in lucem editum*, ed. J. P. Lacaita (1887).
6   *Inferno*, XXVII, 85–7.
7   The manuscripts (Paris, B. N. lat. 6064; Rome, Vat. lat.

4072 and Oxford, Bodleian Library, Laud misc. 390) were first mentioned in connection with Dante by V. Monneret de Villard, *Lo studio dell'Islam in Europa nel XII e nel XIII secolo, Studi e Testi,* CX (1944). For the controversy which was stimulated by the discovery and publication of these translations, see E. Cerulli, *Il libro della Scala e la questione delle fonti arabo-spagnole della Divina Commedia, Studi e Testi,* CL (1949); G. Levi della Vida, 'Nuova luce sulle fonti islamiche della Divina Commedia', *Al Andalus,* XIV (1949) pp. 377–407; E. Cerulli, 'Dante e l'Islam', *Al Andalus,* XXI (1956) pp. 229–53. The translations were edited by J. Muñoz, *La Escala de Mahoma* (1949).

8   T. Silverstein, 'Dante and the Legend of the Mi'Rāj', *Journal of Near Eastern Studies,* XI (1953) pp. 89–110, 187–97.

9   On the links between Dante and this literature, see E. Bossard, *Alani de Insulis Anticlaudianus cum Divina Dantis Alighieri Comoedia collatus* (1885).

Index

Byzantine names are given in the style of the *Cambridge Medieval History*, IV (Cambridge 1966)

Abbasids, 37
Abelard, 75 n.4
Abdul-Rahman al-Nasrani, *see* Christodoulos
Acacian schism, 11, 17ff, 22
Acacius, patriarch of Constantinople, 17, 18, 19
Achaea, prince of, 103
Acre, 86, 109-32 *passim*, 139
   Mer de la Riviere, 112, 124 n.34
Adalbert of Ivrea, 30, 48, 50 n.9
Adalbert of Prague, St, 45
Adalbert of Tuscany, margrave, 36
Adelaide (Adelheid), empress, 41, 45
African church, 24-5
Agnes of France, daughter of Louis VII, 5, 9 n.5, 85
Alberich, prince of Rome, 37, 38, 39, 55 n.49
Aleppo, 68
Alexander, count of Gravina, 85
Alexandria, 2, 14, 16, 115
   patriarch, 101, 104
Alexius I Comnenus, emperor, 79, 89
Alexius II Comnenus, emperor, 5, 85
Alexius III Angelus, emperor, 95, 101
Alexius IV Angelus, emperor, 96, 101, 105
Alexius V Murtzuphlus, emperor, 105
Alexius Axouchos, *see* Axuch
Alfonso X of Castile, king, 140
Alfred, king, 41
Ali, son-in-law of Mahomet, fifth caliph, 72, 134-8
Al Muqtafi, caliph, 37

Amalfi, Amalfitans, 110
Amaury I of Jerusalem, king, 64, 68, 69, 70, 71, 112, 116, 127 n.68
Ambrose of Milan, St, 15
Anastasius I, emperor, 11, 16, 17, 19, 20, 21,
Anatolia, 6, 84, 88-90
anchoragia, 112
Ancona, 110, 111, 120
Andravida, church of Hagia Sophia, 86
Andronicus I Comnenus, emperor, 5, 85, 88
Anna Comnena, 87
Anne of Byzantium, *see* Agnes of France
Anselm, St, 78, 79
Antapodosis, 47, 48, 50 n.7
Anthimus of Trebizond, 23, 28 n.37
Antioch, 2, 68, 110, 116
   patriarch, 101, 104
Aphthartodocetism, 23
Appian, 1, 9 n.2
Apulia, 36, 54 n.42
Aquileia, march, 35
Aquinas, St Thomas, 8, 81
Arab histories, 64, 71
Arabic, knowledge of, 69, 73
Arabs, *see* muslims
archontes, 34, 39
'arif, 116
Argyros, family, 31, 51 n.15
Argyrou, Mary, *see* Mary Argyrou
Aristippus, Henry, *see* Henry Aristippus
Aristotle, 79, 80
Arles, Hugh of, *see* Hugh of Arles
Armenia, 16, 18, 101
Arnolf, emperor, 35, 40
Arnulf, duke, 35, 54 n.36
Arnulf of Milan, archbishop, 32, 38, 57 n.64